A SURVEY OF INDIAN HISTORY

A SURVEY OF INDIAN HISTORY

K.M. Panikkar

First Published 1947
First LG Edition 2018

ISBN 978–93–83723–34–8 (Hb)

Published by
LG PUBLISHERS DISTRIBUTORS
49, Street No. 14, Pratap Nagar,
Mayur Vihar Phase I, Delhi 110091
Email: lgpdist@gmail.com

Printed at
D.K. Fine Art Press, Delhi 110 052

CONTENTS

MAPS

INTRODUCTION TO THE SECOND EDITION

THIS *Survey of Indian History* was published originally on the 15th August 1947, the date of India's independence. Since then, it has been reprinted nine times within a period of seven years* and may, therefore, be said to have achieved the position of a popular favourite, an unusual distinction for a historical work. Unfortunately, however, owing to my continued residence outside India, it was not found possible to bring out a revised edition till now.

A distinguished Chinese scholar, Dr. Yu Ta-wei, once remarked to me that whenever he tried to read a book on Indian history he was constrained to give it up after a few pages as it looked to him less like a historical work than a telephone directory—an enumeration of names unconnected with each other. Though the criticism is no doubt exaggerated, it is undoubtedly true that text books of Indian history are generally written more from the point of view of dynasties and kings and they have but little to say about the growth of civilisation, the change in national attitudes, the development and decay of social organisations and religious beliefs and such other matters which constitute the stuff and substance of national History. Up to a point this was inevitable as, at the time when Indian history became a subject of serious study, there was no framework of dynasties and chronology within which the growth of the Indian people could be historically traced. The efforts of researches were therefore mainly directed towards the deciphering of inscriptions, the discovery of local and imperial dynasties, the study of coins, and the rehabilitation of forgotten kings. These are undoubtedly important, for they provide the background to history, though they do not constitute history.

Though there are still wide gaps in our knowledge and the gulf between the Harrappa period and the period of the Buddha remains to be bridged, the material now available is sufficient to enable a historian to write a continuous narrative of the political and social life of India at least from the 6th century B.C. At times the political background may still be hazy, but the social organisa-

Publisher's note: The book has now been reprinted twelve times during the last fifteen years.

tion, the development of the mind and the general features of Hindu life can be traced clearly not only through the genuinely historical material available from inscription, records of foreign observers and allusions in the annals of neighbouring countries but also through Hindu, Buddhist and Jain literatures which cover the whole period and throw a great deal of light on the living conditions of the period at different periods.

Ever since India became conscious of her nationhood there has been a growing demand for a history of India which would try and reconstruct the past in a way that would give us an idea of our heritage. Brought up on text books written by foreigners whose one object would seem to have been to prove that there was no such thing as "India," we had each to "discover" India for ourselves. I do not think it is an exaggeration to say that it was a spiritual adventure for most of us to gain in some measure an understanding of the historical processes which have made us what we are and to evaluate the heritage that has come down to us through five thousand years of development. This has led to some strange results. The orthodox think of India in terms of the Vedic age and emphasise the Aryan character of our life. The Hindu nationalists recreated an India of their own imagination, based on the glories of the Gupta period, while the Muslim vision of India hardly went beyond the days of Mahmud of Ghazni and equated Indian culture with the achievements of the Moghuls. To read most of the earlier Indian histories one would think that India south of the Vindhyas did not exist, and if it did, only as an appendage to the empires of the North.

A further complication from which we have not yet fully recovered was introduced by European historians, and following them, our own writers, of dividing India into "periods," Buddhist, Muslim, British etc. Now a moment's thought would show that there were no such clearly marked periods. No serious student of Indian history could talk of a Buddhist period, for though, no doubt, some Emperors and Kings professed the religion of the Buddha the vast majority of the people of India, even in the time of Asoka were Hindus as they are today. Asoka's own inscriptions bear witness to this fact and his ethical preaching is addressed as much to the Hindus as to the Buddhists. So far as the "Muslim period" is concerned, we know that while the Gangetic Valley, Bengal, Gujerat and the northern portion of the Deccan Plateau were ruled by Muslim monarchs, vast areas of Central India and Rajasthan never came under Muslim rule, and the South organised itself into a powerful empire after the first shock of Malik Kafur's raid on the southern kingdoms. Moreover after the first generation, these Central Asian invaders whether Khilji, Tughlaq or Moghul lost their contacts with their homelands and ruled their territories as Indians, with the seats of their power in India. They had little or no contact with the Islamic powers of the West. In fact, the only time when India was ruled from a foreign country was during the hundred and fifty years of British authority. It is, therefore, legitimate to speak of a British period, i.e. of a period when the policies relating to India were determined by the interests of another country situated far away; but even that would only be partially true, because the true history of India during the period was not made at Whitehall, or even by the Governors-General and Viceroys in Calcutta and Delhi and the bureaucracy which administered the country, but by the people of India, who quietly and unobtrusively reorganised themselves and called forth from their ancient heritage new sources of strength which enabled them to keep their spirit alive and finally to reassert their indépendence. The true history of India during the British period does not consist of the activities of the East India Company or of its successor, the British Crown, but of the upheaval which led to the transformation of Indian society, through the activities of India's own sons.

There is undoubtedly a history of the British in India, starting from the establishment of the first factories to the withdrawal of the last British soldier from the Indian soil. It is connected with India, as it happened on the soil of India, but it is hardly a part of Indian history. It is an important chapter of British history and as such deserves to be studied by those interested in the history of British achievements overseas. But in relation to India it never became true history, as the government attempted at no time to become national, but always deliberately remained foreign. This is what differentiates such a period as that of Moghul power in North India from British Rule. The Moghul might have been a foreign dynasty, but with their capital in India, and with but little connection with their homelands, they became truly Indian and their government national. The history of the great Moghuls is, therefore, a part of Indian history. The position is very different in the case of the British. Only by the resistance it gave rise to and the forces it generated either by contrast or by reaction did British authority touch the inner life of the Indian people. It will thus be seen that the importance attached to the British period, and the disproportionate space which it takes up in our text books are altogether unjustified and can only be considered as the survival of British propaganda. I have attempted in the present volume to deal with the period of British rule—a period of the utmost importance to us—from the point of view of the Indian people.

The scheme I have followed in this *Survey* is as far as possible to portray the life of the people against a continuous political background, and to deal with dynastic history and with the wars and conquests of different kings, only to the extent unavoidable for the creation of that political background. I have also tried to work into the pattern the major strands of South India's evolution for it is obvious that any attempt to interpret the history of India in terms of the evolution of Indo-Gangetic Valley is bound to be partial and unbalanced. It is the Aryo-Dravidian synthesis which begins at the end of the Rig Vedic age, with the Battle of the Ten Kings, that creates Indian civilisation, and that synthesis, while it was perfected in the philosophical thought, the religious institutions, and the social organisation of the Hindu people was never attempted on the racial level in the areas to the south of the Vindhyas. Thus, the South has continued until today to be different racially, and the geography of India, dividing the sub-continent into two with the Deccan *massif* as a barrier has effectively prevented an intermingling of races. The Deccan continues, therefore, to be predominantly Dravidian in racial characteristics, though the composite life of Hinduism and the dominance of the Sanskrit language unite both the North and the South in unbreakable bonds, proclaiming the cultural unity of India.

In a survey of developments, so extensive in space and in time, meant for the general reader I have not considered it necessary to go deeply into matters which are still controversial. Apart from such questions as the origin of the Dravidians, the relations of the Aryan invaders to the Indus Valley people and other highly speculative subjects, about which a definite opinion is not possible, there are numerous others, no doubt of much less importance but favoured as subjects of heated controversy among scholars, which I have deliberately avoided in the course of my narrative. Thus, for example, I have merely stated my view that Kalidasa lived and wrote during the period of Agnimitra. There are many historians who hold firmly the view that the poet lived at the court of Chandra Gupta Vikramaditya in the fourth century A.D. To enter into a detailed discussion of the topic, which would at least require a lengthy appendix to itself would have been against the scheme of my work. Again many books have been written about the date of Kautalya's *Arthasastra*. Whether the text which is available to us through Shamasastry's edition is by Kautalya himself or is a later rendition of his original work, I have no doubt that the structure of the State that is described in it is that of the Mauryan Empire under Chandra Gupta and, therefore, the question of its authorship seemed to me to be of secondary importance.

The geographical factors which have moulded the history of India are of unusual importance. No one could understand Indian history properly without a correct appreciation of these factors. I have only alluded to them in this *Survey* as it was my intention to deal with the subject separately in a popular volume which has now been published under the title of *Geographical Factors in Indian History*. The influence of the sea on India is also only treated very briefly but those who are interested in this important subject may find it discussed in some detail in my *India and the Indian Ocean*.

Also, there are many unsolved problems in Indian history which I have not even attempted to indicate. I might mention a few here. What were the causes which led to widespread decadence in Hindu life in the 9th, 10th and 11th centuries which made North India break down so easily before the onslaught of the Turks when three centuries before they had valiantly resisted the invasion by the mighty Empire of the Khalifs? The fact of decadence is undeniable. One has only to look at the temple sculptures of this period and to read the literature, and to study the religious trends which led to the extravagances of the *vama marga* to realise that something had snapped which undermined the national vigour, which at one time resisted so valiantly the Sakas, the Hunas and the Arabs. Equally, what were the causes that led to the remarkable revival in the 14th and 15th centuries, which led not only to the establishment of Vijayanagar, but to the aggressive nationalism of Rajasthan under Kumbha and his successors? What lay behind the great revival of Hindu thought during the same period of which the outstanding instance is Sayana's commentary on the Vedas, but which is equally witnessed by the profusion of Dharma Sastra literature and the growth of new religious movements? Again what was the cause of the sudden and unexplained failure of intellectual curiosity which is evidenced by our arrested progress in scientific work? After the 6th century, there are no more Varahamihiras and Bhadanta Nagarjunas in Indian history. The solitary name of Bhaskara illumines a dark age for sciences. The phenomenon of arrested growth after so brilliant a period of achievement requires explanation. Alberuni noted that the Indians had in his time become overweening in their pride and firm in their conviction that they knew everything that had to be known. When did this attitude—surely the clearest evidence of national decadence —gain its hold on the mind of India, for such was not the case when the Hindus accepted Romaka Siddhanta and freely learnt from others?

These and other questions remain to be scientifically studied before a comprehensive history of India, which seeks to interpret the evolution of the Indian people, could be undertaken. All that has been attempted here is to present the known facts in perspective so that the reader could have a bird's eye view of India's historical evolution.

K. M. PANIKKAR

"Śudarsana"
Bangalore
1 June 1954

CHAPTER I

THE MAKING OF INDIA

THE geography of India, its physical configuration, its mountains and rivers have had a decisive influence on its history. Walled off by the impenetrable Himalayan range in the north and flanked on the sides by lesser ranges, India enjoys a practically isolated position in relation to the continent of Asia. A peninsula, washed on its three sides by the Indian Ocean, she was from the earliest period of her history a country with a dominant interest on the sea. With the waters of the ocean separating her from Africa on the one side and Malaya and the islands of the Indonesian Archipelago on the other and cut off by mountains on her land frontiers in the north, east and the west, India was, from the beginning of history, isolated to a large extent in her evolution and was individual in her life and development.

An area so walled off and isolated inevitably develops peculiarities and special characteristics which constitute the differentiating marks of a civilisation. The fact that the area so isolated was large and contained at all times a variety of racial elements, wide differences of climate, great diversities of soil and different physical characteristics, not only prevented it from becoming stagnant but gave it a continental character capable of generating the forces of action and reaction which lead to the development of civilisation. Every kind of climate is met with in India, from the scorching heat of the deserts of Rajputana to the snowy cold of the Himalayan ranges, from the dry rocky tablelands of the Deccan to the moist tropical luxuriance of Bengal and Malabar. The continental character of India is an essential factor in her history.

The outstanding feature of Indian geography is of course the Himalayas. "These are," says an English writer, "the supreme mountains of the earth, tossed high in some convulsion of the primeval age and stricken immobile, a frozen ocean of lava waves, whose crests are on the outer fringes of space, whose depths and hollows are the secret places of the earth, unknown and inaccessible; rock-cut gorges set about by forest swamp and interlocking jungle within whose grim recesses life may pullulate shut off for ever from the outer world. Himalaya—the abode of snow. At least forty heights exceed 24,000 feet. This mountain continent makes its own weather conditions."*

The incalculable influence of the Himalayas on India may be imagined from the fact that the Indus and its great tributaries, the Ganges and its major tributaries and the Brahmaputra, the three river systems on which the life of Hindustan depends, take their rise on the Himalayas.

It is the protective wall of the Himalayas that has given to India the continuity of its civilisation and social structure from the earliest times to our own days. The society described in the *Mahabharata* is not essentially different from what holds sway today in India. The life that the Buddha witnessed 2,500 years ago continues over the continent with no fundamental modifications. People argue about the same questions of *karma* and *maya,* believe in the same doctrines and lead the same lives. The rules of marriage, the rituals of burial, and the organisation of social relationship are not basically different. The Buddha born today would recognise the people of India as his own. This continuity of Indian life is the supreme gift of the Himalayan range.

The great Indo-Gangetic plain lies to the south of this range. Washed by the waters of the great rivers, it has always been the core of the Indian continent. The fertilising waters of the Panchanad—the five rivers—and the Jumna and the Ganges led early to the development of agriculture and the consequent growth of populations in this area. Town and village communities grew up along the river valleys and converted this area into a seat of civilisation. Aryavarta has always been the centre of Indian life, and its gradual expansion to cover the whole continent is the central fact of Indian history. It is the true making of India.

The next important feature in the physical configuration of India is the Vindhya range which divides the Deccan, the peninsular India, from Aryavarta. Geographically, the Vindhyas divide India into two, and normally there is no reason why the separation should not have led to two different evolutions. The much lesser ranges of the Cheviots led to the separate development of Scotland; the Pyrenees isolated the Iberian peninsula. Indeed originally the conception of Aryavarta and the Dakshinapatha was that of two different countries. If the Vindhyan range does not now separate, and the unity of India and its culture is undeniable, and if the Hindu view of India is unalterably defined as *Himvat-*

* M'Cintre: *Attack on Everest,* p. 10.

Setu Paryantam—from the Himalayas to Rameshwaram—it is due to Agastya, the great saint and missionary, who was the pioneer of the movement towards the south. In Hindu legend Agastya is spoken of as having humbled the pride of the Vindhya Mountains and obtained for all who followed him the right of way. To this day he is patron saint of the South.

Peninsular India, though thus finally incorporated in the conception of Bharata Varsha, has its own separate characteristics. Essentially, it is maritime in its outlook. The ocean, while it separates, also provides the highways of commerce and contact. From the earliest days, the ports of the South, from Bhrigu Kacha to Cranganore on the west coast, were in close commercial contact with the civilisation of the Middle East. The ports of the eastern coast maintained from times immemorial contacts with the nations of the East.

It is necessary, therefore, to emphasise that India as a concept comes into existence only with the development of Hindu civilisation. This does not, however, mean that India had no history before this. What it does mean is that the unity of India is a conscious achievement of Hinduism *after the great Aryo-Dravidian synthesis had taken place*. Before that time civilised communities existed in India in different and perhaps in isolated areas; the people who created the Indus Valley Civilisation, the Aryans in Panchanad and later in the Gangetic Valley, and the communities in the South. The creation of one civilisation and social structure out of the varied elements of India's population and its establishment over the whole of the land was the supreme achievement of the early Hindus.

The evidence now available of pre-historic man in India shows that the use not only of implements of stone, but of iron, copper and other metals was widely prevalent. The Deccan megaliths contain many objects of iron. Bronze and gold objects have also come to light, showing a great advance in material civilisation. But pre-history, much light as it may shed on the origins of civilisation, can provide us with but little on which the story of a people can be based. All that we can say is that for ages before Indian history comes to light, human effort was being directed in different parts of India towards a better life, and a more settled society.

The first direct evidence we have of civilisation as we know it today came from the excavations in the Indus Valley. The date of this civilisation has been provisionally fixed at 3000-2500 B.C. It is undoubtedly pre-Aryan, as the culture it discloses is essentially urban while that of the Vedic Aryans is pastoral. A very high stage of civilisation had been reached by the people of the Indus Valley as is evidenced by the excellence of the materials used in the construction of houses, the commodious nature of residences, the planning of cities, great hydropathic establishments and the beautiful personal ornaments discovered at Mohenjo-Daro. The humped bull, the buffalo, the sheep, the elephant, and the camel had been domesticated. Gold, silver, lead, copper, tin and alloys were in common use. For ornaments many kinds of precious stones were in use.

This civilisation, it is clear from the recent excavations at Rupar and in Bikaner, extended far into the interior and may have had its centre in the valley of the Saraswati, the river which disappeared in historic times in the sands of Rajasthan. The people who developed this civilisation used both cotton and wool. The cotton industry seems to have flourished from the earliest days in India. Arts and crafts also flourished greatly as the numerous specimens of pottery, seals, beads and bracelets clearly prove. In fact, the Mohenjo-Daro excavations show a state of social and economic life which could only have been the result of many centuries of development.

Many problems relating to this civilisation remain unsolved. The script on its seals has not yet been deciphered. The area and extent of this culture has not yet been determined. Was it confined to North India or did it extend to other parts? Recent discoveries in the valley of the Narbada would seem to indicate that other equally ancient civilisations existed in different areas. One thing, however, is certain and can no longer be contested—civilisation did not come to India with the Aryans. This doctrine of the Aryan origin of Indian civilisation which finds no support in Indian literature, which does not consider the Dasyus as uncivilised, is the result of the theories of the "Indo-Germanic" scholars who held that everything valuable in the world originated from the Aryans. Not only is Indian civilisation pre-Vedic, but the essential features of the Hindu religion as we know it today were perhaps present in Mohenjo-Daro. "There is enough in the fragments we have recovered," says Sir John Marshall about the religious articles found on the sites, "to demonstrate that . . . this religion of the Indus people was the lineal progenitor of Hinduism." In fact, Siva and Kali, the worship of Linga and other features of popular Hinduism were well-established in India long long before the Aryans came.

How this civilisation was absorbed by the Aryans is not known to us. That it was not destroyed and did not wholly disappear is clear from the survival of the Indus Valley religious ideas in the Hinduism of today. The clearest evidence of this is afforded by the Aryan attitude towards Linga and the God whom it symbolises. In the *Rig Veda* (vii), 21-5, we have this significant statement: "Let those whose deity is the phallus not penetrate our sanctuary." This fear of the phallic worshippers is replaced in the *Yajur Veda* by its recognition in the official ritual, the Linga finding its place even in the Aswamedha. Siva also gains increased importance in the later *Vedas,* and from the period of the *Yajur Veda* Siva definitely assumes the aspect of Maheswara—or the Great God. Perhaps the script which the Indo-Aryans evolved was also based on the script of the Indus Valley. Obviously, the pastoral Aryans who slowly conquered the indigenous population assimilated their civilisation and Hinduism, as we know it, was the outcome of this assimilation. The doctrine of the Aryan origin of Hindu civilisation has clearly to be greatly modified.

The Aryan migration into India was a gradual overflow from Iran, as is clear from the similarity between Zend Avesta and Sanskrit and the identity of many Avestan and Vedic gods. Indra, Vayu and Mitra are common to both. As the movement of the Vedic peoples was towards the Punjab, there can be no doubt that, wherever the original home of the Vedic Aryans was, their migration into India was from Persia.

These Aryans were a vigorous nomadic people. They entered India not as invaders but as peaceful emigrants, with their flocks of cattle, their household goods and gods. Soon, however, they seem to have come into conflict with peoples living in fortified areas (puras and durgas) under their own kings and chiefs. The *Rig Veda* itself speaks of hundred pillared forts of the enemies that the Aryans had to contend with. Many of the hymns of the *Vedas* are addressed to the gods for assistance in fighting the enemies and it is significant that the high god of the *Vedas,* Indra, is described as Purandara, the shaker of cities. There is also an interesting statement about an attack on a hundred towns of an aboriginal king.

The original idea that the people of these fortified towns could not have been the people of the Indus Valley civilisation because no fighting implements or fortifications were seen in Mohenjo-Daro or at Harappa, has now been disproved by the recent excavation of fortified places in the same strata as the Indus Valley civilisation. The people who created that civilisation were no doubt urban and commercial: but they were not pacific or unaccustomed to warfare. The puras (towns) and durgas (forts) which the Vedic gods were asked to help in destroying were the outposts and fortifications of the Indus Valley people.

It is obvious from the evidence available in the *Vedas* that the civilisation that existed in pre-Aryan India, which had no doubt reached a state of decadence, was overwhelmed by the continuous onslaught of the newcomers, who were more vigorous and, perhaps, better equipped. The organisation of the pre-Aryan peoples went down before the Aryans, another example of the recurring fact in history that decaying civilisations, whatever their material advancement, cannot stand up to barbarian invasions. China and the Khalifate before the Mongol hordes, and Byzantium before the Turks are parallels to what happened in India also.

What kind of people were the Aryans? That they were fair-skinned they themselves declare. For the "dark-skinned," they had only contempt. Believers in magic and sacrifice, they claimed to be the favoured of the gods. It is possible to trace the seeds of philosophical speculation in the *Vedas* but the theory which derives the metaphysical thought of the Hindus from the hymns of the *Vedas* is unhistoric and arose from the doctrine that *sruti* (*Vedas*) alone being revealed, all orthodox systems of thought must trace their origin to the *Vedas.* Though in ritualistic life the *Vedas* were supreme, systematic religious thought is embedded only in the later literature connected with the *Vedas,* by which time the Vedic gods were themselves 'dead' and nearly forgotten.

Vedic Aryans (of the *Rig Veda* time) were confined to the Punjab. The Jumna and the Ganges are mentioned but the geographical expansion of the Aryans did not extend further east. Since there was no continuous migration of the Aryans, the theory cannot be maintained that the rest of the country came gradually to be peopled by the Aryans. The expansion from the Punjab was that of a civilisation which had been evolved and which came to be known as Aryan but was predominantly that of the conquered people.

The clearest evidence of this fact is the gradual disappearance of the Aryan gods in the post-Vedic civilisation. Varuna, to whom so many prayers had been addressed, disappears altogether from the pantheon and becomes a mere dikpala. The only temple dedicated to him is in the island of Bali. Vayu is also reduced to the same position, while the great god Indra, the lord of the thunderbolt, the mighty destroyer of cities and the chief eater of sacrificial offerings, is merely a super-king of the lower heavens where he holds luxurious court and is pictured as a debonair debauchee. He is, moreover, made a constant petitioner for protection to the new gods, Siva and Vishnu. The Vedic gods died soon after the Aryans conquered the Dasyus and were reborn as minor figures in a wonderfully elaborate mythology.

Nothing demonstrates so clearly the gulf between the pastoral Aryan people and the Hindu civilisation that emerged from the synthesis of the Aryan and pre-Aryan people as the 'death' of the Vedic gods. The same sacrifices were performed but to gods who had ceased to be potent; the same mantras were repeated but to gods who were no longer worshipped. Even today, the same rituals are followed: the same Gayatri is chanted. Sacrifices are performed to Indra even now for rain; but neither Agni (fire) nor Mitra (sun), nor even Indra is recognised as having divine powers.

This transformation came early enough. The rishis of the *Upanishads* were not concerned with Vedic gods. In the later Vedic literature allusions to the mother goddess also occur, evidencing the influence of the indigenous religion. Many of the rishis are alluded to by their mother's names. As the Aryan society was patriarchal, this method of identification may perhaps indicate the influence of a matriarchal system. In fact, the system which had been evolved through the contact between Aryans and the indigenous inhabitants was a synthesis in which, while the forms of the conquerors predominated, the thought and tradition of the conquered found new expression.

With a settled society the political life of the Aryans also developed. Against the Dasyus, the Aryans had fought under their chiefs. When territorial authority developed, the chiefs in turn became kings. When the Aryan settlement expanded to the Indo-Gangetic plain, a new monarchy—that of the Bharatas—came into existence. As the kingdom of the Bharatas contained a much larger percentage of indigenous people, the new monarchy was organised on a different basis and had little in common with the chiefships of the Aryan settlements of the Punjab. A struggle for supremacy between the two political systems are unavoidable. Thus was fought the great Battle of the Ten Kings, described in the *Rig Veda,* the first recorded event of importance in Indian history. The Bharata king, Sudas, met in battle the ten allied kings of the earlier Aryan settlements. It is important to note that the Battle of the Ten Kings was not a battle solely of Aryan peoples. Non-Aryans under their own kings were ranged on both sides.

The results of Sudas's victory in this great battle, which justly became a central theme of later Vedic literature, were far-reaching. In the first place, Sudas by this achievement became the paramount king, a conception which was destined to have a permanent hold on the mind of India. The idea of the victorious king becoming an overlord and exercising paramountcy over subordinate kings rather than annexing the states to form a bigger kingdom became one of the permanent features of the Hindu political system. Rulers who annexed the enemy's kingdoms were considered to have gone against Dharma. The normal process was for the ruler who was defeated to pay tribute and accept the paramountcy of the overlord. The dig-vijayas of later times which left the local rulers undisturbed was the logical outcome of the theory of the paramount king—the Samrat.

The Battle of the Ten Kings also witnessed the end of the "pure Aryan." The earlier settlements in the Punjab were at least predominantly Aryan. But the new kingdom of Sudas to the east of the Jumna was naturally a composite state where the Aryan population, though dominant in influence, was numerically small. The victory of Sudas was the victory of a combination of Aryans and the indigenous people. The Yakshus and other tribes who were led into battle on the side of Sudas by their own king, Bheda, were non-Aryans. This victory established, therefore, the political assimilation of Aryans and non-Aryans in the new colonies of the Gangetic plains.

In the *Rig Veda* one can see the gradual transformation of the Aryans from a pastoral to an agricultural state of society. The economic life of the people was originally centred round their cattle. Wealth was counted in herds. With their settlement in the Indian plains, watered by the great rivers, the emphasis shifts to agriculture. Krishi or cultivation of land is emphasised in the *Rig Veda* and there are allusions to ploughing by teams of six, sowing, reaping and threshing. Well irrigation was also known.

An agricultural society necessitates occupations of different kinds, e.g. metal workers for the making of ploughs and other implements, tanners, carpenters, etc. Vedic literature alludes to carpenters, blacksmiths, tanners, goldsmiths and other craftsmen. Weaving of course was generally practised. Money economy does not seem to have been generally known, but the mention of the vanik or the merchant shows that the bania was known even in Vedic times. Prices were calculated in head of cattle. Dicing was a popular amusement, so was chariot racing. Dancing and music were cultivated from the early days—in fact, music in its more elaborate forms is said to have its origin in the *Sama Veda*.

With the transformation into an agricultural society the village comes again into prominence. Whether the self-contained village is an Aryan system or is merely a continuation of the organisation of the earlier peoples, it is difficult to say. Obviously, cities like Mohenjo-Daro could only have flourished on an elaborate system of agriculture and a rural economy based on villages. It is more reasonable to assume that when the Aryans became an agricultural people they took over the village organisation as they found it in existence.

Indigenous to India or introduced by the Aryans, the village has remained the unchanging backbone of Indian life. From one end of India to the other, the system prevails with but little local variation. It is the one foundation on which every empire in India has been reared. Even the British used it as the unit of their revenue system.

These and other aspects of Vedic civilisation were perhaps not new. The emphasis that the earlier writers placed on the civilising mission of the Aryans is naturally reduced greatly by the discovery of a much superior earlier civilisation. It is not possible now to look upon the Aryans as the harbingers of cultural life in India; but their contribution is none the less of fundamental importance.

The Aryans introduced into India the ideas of racialism and colour. Their sense of being fair-complexioned in comparison to the indigenous people, who were dark-skinned, dominated their whole thought. To this was added their conviction that God had revealed Himself to them through the *Vedas* and that the power which enabled them to conquer the Dasyus was derived from their mystical rites and magical practices which had to be kept inviolably secret The sense of colour (varna) together with the sharing of sacred knowledge led to the perpetuation of distinctions between Aryans and non-Aryans, between the twice-born and the once-born. The dvijas or the twice-born were people who, after certain mystical rituals, were entitled to receive sacred knowledge, and share in the mysteries of Aryan worship. This was the beginning of caste, the theory of which, as chaturvarnya, came to be elaborated by the *Dharma Sastra* writers at a later stage.

It is, however, necessary to emphasise that this colour distinction, this theoretical relegation of the dark-skinned to an inferior position, was never wholly effective. There is ample evidence of the mixing of races and the acceptance by the Aryans of the dark-skinned even among their rishis or sages. Badarayana Veda

Vyasa, who edited the *Vedas* and arranged them, was himself the dark-skinned son of a fisherwoman, the illegitimate progeny of an Aryan saint, and was known as Badarayana the Black. The doctrinal declaration that the non-dvijas are inferior in no way affected the position of indigenous rulers whose support Sudas, for example, had to invite. The marriage of kings and even priests with the local population is frequently alluded to.

Besides, there is ample evidence to establish the fact that before the caste system took shape much intermixture of blood had already taken place. Though racialism remained in the doctrine of the Aryans, the initiation into the secrets and mysteries of Vedic mantras became the test of the dvija and the non-dvija and the conception of Aryanhood became in course of time one of status and culture, rather than varna or colour.

The early Vedic period cannot be clearly defined in time. As Winternitz says, "Centuries must have elapsed between the composition of the earliest hymns and the completion of the *Samhita* of the *Rig Veda*." As a literary document of the Indo-Aryan people, it is of unique significance. The gradual evolution of ideas is also a matter of great interest to the thought of India. What is perhaps more important from the point of view of the development of Indian people is the extraordinary steps taken to preserve the text in such a way that a unique degree of verbal authenticity has been maintained up to this time in the form, the utterance and the mantras of this sacred text.

The pre-eminence that was conceded to the *Rig Veda* has had also another effect. It clothed all later thought in an Aryan and Vedic form. Even the Saktas have been at pains to claim a Vedic origin for their religion. Apart from Buddhism and Jainism, which are frankly non-Vedic, all systematised thought tried by a fictitious genealogy to trace its descent to the interpretation of some obscure Vedic mantra. It gave to the thought forms of India, even so late as the nineteenth century (e.g., the Arya Samaj), a Vedic framework and thereby kept up the fiction of an Aryan India.

CHAPTER II

THE CONQUEST OF INDIA

THE organisation of Hinduism is the main achievement of the later Vedic period. The geography of Aryan colonisation extended gradually to the whole of the Indo-Gangetic Valley and new kingdoms—Kuru-Panchalas (Delhi-Meerut area), Kosala (Oudh), Kasi (Banaras) and Videha (North Bihar)—began to appear. Side by side with this geographical and political expansion, the later Vedic literature witnesses the development of higher metaphysical and religious thought. The later *Vedas,* the *Brahmanas,* the *Aranyakas* and the *Upanishads* constitute a body of literature which is supremely important for the organisation of Hindus as a society. The *Brahmanas* are the books which explain the sacrificial ritual. They are in vogue all over India even today, for the ritualism of the *Vedas* has remained unimpaired while the Vedas themselves have become important only for recitation. The *Brahmanas* also contain a great deal of secular ritual, for example, the *Aitareya Brahmana* lays down the royal coronation ceremonies which are gone through not only by kings in India but even in Siam.

From the *Brahmanas* the transition to the *Upanishads* is clearly marked. In the *Upanishads* we have Hindu metaphysical thought in its developed form. Hinduism—as apart from the religion of the Vedic Aryans—has come into existence, not as vague yearnings towards a higher realisation but as a systematised body of dogma and doctrine. While some of the *Upanishads* are of a later date, it is obvious that the main body of Upanishadic doctrine about the Atman, about the Absolute (Brahman), about the relationship of God and man, the theory of direct realisation and the conception of *Dharma* were evolved and stated with clarity in the later Vedic period. It is these doctrines, interpreted anew in each period, that have dominated Hindu thought till today. Equally, the doctrines of karma, maya, mukti, transmigration and other special features of Hindu thought which continue to mould the life of every Hindu are found fully elaborated in the *Upanishads.*

It is, however, not only the doctrinal basis of Hinduism that we find established in later Vedic times. The social basis of life is firmly and solidly laid. The *Vedangas,* of which the most important is the *Kalpa,* contain the *Srauta, Grihya* and *Dharma Sutras.* Of these, the most fundamental to the unity of Hindu society are the *Grihya Sutras* which determine the secular life of the Hindu householder. The *Grihya Sutras* prescribe in the minutest detail the duty of man from birth to burial, laying down the ceremonies for each occasion. Pre-natal ceremonies, ceremonies at birth, on such occasions as naming, initiation, education, marriage—are all prescribed with meticulous care. It is this body of domestic ritual which makes a Hindu. The dogmas of Hinduism can be adopted by others. Karma and transmigration find acceptance among an increasing number of followers of other religions in modern times. Hindu law can apply to others. There are indeed sects of other religions who are subject to Hindu law. The acceptance of domestic ritual alone makes one a Hindu.

The Hindu community was created by the *Grihya Sutras*—or the discipline of domestic ritual. It exists today wherever Hinduism exists. In Indian history, the most important fact, therefore, is the formulation of the discipline of the household—the *Grihya Sutras*—for it transformed the peoples of India who came under the influence of Hinduism into a single civilisation.

The *Srauta* and *Dharma Sutras,* though less fundamental from the point of view of historical development, are also of great importance. The *Dharma Sutras* deal with social customs and usages. They are the work of different ages but are valuable as showing the tendency to organise society on a conscious basis. A common civil and criminal law, no doubt reactionary from our present point of view, a code of social behaviour and relationship, theories of property, etc., came into being.

Perhaps more important than all this is the social doctrine of Varnashrama Dharma. This is a concept which, holding to the division of society into castes, prescribes the suitable activities of different stages of life. Life is divided into four periods. brahmacharya, the period of celibate education, grihastha, the period of domestic life, vanaprastha, retirement, and tapasya, ascetic search for divine life. This is an over-all concept, the ideal which the Hindu householder should follow. Is is doubtful whether it was ever generally practised, but all the same as an ideal it has maintained its hold on Hindu society until the present time.

The development of chaturvarnya, or the doctrine of four colours, known to us as caste, also belongs to this period and can be related to the conscious organisation of Hindu society. The original division, as stated before, was between dvijas and non-dvijas, the twice-born and the once-born, i.e. those entitled to initiation and the sacred thread and those not so entitled. In the later Vedic period, the doctrine of the four castes, the Brahmin, whose duty is to learn and guide; the Kshatriya, the warrior, the protector; the Vaisya, engaged in economic pursuits; and the Sudra, the common man, the tiller and the cultivator, comes into being. This is what may be called the Neo-Aryan society, for outside its pale were the Avarnas or the Panchamas (the non-coloured or the fifth), a large mass of people who were denied social rights and were held as unclean.

In practice, the four castes were not so clearly defined as they were in theory. The admission of non-Aryans into the Aryan fold finds clear Vedic sanction. The *Vratya Stoma* in the *Sama Veda* lays down even the process of such admission, and we have also instances of such admission in many of the tribes which came to be known as Vratya Kshatriyas. Of changes in caste also we have instances. Besides, we have the recognised cases of Janaka and Vishwamitra, both Kshatriya kings, one of whom became a royal teacher at whose feet even Brahmins sat, and the other a rishi, a composer of Vedic hymns, who set all caste restrictions at nought, performed yagas for outcastes and generally denied the supremacy of the priesthood. Marriages between people of different castes are alluded to in many places. In fact, the growth of the Neo-Aryan society was preceded both by a considerable intermingling of castes and a wide acceptance of non-Aryan people into the Aryan fold.

Another marked tendency in the later Vedic period is the rivalry between the Brahmins and the Kshatriyas. Pargiter, in his *Indian Historical Tradition* has brought together a volume of evidence which seeks to prove that the claim of Brahmin superiority was for long resisted by the warrior classes—many of whom were non-Aryan—and the later-day idea of unquestioned Brahmin superiority in caste is the outcome of a large-scale re-writing of books and the use of the systems of education for this purpose. Dr. Sukhtankar, the learned editor of the *Mahabharata*, in a masterly analysis of the Bhargava tradition in the epic, traces this process of the conversion of a Kshatriya tradition—the war in which the kings of India are arrayed on two sides—into a book for glorifying a Brahmin tribe. As the epic became the fifth Veda and the general encyclopaedia of knowledge for the people, the effect of this transformation on the popular mind became permanent. But essentially, all through the earlier Indian literature, the conflict of the Kshatriyas and the Brahmins for primacy in the Aryan society can be noticed.

The secure establishment of the caste-society with its doctrine of varna was only possible by accepting into the fold of caste local tribes and assigning to them suitable positions in the hierarchy. We see this process even in historical times. When the caste system was taken by the Hindus across the sea into Indonesia, Champa, Annam and other countries, the territorial magnates of those countries, who accepted Hinduism soon assumed caste names like Varman and were accepted as Kshatriyas. The four castes exist today in Bali. The same system was undoubtedly followed in the South also, as the existence of matrilineal Kshatriyas in Malabar clearly proves.

Another important factor which may also be noticed with regard to the expansion of the caste system is the maintenance of the identity of racial elements powerful enough to resist assimilation and organised enough socially to maintain their separateness. Many racial groups of high social position, e.g. the Reddys in Andhra country, the Nayars in Kerala, the Maravas in Tamil land, and the Marathas, while they accepted Hinduism, could not be effectively assimilated into the four castes. Their social position was too powerful to relegate them to the position of Sudras. They were, however, non-dvijas, who accepted vaguely the superiority of the Brahmins but of no other caste. The theoretical basis of caste was at all times unreal over large areas and over many peoples.

The political evolution of the Hindu community at this period though shrouded in the obscurity of legends can be seen in outline from the literature of the time. Powerful monarchies take the place of the tribal chiefs and kings. Theories of political power are discussed in the *Dharma Sutras.* Danda or enforcement of obedience, and Dharma as law or justice are conceptions explained in the later Vedic texts. A proper ceremony of coronation which emphasised the duties of the king is prescribed. The king is told: "To thee the State is given for agriculture, for commonweal, for prosperity and for progress." While the organisation of the great bureaucratic state is the outcome of later times, the later Vedic kingdoms show a system of government and organisation which was perhaps more 'democratic' in the sense that the authority of the leaders of Aryan tribes was still recognised by the king. The Purohita or the royal chaplain is a person of great political importance; so is the Suta. The dignitaries of the court develop gradually into officials who not only advise the king but also help him in the administration of the state.

The fairly long period covered by the later Vedic literature was marked by a considerable growth of civilisation. Learning became both religious and secular. Apart from the *Vedas* and the subsidiary texts, and the *Upanishads*, grammar and logic and law were included in the courses of study.

With the growth of political life, the range of occupations also grew. The craftsmen (shilpins) of all kinds occupied a high place in society. Architects, navigators, carpenters, bricklayers, dyers and followers of numerous other professions are mentioned and described in the literature of the time. The growth of trade involved the maintenance of highways, and there are allusions to guilds of merchants.

Generally speaking, society during the early days when Hinduism grew out of Vedic religion showed marked advance in every direction. The difference can best be seen by comparing society described in two different ages.

When the story of the *Ramayana* opens, the picture of India as we see it is that of a Hindu civilisation limited to the Gangetic Valley. Once Rama leaves 'the pale' he is in a land of unexplored forests with the Aryan hermits maintaining a precarious existence here and there. Till he reaches Kishkindha—the present area of Bellary—there is no evidence of an organised social life anywhere. Mighty forests extend from immediately south of the Ganges, across the Vindhyas to the Deccan. There are no allusions to kings or countries, though we know that the Narbada valley was the seat of another civilisation at the time, mainly maritime in its interests.

The *Ramayana* is essentially a story of high adventure in unexplored areas. When, however, the story of the *Mahabharata* opens, the whole picture is different. India has become one. The kingdoms of the south are as familiar as the kingdoms of the east and the west. The rulers of southern countries are described as taking part in the historic battle. The home of Krishna, the central figure of the *Mahabharata*, is far away in Dwaraka on the coast of Kathiawad. The great pilgrimage centres are all well established and they are distributed all over India. The rivers, the mountains and the general physical features of every part of India are familiar. In the *Ramayana* the Himalayas are hardly alluded to. Tradition identifies Lakshmana's penance with a spot near Hardwar where the Ganges debouches into the plains. On the other hand in the *Mahabharata*, the Himalayas are well known. In the *Mahaprastana* portion there is a description of the country on the northern side of the Himalayas as seen from a mountain top. The Kailasa peak and the Manasarowar lake are known.

In fact, the whole of India had been explored. The conquest of India had taken place.

Similar is the case with society. The social life as pictured in the *Mahabharata* is of India as we know it. It is true that the recension of the epic as we have it is perhaps not earlier than the fourth century A.D., but the story of the *Mahabharata* war is of a very much earlier tradition as Panini (sixth century B.C.) mentions the more important characters. While numerous additions and alterations were no doubt made in the last recension, the setting of the story itself and the main incidents could not have been changed.

The structure of society in the *Mahabharata* is based on caste but the difference between the *Ramayana* and the *Mahabharata* in this matter is most significant. In the *Ramayana,* Rama is bound by his Kshatriya duty to kill a Sudra who performs tapas or asceticism and though with reluctance he performs his duty. The Sudra scholar and ascetic is a conception which the Aryans of the *Ramayana* days found hard to accept. In the *Mahabharata,* how different is the story. It is Vidura, the dasiputra, who is the guide, philosopher and friend of King Dhritarastra. The kings themselves are Kshatriyas only by theory. Both Dhritarastra and Pandu are actually the sons of Veda Vyasa, himself the son of a fisherwoman, and Krishna does not hesitate to say so when challenged in open Durbar. Salya, the uncle of the Pandavas and one of the leaders of the Kuru hosts, is a non-Aryan, and is roundly abused by Karna for all the non-Aryan customs which he follows. Considering that his sister was the mother of two of the Pandava brothers, the allegations made against Salya, the king of the Mādrās, are particularly significant. Other non-Aryan kings like Susarma of Trigartha and Bhagadatta take their place in the hierarchy. The children of Pandavas by aboriginal women play a notable part in the battle.

Brahmin warriors (Drona, Kripa and Aswathama), Brahmins living in the houses of potters, lower caste heroes appearing as claimants for the hands of Kshatriya princesses and numerous other facts in the *Mahabharata* show that the system of the four castes had ceased to have any rigidity. It was no doubt accepted as the ideal doctrine but the facts of life did not fit into the Chaturvarnya—the four-caste system.

From what has been briefly stated above it may be seen that the interval between the Rama story and the Kuru-Pandava battle is the formative period of Indian civilisation. Unfortunately, it is also the great gap in our knowledge. Little is known of the intervening period, except that this great transformation took place and we have the fully evolved Hindu society when the events of the *Mahabharata* are enacted.

The geographical conquest of India is the first factor. How this took place we are in no position to say. The hermitages in the forests to which the *Ramayana* alludes must in due course have become colonies—centres from which Hindu life radiated. Slowly the forests must have been cleared, the rivers navigated, and the land brought under cultivation. The aboriginals were slowly assimilated into the social life, and, where that was resisted, pressed further into their mountain fastnesses.

Some idea of the expanding geographical knowledge may be gathered from books. The Vedic Aryans knew only of the Punjab and the Jumna-Ganges area. The *Dharma Sutras*, however, mention many different countries and local customs and Baudhayana alludes to the mixed character of castes in the Dakshinapatha or the Deccan and in the time of the *Grihya Sutras* the geography of India was perhaps fully known. The assimilation of local tribes into the loose framework of caste and the imposition of Hindu civilisation on them was the process by which the Neo-Aryans established Hindu civilisation in India. This historic process, it may be noted, has by no means come to a stop even now. It is by this method that the Hinduisation of aboriginal tribes goes on even today.

The picture of society that one gets at the close of the period (seventh century B.C.) is one of growing kingdoms, side by side with powerful tribal organisations keeping their independence. The Indo-Gangetic plain—the heat and core of Indian civilisation—contained many such tribes who neither conformed to the theoretical political organisation of the later Vedic books, nor fitted into their social organisation. The Vrishnis, Bhojas and Andhakas for example maintained a non-monarchical form of government from the earliest days. The Lichchavis, the Mallas and other important tribes are also mentioned. Among the castes, the Vaisyas had not yet acquired the importance which the next age was to bring to them. In a predominantly rural civilisation money, credit and trade, which the Vaisyas represented, take but a secondary place. With the monarchies established firmly, towns were becoming more important. The social bonds were firm. The family was the centre of that society and it was governed in the minutest detail by the regulations of the *Grihua Sutras*.

The sixth century B.C. is a highly significant period in Indian history. For the first time we are able to establish with some certainty a chronological order for events. On the basis of both Jain and Buddhist traditions which generally do not accord with each other, we have a very significant synchronism of Bimbisara, king of Magadha; Udayana, king of Kausambi; Prasenajit, king of Kosala; Pradyota, king of Avanti; Buddha and Mahavira. The accepted date for the Buddha is 567-487 B.C. Mahavira was his senior contemporary. The Puranic succession lists also mention these kings, and give their genealogies. We have therefore the political picture of northern India in the first half of the sixth century B.C. Avanti with Ujjain as its capital was ruled by Pradyota or Prachanda Sena, whose son-in-law was Udayana of Kausambi, the hero of Indian legends—of the *Udayana Kathas* alluded to by Kalidasa, and celebrated in dramas by Bhasa, and in stories by Gunadhya, Somadeva and others. Prasenajit, the king of Kosala, a ruler educated at the university of Taxila, is known to us by the magnificent sculptural representation of his visit to Buddha. Magadha, the seat of a great empire from the time of the *Mahabharata*, was under king Bimbisara with whom Buddha had established contact even before he became the Enlightened One, and who later became one of his disciples. The capital of Magadha at the time was Rajagriha. It is especially interesting to note the alliance between the Lichchavis—the great republican tribe—and the Magadha kings even in Bimbisara's time, one of the recurring and central facts of north Indian history, up to over a thousand years later.

It is a society so organised that witnessed the ministry of Gautama and Mahavira. A great religious discontent was clearly abroad at the time. The old sacrificial religion of the Vedas had, as we noticed before, lost its appeal and the Vedic gods had long ceased to satisfy the spiritual needs of the people. The *Upanishads* taught the doctrine of the direct realisation of God but such a teaching, postulating as it did a high evolution of the individual, could neither become the basis of a popular religion nor satisfy the cravings of the ordinary man. The Brahman, the Atman and other conceptions of the *Upanishads* remained highly scholastic and in time led to the development of metaphysical doctrines which profoundly influenced the Indian mind. But the ordinary man could not be made to order his life according to the doctrines of the *Upanishads*.

A significant result of this philosophy of direct realisation was the popularity that asceticism gained among the religiously minded people. The Aryan rishis were Aranyakas, men who lived away from the madding crowd and led a life of study, contemplation and teaching. Tapasya with mortification of the flesh was also practised, but was not considered essential for the acquisition of spiritual knowledge. The Yoga of bodily austerities was a pre-Aryan spiritual discipline. Siva seated in the posture of a yogi, which is one of the great discoveries at Mohenjo-Daro, and the stone image of a saint in yogic contemplation are clear evidences that the doctrines of yoga came from the Indus Valley civilisation. With the decay of Vedic religion and the importance attached to direct realisation through spiritual discipline and contemplation, asceticism became the dominant feature of religious life—a system which, by its separation of the life of society from that of the religious leader, could only lead to greater spiritual bankruptcy.

The bare facts of Buddha's life are now well established. Son of the Sakya chief, Suddhodana, he was born in 567 B.C. The old tradition that he was born in the Lumbini Gardens has been confirmed by the discovery of the commemorative pillar erected by Asoka in 250 B.C. with the inscription, "Here was born Buddha, Sakya Muni." From the early days of his manhood Gautama was deeply moved by the miseries of humanity and soon he decided to renounce the world in order to find a path for the betterment of man. His first search was for a master who would be in a position to explain the contradictions and mysteries of the world to him. He tried many, some of whom had made a speciality of mortifying the flesh for purifying the soul. Others had some special doctrines. The Alaras and Udrakas taught him the way of penances, but finding that this led him nowhere, Gautama took his normal food, thereby scandalising his five associates. Then he began his lone quest for truth. On the full moon day of the month of Vaisakh, Gautama felt suddenly that the truths regarding life and death were revealed to him. The enlightenment he received he decided to give to the world. To his first masters he repaired to give them the glad tidings but they had passed away. Then he thought of the five companions who had deserted him. To them at Saranath, a suburb of Holy Banaras, he pronounced his first sermon on the working of the Wheel of Dharma (dharma chakra pravartana).

Buddha's teachings, explained by him through many sermons and conversations during an active ministry of 40 years, cannot be dealt with here. In essence it was a call to follow the Middle Path based on the realisation of the four truths, i.e., the Truth of Pain—birth, old age, sickness, etc.; the Truth of the Cause of Pain—trishna, craving; the Truth of the Cessation of Pain—by eradicating trishna or craving; and the Truth of the Way to this eradication—the Noble Eightfold Path, the Sadastanga Marga.

The basic doctrine of Buddha's teaching is that it is only by the right life of the Middle Way that trishna which is the cause of all pain can be removed. The rest of the teaching of the Enlightened One flows from this. Till his seventy-ninth year Buddha travelled and preached, taking only a short rest every year during the rainy season. His message, preached in the vernacular of the day, appealed to all classes—kings, merchants, and teachers of other sects flocked to him. It was not a new religion, but a new revelation which a great teacher was preaching. Many others there were at the time who were doing the same. The only difference was that Gautama's message appealed to a very wide audience. His own very compassionate, loving and human personality, his tireles energy, no less than the striking simplicity of his message, contributed to the extraordinary success of the great ministry. Bimbisara of Rajagriha became a disciple. Prasenajit, the Kosala king, came in pilgrimage to meet the Master. Ajatasatru, the son of Bimbisara, though misled for a time by Devadatta, became an ardent follower. The prophet found honour in his own country. The Sakya leaders accepted the new teaching and Gautama's father, wife and son accepted initiation.

The appeal of Buddha's teaching to the middle classes was even more remarkable. Early Buddhist literature records numerous gifts and endowments made by merchants (e.g., Sudatta's grant of Jetavana, Visukha's gift of Purvarama). To the common man this was indeed the new gospel. There were no secret mantras, no expensive yagas or sacrifices and indeed no difficult doctrines as in the *Upanishads.* The simple truths of Buddha's teaching were explained to him in his own language. Everyone—even a chandala, an outcast—could follow the Middle Way and attain nirvana. More than a religious revolution, the Ministry of the Enlightened One was a social revolution. The foundation of monasteries where monks could live together and later of nunneries constitute a very important change. There is no evidence of any such institutions in pre-Buddhist times. They seem to have come into being almost under fortuitous circumstances. Lay followers placed different parks at the disposal of Buddha where his immediate followers were allowed to reside. As they were by their vows homeless, Buddha gradually laid down rules for the monasteries, and the great monastic orders which spread all over the world under the shadow of different religions arose out of them.

The establishment of the order of female ascetics, an even

greater revolution both in the social and religious history of the world, was but reluctantly permitted by the Buddha. In the fifth year of Buddha's ministry, the widowed queen of Suddhodana asked to be allowed to leave the world under the doctrine of the Tathagata. Buddha refused the request three times but the lady cut off her hair, put on mendicant clothes and followed the train. Finding the queen and the other women who were with her weeping at one of the halts, Ananda the disciple took pity on them and made the request to the Master. This was also refused three times. Then Ananda asked him the straight question: "Is a woman who has gone forth from a house to a houseless life in the doctrine and discipline declared by the Tathagata capable of realising the spiritual truth?" "She is capable," Buddha answered. Ananda pressed home the advantage and Buddha agreed to the ordination of women.

The eight strict rules which the Master laid down show that the decision was taken only after the most careful consideration. Among the conditions of ordination are: (1) a nun shall not spend her retreat in places where there are no monks; (2) twice a month the nun shall under the direction of the order of monks receive admonition; (3) the punishment for offences in serious cases should be by the assemblies of monks and nuns.

The great impression that the Master made during his lifetime may be imagined from the events that followed his Mahaparinirvana. The Enlightened One passed away at Kusinara in the country of the Mallas—a republican people—at the age of 80. His last words were: "Subject to decay are compound things: strive with earnestness." When the news of the Lord's passing away spread, all the people among whom he had wandered and preached sent their representatives and claimed a share of the relics. Ajatasatru put in a claim, the proud Lichchavis, the Sakyas among whom the Lord was born and all others. The Mallas stoutly refused but yielded to the persuasion of a Brahmin and divided the relics into eight parts. The relics of Buddha over which stupas were built by Asoka and Kaniska are said to be from among those which were distributed in this manner.

Mahavira, the last Tirthankara or prophet of the Jains, also lived practically at the same time. The Jain tradition goes back to a much earlier period and Jainism as a sect seems to have existed for many centuries before Mahavira, as the Niganthas are alluded to as a well-established order at the time of Buddha. The twenty-third Tirthankara Parsva seems to have been a historical personage. It was, however, Vardhamana Mahavira who made

Jainism a separate religion. Born of a Kshatriya family and related on his mother's side to the Lichchavis, he took to asceticism and led the life of a wandering teacher for thirty years. The Jain religion which he revived found its followers mainly among the richer mercantile classes and even today it is mainly among the Vaisyas of Gujerat and Rajputana that Jainism has its largest following.

Two features of both the Buddhist and Jain movements may be alluded to here. Buddha especially laid down the procedure of assemblies for his monastic orders. "I take refuge in the Church —Sangha" is one of the prayers of every Buddhist. In his own lifetime the Master laid down the rules of the Sangha and the procedure to be followed. The democratic character which the Master emphasised comes out in every one of the rules. The seating order of every assembly was to be arranged beforehand by a specially nominated senior monk. No assembly was valid unless at least ten monks were present, though in border countries the quorum could in exceptional circumstances be reduced to five. Novices and women were not entitled to vote or to constitute the quorum. The acts of an invalidly constituted Sangha could not be made valid by the assent of absentee members. Questions to be decided at the Sangha had to be formerly presented. Voting, recording of decisions and the other normal procedure of government by discussion were laid down and had to be strictly followed.

In elaborating this extremely democratic procedure Buddha no doubt had the example of the republican tribes of Vajjis, Lichchavis and even Sakyas before him. These communities were no doubt oligarchical and not democratic; all the same, since all public affairs had to be decided by discussion, though limited to the noble families, the procedure of assembly and debate had been developed early among them.

The Buddhist Sanghas were essentially democratic, as the monks were ordained from among all classes of people. More, the movement itself was democratic and the lay community consisted of recruits from all castes. Buddha accepted the hospitality of all—prostitute, low castes, kings and Brahmins. The honoured teacher of Ajatasatru refused an invitation from the proud Lichchavis in order to accept a dinner at the house of a fallen woman. The social upheaval which followed Buddha's teaching in the countries which were traditionally the home of orthodoxy could well be imagined.

Neither the Buddhist nor the Jain teaching claimed to break

away from the Aryan tradition. The popular mythology is not discarded; Brahma, Sakra (Indra) and other gods figure in both Buddhist and Jain stories. The doctrines are presented merely as new ways of attaining the goal of liberation. The social revolution of the teaching was a corollary and not an object which the Masters had in mind. In the result, Brahmin opposition was slow in gathering strength. When Buddha began to preach, orthodoxy could not have foreseen that the doctrine so peacefully preached would grow into a mighty challenge. There were so many heretical sects in existence under teachers, all of whom claimed to know and teach a special way, that the upholders of orthodoxy did not think that danger could come to them from the teachings of one who only preached a way of life. By the time they awoke to a realisation of the dangers of the new party, Buddha had already found the support of powerul kings like Prasenajit and Bimbisara.

The existence of innumerable heretical sects during this period is a factor of great importance. Buddhist and Jain literature speak of numerous ascetic orders teaching variations of doctrines and practice. The Ajivikas were said to be Sudra Sanyasis whose leader was Makkhali Gosala. Born a slave himself, Makkhali was a radical teacher who denied even the basic doctrine of all Hindu thought—the theory of Karma. Another radical sect was that of Ajita Kesakambala who taught that everything ended with death, a precursor of the Sunyavadins Purana Kassapo was a Brahmin teacher whose main doctrine was that action was neither of merit nor of demerit. He was a very popular teacher. Numerous others are mentioned by name. We know very little of their teachings beyond what is given in the literature of their opponents. What is important, however, is that at the time of the ministry of Buddha the number of heretical sects was very large. No less significant is the large number of wandering teachers mentioned as teaching their own doctrines without, however, forming any definite sect. The Hinduism of that time seems to have taken this as a normal growth, even as it does today.

Apart from spiritual discontent which is evidenced by this fact, society seems to have been prosperous and contented. The mercantile classes had become powerful. Both Buddhist and Jain literatures talk of great merchant princes allied to persons of similar wealth and rank in other towns, of commerce on a large scale, of guild masters, of middle classes owning gardens and rest houses, of luxurious mansions and comfortable houses.

Ajatasatru who was a disciple of Buddha was also the founder of Pataliputra, which was to remain the chief city of India for a thousand years. Rajagriha was the old capital of Magadha under Bimbisara, but Ajatasatru, anxious to reduce the power of the Lichchavis, decided to erect a fort on the Ganges from which he could control these turbulent people. The city so founded was built according to a plan and was the wonder of its age. Magadha power continued for another 150 years under the same dynasty, which was replaced by the famous family of Nandas. From the Hathigumpha inscription of Kharavela, we know that the Nandas exercised power over Kalinga also. The last of the Nandas, Mahapadma, was undoubtedly a powerful ruler who exercised sway over the whole of north India. The Nanda kings were so prosperous that the tradition penetrated even to South India and is alluded to in a Tamil poem. In fact, the Nandas seem to have developed a taste for luxury and glory which added to the primacy of the Magadhan kingdom. It was in the time of Mahapadma Nanda that Alexander invaded the Punjab.

CHAPTER III

THE PERIOD OF EMPIRES

THE second half of the fourth century B.C. is one of the most important periods in world history. The breakdown of the city states of Greece before the rising power of Macedon, and the final eclipse of Greece following the break-up of Alexander's empire, the collapse of Persian power in the Middle East, the transformation of the city republic of Rome into a great territorial power, and the organisation of an empire state in India—these great events of far-reaching importance are all crowded into a short period of fifty years. It can well be argued that the whole history of Europe, the Middle East and India was shaped for the future during this half-century, during which period the Mediterranean became organised under one power, the Seleucides established their authority in Central Asia, and the imperial tradition, never again to be forgotten, was established in India.

Alexander's conquest of the empire of Persia in 330 B.C. brought him to the frontier of India. The Punjab had for a time been the satrapy of the Persian kings and it is well to emphasise here that it is not India that the Macedonian invaded but the province included in the Persian Empire. Alexander's so-called wars on Indian soil were not against any organised state but against local chiefs who had acknowledged the authority of the Persian monarch. These he conquered with ease and marched up to the Beas, where the Persian territory ended. From there he ordered his retreat. In the area of the Punjab that Alexander conquered he created three satrapies and placed them under Indian rulers.

The confusion following the death of Alexander gave the opportunity he was seeking to young Chandra Gupta, according to Hindu traditions an illegitimate scion of the Nanda dynasty, then leading the life of an exile in the Punjab. After expelling the Greek garrisons left behind by Alexander, Chandra Gupta, aided and advised by his guru and counsellor Chanakya, attacked and defeated the Nanda king and became the monarch of Magadha.

Thus Chandra Gupta succeeded at an early age to an organised, powerful and rich empire which, through many centuries and under a succession of able kings, had not only developed a tradition of efficient government, but had claimed and occasionally exercised authority over the entire Indo-Gangetic Valley. Under the guidance of Chanakya, Chandra Gupta followed, as we know from the tradition embodied in the play *Mudra-rakshasa*, a courageous policy of conciliation. The whole story of the play is based on the steps the great counsellor took to reconcile the unbending minister of the last Nanda and to force him to accept service under Chandra Gupta. Then alone, Chanakya claimed, were the Nandas finally overcome and the empire of the Mauryas established. This wise policy enabled Chandra Gupta to consolidate his empire and, within a short time, to have his supremacy accepted over the whole of Hindustan from the Indus to the Brahmaputra and from the Himalayas to the Vindhyas. For the first time Hindustan was organised under one effective imperial authority.

The results of this consolidation soon became apparent. In 305 B.C., Seleucus who was called by the Greeks the Nikator or the victorious, and who was the most successful among the generals of Alexander, after having established himself firmly in Bactria, crossed the Indus in the hope of repeating the success of his Macedonian master. This time, however, it was not the weak feudatories of an outlying Persian satrapy that he encountered but the armies of a great empire. The Greek phalanx which had won so many wars gained no success in the contest that ensued, and the boastful Greek had to accept a humiliating peace by which, apart from the gift of a daughter, the provinces to the west of the Indus up to Kabul had to be surrendered to the victorious Indian emperor. Seleucus also sent to the Maurya court an ambassador, by name Megasthenes, fragments of whose descriptions of India have fortunately come down to us.

Chandra Gupta's provinces seem to have been governed directly by officers appointed by the central government. We know of such a governor, Pushyagupta, who administered the distant province of Kathiawad, through a great work of irrigation which he carried out there. The Sudarsana lake at Girnar was formed by damming up a river by great walls of masonry and the inscriptions testify to the care with which this great work was undertaken. It is a feat of engineering and is one of the most notable examples of irrigation in ancient India that has come down to us. It is also clear that Chandra Gupta had a fully staffed department of irrigation for major works such as the construction and maintenance of canals and reservoirs undertaken from provincial or imperial revenues, and the minor ones undertaken by village communities. The system of measuring out water for irrigation purposes and charging a rate for it which is still prevalent in India was in operation in Chandra Gupta's time. Kautalya in his *Arthasastra* specifies the rates and the punishment for the neglect of irrigation regulations.

The direct government of the provinces under viceroys which is the basis of the imperial system of India is first alluded to in the Mauryan inscriptions. It might have been inherited from the Nandas but its extension to distant areas and its conversion to a system of government controlled by regulations issued from the centre and supervised by great imperial departments seem to have been the work of Chandra Gupta.

The reign of Chandra Gupta extended to twenty-four years. He died in 301 B.C. leaving to his son Bindusara an empire which in extent, power and glory exceeded that of any king of earlier days. He has remained a hero of legend, poetry and drama.

Of the organisation of the state under Chandra Gupta we have very detailed information. The *Arthasastra* of Kautalya, whether by Chanakya himself or by one of his school, undoubtedly represents the system of administration prevalent under the Mauryan emperor.

The Mauryan state organisation was bureaucratic. Numerous departments regulated and controlled the activities of the state. The more important departments that Kautalya enumerates and discusses are: accounts, revenue, mines, arsenal, customs and taxation, agriculture, trade, navigation, excise and animal husbandry.

The state was conceived as a complex of the activities of its arms—the executive departments—which covered every sphere of the life of the people. The villages were grouped for revenue administration. For purposes of defence, they were grouped separately around a central fortified village. Inter-village communications were carefully organised. The organisation and security of the empire depended on highways and the Mauryan officials devoted special attention to them. The Great Royal Highway, precursor of the Grand Trunk Road, was one of the wonders of the world. Megasthenes, who travelled down to Pataliputra by that road, has left us a description of it. The first stage was from the frontier of the empire to the provincial capital of Taxila. From Taxila, crossing the five rivers of the Punjab, it reached the Jamna and passed via Kanauj to the town of Prayag, then, as in later times, a town of the greatest strategic and political importance. From Prayag it went to Pataliputra and thence to the mouth of the Ganges. This central road was under an imperial department which was responsible for its upkeep, for the maintenance of the necessary ferries and for the erection of milestones. Planting of trees on roadsides had always been considered an act of great religious merit. The *Arthasastra* mentions different kinds of roads and the obligations of the state and the people to maintain them.

Maritime navigation and river traffic were the special concern of the department of admiralty. The board of shipping was one of the great departments of state. At the head of it was the minister who dealt with all matters relating to shipping, including navigation of the seas. Under him there was a staff of commissioners, harbour masters, etc., whose duty it was to look after ships in distress.

The revenue system of the Mauryas was based on a land tax, income from the working of mines and minerals, tax on trade, salt monopoly, customs and excise. The cultivator paid one-sixth of his produce, the merchant one-fourth of his profits. Licensing of gambling houses and liquor shops brought large revenues and the monopoly on salt must have yielded a large income. The extraordinary character of the taxation system of the Maurya Empire is that, fundamentally, it is not different from what exists in India today. It is Chanakya's revenue system that came down to the British and was perfected by them. The descriptions in the *Arthasastra* are in no way of a system that has vanished but of one which is recognisably the same as the system under which modern India lives.

The Mauryan Empire was a police-state. The power of the state was built upon a system of espionage. The use of spies was known in the time of the *Vedas*. A passage in the *Rig Veda* says:

> Send thy spies forward, fleetest in their motion.
> Be never deceived.
> From him who near or far is bent on evil (gather information).

In the *Ramayana*, it is on the report of a spy that the public are abusing Sita for her conduct that Ramachandra decides to put her away. In fact, in India spies were always looked upon as the eyes and ears of the king. The pre-Mauryan kingdoms had their spies but the organisation of espionage as one of the great activities for the safety and security of the state seems to have been perfected by Chanakya. There are five different classes of spies enumerated in the *Arthasastra*—idlers who give the impression that they are not serious; astrologer, palmists and others in whom people confide; ascetics who have access to all classes; those directly concerned with the two main professions of agriculture and trade. These five may be classed as informers as they were not in departmental service. Nurses, cooks, prostitutes and mendicant women were regularly trained and employed by the state. Also the police had at their disposal *agents provocateurs,* toughs and poisoners. Chanakya even gives illustrations as to how the spies should set about their work.

The police-state which the *Arthasastra* depicts was awe-inspiring to the individual. But its limitations were clear. The normal life of the people, though watched and reported upon, was not interfered with. The object of espionage as laid down in early books was to keep the king informed of public opinion by direct reports of people moving freely among all classes and, secondly, to ensure security. By a system of quick communication, developments in the farthest provinces were communicated to headquarters. The provision for toughs, poisoners and others clearly shows that the Mauryan state had no compunction in dealing with its enemies in an unorthodox manner.

The system that Chanakya perfected or inherited, or in any case, described, endured without much change through ages. The Hindu kings, to the last, followed the organisation of the Mauryan Empire in its three essential aspects, the revenue system, the bureaucracy and the police. The organisation, as it existed, was taken over by the Muslim rulers and from them by the British. If Indian administration today is analysed to its bases, the doctrines and practice of Chanakya will be found to be still in force.

Chandra Gupta was succeeded by his son Bindusara. In his time the authority of the empire was extended over the Deccan, perhaps by conquest or more probably by the acquiescence of local rulers. The empire extended as far down south as Mysore and all India, except for the powerful kingdom of Kalinga, seems to have come either under the direct administration or the paramountcy of the Mauryas. Antiochus, the son of Seleucus, maintained at the Mauryan court the diplomatic mission originally sent by his father. Even the king of Egypt, Ptolemy Philadelphus, sent an ambassador, Dionysius to Pataliputra. Bindusara is also said to have asked Antiochus to arrange that he may be supplied with a really good Greek philosopher. It was an era of peace which contributed greatly to the prosperity of the empire and when Bindusara's son, Asoka, ascended the throne in 269 B.C. he succeeded to an empire which was not merely rich and powerful but whose internal peace was undisturbed.

As crown prince, Asoka had been viceroy of the frontier province of Taxila, and later of Ujjain. The first years of his reign seem to have been devoted to the peaceful administration of the empire. In 261 B.C., he embarked on a war against the Kalingas, the great maritime power of the time, whose territory lay between the Mahanadi and the Krishna. The Kalingas were the only people who had not accepted Mauryan supremacy. We do not know the causes that led to the war but we know from Rock Edict XII that after a most sanguinary battle the Kalingas were conquered and their territory annexed to the empire.

Asoka was struck with remorse at the useless carnage which this campaign involved and, in a truly human document, he announced his repentence and his faith that the only true conquest was the conquest of self. He set himself out with zeal to establish a commonwealth of dharma in the world, and for this purpose issued a series of proclamations which he got engraved on rocks in different parts of the empire. He was not merely the first royal missionary. He was undoubtedly the first who recognised the importance of propaganda in government. His admonitions to his subjects, his regulations, his pious injunctions in regard to birds and animals, and his zealous preaching of the dharma even to the hill tribes have come down to us as evidence of Asoka's unique conception of kingship, not as an embodiment of power, but as the instrument for the establishment of peace, goodwill and compassion in the world.

Asoka was not content with his success as a propagandist in his own empire and among the tribes on his frontier. The diplomatic connections which had been developed in the reigns of his father and grandfather became useful to him in his desire to propagate the doctrine of Buddha in far off countries. He sent religious embassies to the kings of Syria, Egypt, Macedonia and Epirus. We have but little information about these missions but of the conversion of Ceylon, which was one of the major achievements of the great emperor, we have ample evidence. The first mission to Ceylon was led by Mahendra, the brother of the emperor, who had been ordained as a monk. Mahendra was on a mission to South India and crossed to Ceylon from the Pandya country. The royal missionary met with success at the court of the Ceylon king who accepted the Noble Eightfold Path from the brother of Asoka himself. The second mission was led by Sanghamitra, the emperor's sister, who voyaged down along the east coast of India.

She took with her a branch of the sacred Bo-tree which still flourishes in Ceylon. The sculptures of Sanchi attest the fact of the carrying of the Bo-tree to Ceylon.

Asoka is spoken of as a Buddhist emperor and his reign as a kind of Buddhist period in Indian history. The distinction between Hinduism and Buddhism in India was purely sectarian and never more than the difference between Saivism and Vaishnavism. The exclusiveness of religious doctrines is a Semitic conception which was unknown to India for a long time. Buddha himself was looked upon in his lifetime and afterwards as a Hindu saint and avatar and his followers were but another sect in the great Aryan tradition. Asoka was a Buddhist in the same way as Harsha was a Buddhist, or Kumarapala was a Jain. But in the view of the people of the day he was a Hindu monarch following one of the recognised sects. His own inscriptions bear ample witness to this fact. While his doctrines follow the Middle Path, his gifts are to the Brahmana, Sramanas (Buddhist priests) and others equally. His own name of adoption is Devenam Priya, the beloved of the gods. Which gods? Surely the gods of the Aryan religion. Buddhism had no gods of its own. The idea that Asoka was a kind of Buddhist Constantine declaring himself against paganism is a complete misreading of Indian conditions through the eyes of Christian Europe. Asoka was essentially a Hindu, as indeed was the founder of the sect to which he belonged.

Asoka's contribution to Indian culture was unique. He built numerous stupas all over North India, erected pillars of great architectural beauty and gave to his empire a visible unity of culture. His inscriptions, which include regulations and edicts as well as sermons, constitute a literature which must have been a source of great inspiration to his people. With Indian kings outside the boundaries of his empire, the four southern kings—the Cholas the Pandyas, the Satyaputras and the Keralas, he maintained a constant and friendly intercourse. The conversion of Ceylon brought the southern island definitely into the orbit of Indian life

From the inscriptions, we are able to know something of the provincial administration of Asoka's empire. The four vice-royalties were Kalinga (capital Tosali), Avanti (capital Ujjain), Uttrapatha (Punjab, etc., capital Taxila) and Madhyadesa (capital Suvarnagiri). The centrally administered areas were Magadha and the Gangetic Valley, which were governed under a system of district officers. The areas on the boundaries were under feudatories who recognised the paramountcy of the empire.

cultural unity of India. The Mauryan conquest of the South was an extension of northern authority which no doubt was accompanied by a penetration of northern culture and ideas. But the Mauryan hold weakened after Asoka and the authority of the imperial government was too short-lived to have brought the North and the South together in ideas. This was the historic mission of the Satavahanas, and the geographical position of the empire, placed as it was at the centre of India, enabled them to fulfil it with success. The South India we see in the fourth century, has been Aryanised in thought and ideas. The Pallava empire at Kanchi is Sanskritic in its outlook, and even the Pandyas and Cheras have come [illegible] into the composite structure of Hindu civilisation. The credit for this great transformation belongs to the Satavahanas.

[illegible] became one of the great centres of civilisation [illegible] reflected in literature. [illegible] the capital [illegible] Gunadhya, the author of *Brihatkatha* lived here, and the story of the rivalry between [illegible] (the [illegible] of the barbarous [illegible] in which the story of *Brihatkatha* is said to have been [illegible]) is a clear indication of the [illegible] Sanskrit as the vehicle of civilisation and culture.

Under the Satavahanas Hinduism and Buddhism seem to have flourished equally. "In the first centuries of our era," says Grousset, "when northern India was being subjected in art as well as in politics to the domination of foreign peoples—Greeks and Scythians—Andhra has preserved [illegible] as well as its political independence [illegible] of Indian aesthetics." [illegible] Nagarjuna Konda [illegible] in the fourth century A.D. [illegible] link between the [illegible] Buddhist art of Sanchi and [illegible] workshops of the South [illegible] establishments, temples, monasteries and [illegible] all over the country both by royal bounty and by the munificence of private donors. The foreman of the artisans of Sri Satakarni is recorded in an inscription in Bhilsa tope as having made a grant. In the Nasik inscription, which records the dedication of a great Buddhist cave monastery excavated at his own expense, Ushavadata speaks of his numerous charities to Brahmins also. This Buddhist merchant fed a hundred thousand Brahmins. Gautamiputra Satakarni who declares himself to be the sole protector of the Brahmins records a benefaction for the Buddhists.

CHAPTER IV

LIFE UNDER THE MAURYAS

FOR a survey of Indian life under the Mauryas we have ample evidence of a varied character. The *Dharma Sastras*, especially Manu, give us a picture of life as the legislators of the time saw it. In the *Arthasastra* we see society described as it came under the view of an administrator who was concerned mainly with the problems of the day. In Vatsyayana's *Kamasutra* we have a description of the social life of the period. From the meagre foreign sources now beginning to be available the composite picture can be checked and corrected.

The Mauryan state, as we saw in the previous chapter, created a machinery which attempted to govern vast areas directly and to enforce rules and regulations in respect of agriculture, industry, commerce, animal hubandry, etc. Though it is obvious that, except in the areas under the immediate charge of the central government or of the imperial viceroys, these regulations could not have been very effectively enforced, the very fact that the government devoted itself not merely to the collection of revenues but to the control of productive and commercial activities was a significant change from the earlier system of government.

Industrial life seems to have developed early through guilds and unions of craftsmen. The srenis or trade guilds were powerful institutions. The Sanchi stupa inscriptions, for example, mentions that the carving was done by the guild (sreni) of the ivory workers of Vidisa. The Junnar cave inscription testifies to the gift of a cave by the guild of corn dealers. We have also allusions to the guilds of gold and silver smiths, and silk cloth weavers. The Nasik cave inscription (circa 200 B.C.) mentions that the endowments given for a temple were invested in perpetuity with two weavers' guilds who were to pay only interest on the capital. This is probably the earliest allusion to collective banking practices and is noteworthy in that respect.

The organisation of industry in guilds gave to craftsmen great political and economic power. It also broke down the restrictions of caste which the smriti writers had laid down. The power of the guilds which exercised many governmental functions is one of the factors which the social historians of India, basing their judgments on the symmetrical classification of smriti writers, have been inclined to underestimate. The craftsmen always enjoyed a high place in society, but according to the unreal classification of castes they were only sudras. The smriti disabilities in regard to sudras could not be enforced against the craftsmen organised in guilds, enjoying royal favour, employing vast resources and exercising effective power.

The Bhita excavations have led to the discovery of numerous seals belonging to such corporations. One of these terracotta seals is written, according to Sir John Marshall, "in the letters of the third or perhaps the fourth century B.C." The house of the guild which Marshall excavated is claimed by him to be the headquarters of an organisation of craftsmen. Dr. Block even comes to the conclusion that at big centres like Pataliputra, "something like a modern chamber of commerce existed."

The failure of the Chaturvarnya in relation to the organisation of industrial crafts is emphasised by the fact that the non-productive craftsmen were subject to a social stigma. Actors, jugglers, jesters, bird fanciers, snake charmers, etc., seem never to have obtained social recognition. Among the professions which were actively pursued at the time are dyers, weavers, mechanics (Mahayantra pravartakas, literally those who work great engines), miners, architects, carpenters and metal workers, stone masons, gem cutters, engineers, mariners, etc.

The rise of capitalism even in the time of Buddha has already been alluded to. We have epigraphic record of the great growth of wealth in Mauryan India. The inscriptions on the Sanchi stupa record numerous gifts by very wealthy merchants. They are all described as merchants (srestin). Merchants who undertook expensive repairs are also mentioned by name. Great endowments for monasteries and temples were also common. The Buddhist and Jain chronicles relating to the early period of these two religions also bear witness to the great wealth of the mercantile classes.

Perhaps one reason for this growth of material prosperity, apart from the general tranquillity and the increase of trade and commerce inside the country, was the development of maritime traffic and overseas trade. The Magadhan monarchy till the time of Asoka did not probably have much maritime intercourse. Chandra Gupta undoubtedly maintained a separate department of admiralty, which looked after harbours, maintained waterways and otherwise encouraged shipping. But it is doubtful in view of the geographical position of the empire whether the subjects of

Chandra Gupta and Bindusara were interested in maritime traffic. The upkeep of internal harbours on the Ganges and the use of the great waterways for commerce together with the encouragement of such shipping as ventured into their harbours seem to have been the activity of Chandra Gupta's admiralty. But with the conquest of Kalinga and the control of the great ports of that country maritime activity clearly gained greater importance as is evidenced by the fact of Asoka's own sister Sanghamitra being allowed to travel by sea to Ceylon. The routes were well known and voyages must have been frequent for the emperor to have permitted such a journey. Besides we know that the Kalingas were traditionally a great naval power and the extension of the empire to the Kalinga coast should have added to the material prosperity of the trading classes of the time.

Internal trade was carefully regulated and encouraged. Ferries were maintained and a system of safe communications developed all over the empire. The regulations which Chanakya laid down were clearly meant to encourage trade, and the provision of warehouses, godowns and transport arrangements indicated that with the union of north India under one authority there was a remarkable development of economic life. In the Hathigumpha inscription it is stated that a canal which an earlier king had constructed was extended by Kharavela. Internal transport was a matter of interest to government, and special arrangements were made for the protection of the trade routes.

Pataliputra was the main city. Founded by Ajatasatru on a bend of the Ganges in the sixth century B.C. the city had become one of the most famous in the world. The Sugangeya palace, which is named in Indian texts as the seat of the king, occupied a central position and is stated by Megasthenes to have been more splendid than the palaces of Susa and Ecbatana. The excavations on the site have borne out the description. The city had a long river frontage of over nine miles and the beauty of its parks and the regal splendour of its buildings were proverbial in India. *Kathasarit Sagara*, embodying the views of Gunadhya's time (first century B.C.), consistently speaks of Pataliputra as the home of culture, learning and fine arts and the queen of the cities of the world. It is interesting to note that the city is spoken of as the city of the Nandas. It is the home of learning and wealth. Known as the "city of flowers," its prestige in imperial times was something unique and it seems to have been completely cosmopolitan in its character. Undoubtedly it dominated the intellectual life of India for many centuries, as we have continuous allusions to students flocking to Pataliputra for study. Patanjali speaks of its towers and the Sugangeya palace (or the golden palace) is as familiar in Indian literature as Versailles, Quirinal or Windsor is in European literature. The Hathigumpha inscription of Kharavela mentions the palace by name and claims that a miraculous image of Jina, which one of the Nanda kings had taken away from the Kalinga capital and installed there, was brought back by him.

The city seems to have been built mainly of wood which no doubt explains why the destruction caused was so complete that only the archaeologist has been able to determine the site. Other cities, only less important than Pataliputra, like Vaisali of the Lichchavis, Ujjain, the capital of Avanti, where Asoka was once viceroy, Banaras, the eternal, and Taxila, the seat of the famous university and a provincial capital of special importance, shared equally in the prosperity of the period. Vaisali was even older than Pataliputra. The *Ramayana* alludes to it and ascribes its foundation to Ikshvaku, the ancestor of Rama. Mahavira was claimed by Vaisali as one of her citizens and Buddha's association with it was intimate. The chaityas, temples and garden retreats of the city are alluded to frequently in early Buddhist and Jain literature. According to the *Jatakas* the city at the time of Buddha was encompassed by the three walls with gates and watch towers. The growth of towns independent of royal residences has been gradual and we have one very remarkable example at Bhita where the excavations have proved the existence of a great commercial and industrial centre and perhaps a river port on the Ganges.

The growth of towns and the amenities of life in the cities led to the popularity of urban life among the richer classes. The nagarika or town-man became a type with well-developed tastes, special codes of conduct, leading a life of luxury and devoted to a life of enjoyment. Vatsyayana, who describes the life of the nagarika, gives us a picture of the state of urban culture at the time. To Vatsyayana the only place where a young man of wealth and culture can properly stay is the city, a view contrary to that enjoined by Baudhayana that a good man should avoid living in towns. Vatsyayana recommends that a man who desires civilised life should build his house near a city or town so that he can consort with people of his own class. The house of the town-man as we find described in *Kamasutra* is divided into two parts, the women's apartments and the men's—a division that is still to be found in India. The house is surrounded by a garden, where flowering plants and fruit trees are planted. In the centre of the garden there is generally a pond. The garden is meant both for household use and for recreation, for Vatsyayana mentions seats and bowers where the nagarika is to find repose and amusement. Terraces are recommended for the enjoyment of moonlight parties.

The description of a young man's apartments gives us an insight into the intimate life of this class of people at the time. The rooms are elegantly furnished both for comfort and for enjoyment. Ivory brackets are provided for keeping such articles as painting boxes, musical instruments and also a table for toilet articles. Chairs are not in fashion and the nagarika sits on carpets spread on the floor. The room is decorated with flowers, and outside on the verandah pet birds and animals are kept.

Housed in this elegant fashion the nagarika spends his time in suitable amusements and occupations of interest. His toilet which is described in detail is specially interesting. After his daily bath fragrant ointment is applied to his body; his clothes are mildly perfumed. Collyrium is applied to his eyes; his lips are reddened by a dye which is rubbed with wax in order that it may not lose colour. His dress consists of two garments, an uttariya covering the upper part of the body. The *Dharma Sastras* lay down that one who has finished Brahmacharya, or the life of a student, must wear an upper garment. We have allusions to Lichchavi young men going to see Buddha wearing garments of blue, red and yellow. The upper cloth could be of coloured silk, laced or otherwise, and was generally of fine texture. The quality of the garment was often a test of a man's culture and standing; Vasantasena, the courtesan in Bhasa's play, for example, noticing the garment of her impoverished lover, infers that he was still a man of fashion.

Massaging of body seems to have been extensively practised and the nagarika does not neglect active exercises which keep his body vigorous and shapely. He takes two principal meals daily. The description given by Vatsyayana of the different kinds of food taken by the men of the leisured classes is particularly interesting. Apart from such staple foods as rice, wheat, barley, and milk, Vatsyayana speaks of meat as an important article of food. Taken as soup, roast and in other forms, meat seems to have been a popular article of diet. The *Mahabharata*, it will be remembered, mentions the different kinds of animals (including buffaloes) killed for the feasts on the occasion of Draupadi's wedding and Buddhist literature also alludes frequently to the eating of meat. Different kinds of wine—sweet (madhu), dry (asava)—were also in common use. In fact, wine-drinking seems to have been very popular for Chanakya provides for definite rules for the control of liquor shops.

Clearly the picture that Vatsyayana presents us with is that of the leisured cultivated class of young men who had plenty of money to spend and time to spend it. It is a class that loved the pleasures of life, enjoyed festivals, went to cock-fights, betting games, diverted itself with music and arts and patronised public places of amusement. The life of the ordinary man in the village bore no relation to this, but Vatsyayana's description is significant of the highly sophisticated civilisation that had developed in the cities as a result of centuries of prosperity and settled rule.

We have also some idea of the festivals and enjoyments of the people. The festival of the Sabbarattivars which the Lichchavis celebrated with great rejoicings is specially mentioned in the *Samyutta Nikaya*. The whole population seems to have taken part in it. The Hindu love of seasonal festival is evidenced in the earliest literature and we have allusions to Vasantotsava (the spring festival) and other such celebrations from early times. The Jains claim that Dipavali, or the festival of lamps, originated when the eighteen kings who were present at the nirvana of Mahavira lighted torches. Hindu tradition in fact connects it with the return of Rama from his exile. Whatever the origin, Dipavali seems to have been celebrated from very early times under different names. We have also allusions to other local festivals such as the Giri Puja of the Yadavas who seem to have been particularly fond of festivals for which they transported large numbers of people to the mainland. Flower festivals are also alluded to. In fact, the change of seasons was always an event to be celebrated with appropriate amusements.

Dicing was almost a universal habit. Gaming houses were licensed and controlled—according to *Arthasastra.* Vatsyayana provides for dice in the apartments of a nagarika and even in villages primitive forms of gambling seem to have been widely prevalent. Ball games were favoured by women and in the women's garden Kanduka Krida or playing at balls is often alluded to. Young men of the higher classes hunted game and we have the statement that while Buddha was resting under a tree near Vaisali, a large number of Lichchavi young men arrived there with hounds all ready for chase. Kings and princes were supposed as a part of royal duty to hunt in order to keep down the ravages of wild animals; but hunting as a pastime seems also to have been popular. Boating, swimming and archery were the other manly games in which the young men frequently tried to excel each other.

Music and dancing were widely cultivated. The nagarika amused himself with music, and Vatsyayana asks him to keep the veena on a special rack Teachers of natya or dancing suffered a social stigma from the point of view of caste but the *Malavikagnimitra* shows that the teachers employed by kings held an important and influential position at court. It will be remembered that during the last year of the exile of the Pandavas, the hero Arjuna spent his time as a teacher of dancing and music to the princesses at the Virata capital and Bhasa's play *Pancharatra* alludes to the social stigma attached to the profession. Among the sixty-four arts which a well educated man was supposed to know dancing and music ranked high. Baudhayana (500 B.C.) mentions natyacharya or teacher of dancing. Bharata's *Natyasastra*—undoubtedly of high antiquity—shows a long and systematic cultivation of the art of dancing and music. Even by the time of Bharata, the professionals in these arts had fallen into social disrepute as a long story of the curse on actors is introduced to explain their low position in society. But the arts themselves were held in high esteem and men and women of all classes were enjoined to study them.

Education was fairly widely spread. *Dharma Sastras* condemn all illiterate Brahmins. The varnashrama dharma rules provided for a period of intensive study for the three higher castes. Teaching was mainly the duty of Brahmins but after Buddha's time the Buddhist monks, because of the convenience provided by monastic institutions, seem to have assumed a large share in educating the people. But the orthodox system was of studying under a suitable teacher or, in the case of nobility, of employing a private tutor. The higher classes looked upon literacy as essential. The universities of Taxila, Ujjain and Banaras were famous from the earliest times, King Prasenajit himself having gone as far as Taxila to study at the university there. In *Dhammapada* there is mention of a Lichchavi youth named Mahali who, after finishing his education at Taxila, devoted his life to educating his people.

Education in schools and universities seems to have been mainly literary and religious. The *Dharma Sastras,* grammar and rhetoric, and artha and varta (economics and politics) were widely studied and are mentioned as the necessary course. From the time of Panini (sixth century B.C.) at least great importance was attached to grammar and it was a primary course of study. Popular education must have been based on the *Mahabharata* and the *Puranas*—early versions of which existed in Panini's time also, as there are numerous allusions to *Mahabharata* incidents in the grammar and the *Puranas* are alluded to in *Dharma Sastra*. That education was widely spread in Maurya times is witnessed by Megasthenes and the enormous army of civil servants that the empire required could only have been based on an educated middle class.

Of women's education we have not much direct evidence. The establishment of nunneries must, however, have been a great step in this direction for the wandering parivrajikas, who seem to have been held in great respect by the people, carried education to the villages.

Technical education was through guilds. The allusion to engineers and people who look after machinery, state control of mining, metallurgy and other professions requiring high technical skill apart from weaving, dyeing, carpentry, show that training in such professions requiring high skill was undertaken on a large scale. Manu and other writers lay down the obligations and conditions of professional apprenticeship and the organisations of craftsmen already alluded to seem to have had authority to insist on standards in the case of apprentices under training.

The growth of medicine in this period is also an important factor. Medicine is an ancient science in India and physicians are alluded to frequently in the earlier Buddhist texts. Buddhism and Jainism, with their care of all living beings, gave a great impetus to organised medical treatment and Asoka's hospitals form a new departure in the care of the sick.

Of the position of women generally in Maurya times, it is difficult to speak. But considerable freedom seems to have been permitted, for the nuns—both Buddhist and Jain—were freely initiated and wandered about all over the country with free access to palaces and cattages. Gunadhya's stories also testify to the freedom of women of all classes. The dress which the women wore is a matter of special interest. We do not know when the sari came into fashion, but the recent Arikamedu excavations have brought to light the torso of a female figure draped in sari and wearing it as Hindu women wear it today. As the site and the torso are dated the first century B.C. it is clear that the women at least of South India wore saris from the earliest times.

The life of a man of the middle class under the Mauryas was civilised, balanced and materially advanced. He lived in a comfortable house and had cultivated surroundings. He followed a routine laid down by the *Dharma Sastras* which gave him spiritual comfort and an assured position in society. He went through the rituals befitting his station. His domestic and social life was regulated by a code which found general acceptance. Materially he had the benefits of being the citizen of a highly prosperous empire. The necessities and even the luxuries of life —fine muslin, good food and wine—the amenities of civilised life—gardens, amusements, facilities for travel—were available to him.

During the period from the Nirvana of Buddha to the fall of the Mauryas Hindu society was in a measure re-integrated. The great non-Aryan tribes which held power, the Lichchavis, Mallas, and others were integrated into Hinduism as Kshatriyas. Considerable effort has been made by historians under the domination of Aryanism to prove that these were Aryan tribes. The fact that Manu describes them as Vrata Kshatriyas shows clearly the compromise theory had to make with fact. The political power of the tribes could not be overlooked; the fact, however, remained that they were Vratas and by marriage they were related to the great empires. The Mādrās, an undoubtedly aboriginal tribe, and abused as such by a Suta (Karna) in *Mahabharata,* was closely allied by marriage to all royal families, then the women of the Himalayan sub-ranges being popular in the harems of Indian rulers. The assimilation of these tribes into the neo-Aryan society proceeded apace and by the end of the period the claim of these peoples to the privileges of Aryan life was generally accepted.

The birth of new gods is also a factor of great significance. The hold of the older gods not only disappears completely but new deities begin to make their appearance and claim allegiance. Vasudeva is mentioned in Panini and though the Krishna-cult assumes importance only later, Balarama, his brother, was already the object of worship in the third century B.C. According to Mr. Kane (*History of Dharma Sastra,* Vol. I, p. 103) Skanda was worshipped in Mauryan times. Siva of course had regained his ascendancy. The allusion to the early versions of the *Puranas* and the *Mahabharata* also indicates that the Puranic gods had during this period become popular.

The growth of Sanskrit is one of the major factors which make the Maurya period a basic one in regard to Indian civilisation. Panini's (*circa* sixth century B.C.) *Astadhyayi* marks the turning point in Sanskrit. It becomes the "perfected language" and while it is undeniable that Panini provided Sanskrit with a grammar, which remains the model even today for grammarians, it is possible to argue that the attempt to crab and confine the language within the frame-work of rules and regulations was also the cause of the arrested growth of Sanskrit after the classical period. Apaniniya—not according to Panini—became a major offence as time went on. That, however, is a much later development. During the period between 500 and 150 B.C. we have the great works of Katyayana and Patanjali who between them established the supremacy of Panini and gave to Sanskrit the form and shape which it enjoys today. As a result the period witnessed a remarkable literary growth of which but little has come down to us. If we place Kalidasa in the period that immediately follows (during the reign of Agnimitra), Bhasa and Saumilla, alluded to in *Malavikagnimitra* as classics, will fall within this period. *Swapna Vasavadatta* at least would seem to be a work of this period and there are indications that plays like *Pancharatra* and *Oooru Bhanga* are based on a version of the *Mahabharata* different from what we have today.

Of Mauryan art we can speak with greater certainty. The beautiful pillars which Asoka created in different parts of his empire and the sculptures on the stupas of Barhut and Sanchi and the Ajivika caves near Gaya are the surviving examples of Mauryan art. The pillars, according to one high authority, are "distinguished by great nobility of design, a cultured form of expression and the finest technical accomplishment." The Ajivika caves, the precursors of Ajanta, Bagh and other later monasteries are marvels of workmanship. As we know from the edicts, they were carved under orders of the emperor himself. Mr. Havell considers the sculptures of the stupas of Barhut and Sanchi as work which combines non-Aryan and Aryan elements.

Of architecture other than stupas, very little has come down to us from this period. We know, however, of the great architectural beauty of the Sugangeya palace built by the Nandas, which continued, no doubt with renovations and additions, for many centuries. The pillared hall of the palace has been excavated and bears out fully the fame of the great royal residence. In brief, it may be stated that the century and a half of Mauryan rule witnessed a growth of civilisation, arts and culture, which entitled India to rank among the greatest countries of the time.

CHAPTER V

THE PERIOD OF EMPIRES *(continued)*

THE assassination of the last Mauryan emperor by his commander-in-chief, Pushyamitra, did not mean the immediate break-up of the empire. The empire of Hindustan (excepting Kalinga) passed under the control of Pushyamitra, who, however, seems to have been content with the title of Senapati (general) though his son Agnimitra ruled as a viceroy with the title of Maharaja at Bhilsa. Senapati Pushyamitra, though he did not assume the royal title, performed a great Aswamedha, indicating his imperial power, an event which was considered so remarkable that both Patanjali and Kalidasa alluded to it in their works. It would appear, though it cannot be asserted with certainty, that it was at Agnimitra's court at Bidisa (Bhilsa) that Kalidasa lived and wrote his works. The theory that the poet lived under Chandra Gupta Vikramaditya, four centuries later, though still asserted by many, has fewer supporters today. Agnimitra's successors held together the empire in the Gangetic valley and the Punjab.

The eastern provinces, especially Kalinga, which had thrown off the Mauryan authority even earlier than Pushyamitra had done, assumed the imperial role with much greater effect. Under Kharavela who came to the throne of the Kalingas in 183 B.C. the Kalinga revival reached its zenith. The Hathigumpha inscription which records the achievements of this king is the first detailed historical document available to us. In his twenty-fourth year Kharavela became king of Kalinga. His first campaigns were meant to extend his territory to the south where the Andhra Bhrityas had become a major power under Sri Satakarni. In a series of campaigns Kharavela seems to have brought the whole of the Deccan under his sway. In 171 B.C. Kharavela invaded Magadha and captured Pataliputra, which was then under Brihaspati-mitra, the son of Agnimitra, who was probably ruling there as his governor. Kharavela seems to have favoured the Jains.

The north-western frontier was subjected to considerable foreign pressure at this time. The Yu Chi, a barbarian tribe who had their homes in Kaorsu and Sinkiang, were driven out of their homes by Giyu, the Hun conqueror. They in turn drove the Sakas before them, and in the first century B.C. the Saka hordes descended on India threatening, it would seem, Ujjain itself. Their defeat and expulsion in 57 B.C. was according to Hindu tradition the achievement of the great Vikramaditya of Ujjain, who to celebrate this event took the title of Sakari or the conqueror of Sakas and established an era (Vikrama Samvat) which is still the most popular among the Hindus. But though the Sakas were driven off, the Yu Chi who had settled in the valleys of the Hindukush began to make their power felt on the frontier. Known as the Kushans, under an outstanding ruler, Kanishka, they extended their authority at least up to Mathura, taking advantage of the breakdown of imperial power in North India. During the period of their authority in the Hindukush valleys the Yu Chi had themselves undergone a transformation. They had come under the influence of Buddhism and Kanishka who extended his authority into the Gangetic valley was himself an enthusiastic Buddhist. His power was, however, based on Central Asia, and the emperor, while he accepted and championed Buddhism, comes hardly into Indian history. His son Huviska is a shadowy figure, while with Vasudeva the empire may be said to have become definitely Hindu.

It is necessary to emphasise the fact that the Kushan empire in India meant merely the annexation of certain provinces and not the conquest of one people by another. That state already established in what is now Afghanistan merely extended its boundaries further inside with the breakdown of the imperial authority of Pataliputra. Vasudeva's conversion to orthodox Hinduism eliminated whatever foreign character the monarchy had originally. The same is true of the so-called Greek kings. There was no Greek conquest of India; no Greek army marched across the Indus after Alexander's raid. Certain Bactrian monarchs on the boundaries of India extended their authority and less important rulers, no doubt originally governors, set themselves up as local rulers. We have no evidence of Greek populations having settled anywhere within India and this alone should dispel the doctrines sedulously put forward by some European writers that for at least two centuries after the fall of the Mauryan empire north India was under Greek and Kushan kings.

The absence of a central imperial government between the fall of the Sungas in the first century B.C. and the rise of the Bharasivas is, however, noticeable. The authority of the Kushans extended for a very short time up to Allahabad but after Vasudeva in the middle of the second century they disappeared in the same manner as they rose to prominence. Their expulsion is attributed to the revolt of the great republican tribe of Yaudheyas who occupied the area now known as western Rajputana. The Yaudheyas, whose valour is recognised even by their enemies, e.g., in Rudra Daman's inscription, seem to have organised a national revolt, for their coins bearing the legend Yaudheya Ganasya Jaya have been discovered in the Punjab. Other republican tribes, notably the Malavas and Arjunayanas seem also to have helped in the national effort. It is after the Kushan power was effectively broken that the Bharasivas who significantly describe themselves as those who secured the favour of Siva by carrying at all times the symbol of Siva on their shoulders, emerged from the area now known as Bundelkhand and re-established a semi-imperial authority in north India. They are officially described as having performed ten Aswamedhas or horse sacrifices —the traditional ceremony of imperial authority. Virasena was perhaps the greatest of the line. The continuous onslaughts against the receding power of the Kushans seems to have necessitated the establishment of the branches of the family at Bidisa and Mathura. The last of the Bharasiva or Naga kings, Bhava Naga, allied himself with the rising power of the Vakatakas. The formal establishment of Vakataka empire is placed at about 284 A.D. The great Vakataka ruler Pravarasena I assumed imperial titles and his authority was well established all over Hindustan. The *Puranas* recognise the greatness of the Vakatakas, known as Vindhya Sakti. For over a hundred years the Vakatakas with their capital at Nandi Vardhan ensured peace and tranquillity over central India and re-established the orthodox social system which had suffered considerable shocks by the inroad of Kushans and Yavanas. In one of Prithvisena's inscriptions, the dynasty is described as one whose economic and judicial administration had been perfected for a hundred years, a significant if vainglorious announcement of the greatness of the Vakatakas.

Pravarasena's son Sarvasena established a branch of the dynasty at Bassim which in time extended its authority as far south as Karnataka. In fact the Vakatakas in middle India succeeded to the empire of the Satavahanas and held their sway, north and south of the Vindhyas, and fully earned their title of Vindhya Sakti.

The Bharasivas and the Vakatakas cannot be looked upon merely as the bridgeheads to the imperial Guptas. The glory of

Samudra Gupta and his successors has obscured in a measure the great achievements of their predecessors who not only expelled the foreigners from Indian soil but re-established the imperial tradition which had been threatened by Kushan attacks. Even more, it is these dynasties, more than the Guptas, that contributed to the re-establishment of Hindu society and Sanskrit culture over Hindustan, as may be seen not merely from the numerous Aswamedhas performed by the kings of these dynasties but the very orthodoxy which they claim for themselves. The growth of classical Sanskrit literature to its full greatness was also in this period for Harishena's great Prasasti of Samudra Gupta on the Allahabad Pillar bears clear evidence of the evolution and perfection of the Kavya style. Kalidasa who it is claimed lived in Agnimitra's times (150 B.C.) and Aswaghosha who followed him with his *Buddha Charita* and *Saundarananda* were the ornaments of Sanskrit literature in the pre-Gupta period.

The later Vakataka period witnessed a revival of Lichchavi power. The great republic had suffered an eclipse with the rise of Magadha power. The Lichchavis seem to have accepted the imperial authority of the Mauryas but were able to maintain their republican form of government as Chanakya alludes to them as sanghas and united in council. The breakdown of imperial authority in Pataliputra released the republic of its obligations to the paramount power and the Lichchavis continued to grow in strength within their own territories. For a time they seem to have even occupied Pataliputra. The power and prestige of the great republic which had an unbroken tradition of over a thousand years were so great that its alliance was eagerly sought. It was by one such alliance that the Guptas established themselves originally in Magadha. Chandra Gupta I married into the Lichchavi clan and the alliance was so prized that Samudra Gupta, his great son, took pride in announcing himself as Lichchavi Dauhitra—the son of a daughter of the Lichchavis.

No republic except that of the Lichchavis lasted in history for a thousand years. Neither Athens, nor any of the other city states of Greece, nor the great republics of Venice and Genoa can claim a similar greatness. The tradition of non-monarchical states was originally very strong in India as the history of the Yadava confederacy and later of the numerous sovereign communities in northern India clearly proves. But one by one they fell before the might of growing empires or were themselves transformed into monarchies. Only the Lichchavis remained.

Chandra Gupta's ancestors seem to have been local Rajas as

only his father Ghatotkacha and grandfather are mentioned in inscriptions; but it is the occupation of Pataliputra with the help of the Lichchavis, which incident Jayaswal claims to see reflected in the drama *Kaumudi Mahotsava,* which gave to the Guptas their imperial position. Chandra Gupta's own reign seems to have been an unsettled one; but under his son and successor Samudra Gupta —the grandson of the Lichchavis as he calls himself—the Gupta empire was firmly established and attained a supremacy in North India equal to that which the Mauryas had exercised before.

We have full details of Samudra Gupta's conquests and achievements in Harishena's magnificent inscription engraved on the Asokan pillar at Allahabad. Harishena, the composer, was himself one of the leading statesmen of Samudra Gupta's time and the record of conquest and political achievements has been borne out by other evidence also.

By a series of military campaigns Samudra Gupta brought under his imperial sway the whole of North India and a portion of the South. The names of the kings of the Deccan whom Samudra Gupta defeated and conquered such as Mahendra of Pithapuram and Vishnugopa of Kanchi leave no doubt as to Samudra Gupta's southern conquest.

It would seem, however, from the inscription itself that the Vindhya and Maharashtra country, the home domains of the Vakatakas, were not attacked or conquered by the Guptas. The continued existence of powerful Vakataka monarchs and their close alliance with the Guptas, under Samudra's successor, would seem to indicate that Samudra did not challenge the Vindhyan power but satisfied himself with an alliance. Chandra Gupta II's marriage with a Vakataka princess and his own daughter Prabhavati's marriage with a Vakataka monarch are further indications of the fact that the Guptas shared their imperial power with the Vindhyan state.

Samudra Gupta's empire was organised on the basis of imperial provinces, frontier feudatories, and subordinate kings of vassal states, within the empire. The imperial provinces followed the lines of Maurya organisation, but eastern Bengal and Assam (Kamarupa), Katripura (the hill districts of Garhwal and Kangra) and the republican tribes of the Punjab were left semi-independent but "obeying orders and tendering homage." The countries annexed are specially mentioned in the inscription as also those the kings of which were re-instated in vassal state. The formal proclamation of Samudra Gupta's imperial paramountcy through the traditional ceremony of an Aswamedha is testified by coins struck on the occasion bearing the legend "Aswamedha Parakrama." After having vanquished the powers on the frontier, Samudra Gupta assumed titles and dignities imitating the glory and pomp of the Roman emperors.

Samudra Gupta was not only a conqueror, he was a great patron of arts and humanities and is himself described as a prince of poets. The inscriptions speak of him not only as a learned man, but as one fond of the company of poets and writers. One type of his coinage represents him playing on the veena and he is also described as putting to shame divine singers by his musical accomplishments. His chief queen was Datta Devi, the mother of Chandra Gupta Vikramaditya, and the figure which is represented on the Aswamedha type of coin is presumably her's. On one of Chandra Gupta's coins also there is a representation of Datta Devi receiving a gift from her husband.

Samudra Gupta was succeeded by his son Rama Gupta in whose time the pressure of the Sakas began to be felt on the north-west frontier. Rama Gupta tried to buy off the invaders, but this pusillanimous policy cost him his throne which was usurped by Chandra Gupta II, the son of Datta Devi, destined to be known in history as Sakari Chandra Gupta. Consolidating the empire where forces of disruption had begun to show themselves during the weak reign of Rama Gupta, Chandra Gupta expelled the foreigner and gained for himself the title of Sakari—the conqueror of the Sakas. His effective rule extended over the whole of North India, including the maritime provinces of Gujarat and Kathiawad, but he seems to have allowed the authority over the distant provinces of the south to lapse.

Chandra Gupta married a Vakataka princess and thus allied himself with the historic imperial tradition. His own daughter Prabhavati Gupta married Rudra Sena, the Vakataka king. A lady of remarkable ability she seems to have ruled the State as Regent for her son and in her inscriptions we see reflected the pride both of the Vakatakas and the Guptas. Chandra Gupta's firm alliance with this great power based on the Vindhyas enabled him to concentrate all his forces against invaders.

Chandra Gupta's main achievement was the expulsion of the Sakas who had grown into a menace. Apart from this, he seems to have been devoted to the arts of peace. An ardent worshipper of Vishnu—a Parama Bhagavata—he was the patron of the great revival of Puranic Hinduism, which in the course of a century undertook a process of national re-education which in its mighty sweep absorbed even the great Dharma of Buddha and incorporated it, in due course, in the comprehensive re-interpretation of Hinduism. In his court, literature, science and art flourished as never before in India.

Chandra Gupta's son, Kumara Gupta I, had a long reign of forty years, the earlier portion of which was a continuation of the glory of Chandra Gupta. The Huns began to press on the borders of India and this led to disastrous wars which weakened the empire considerably. Under Kumara Gupta's successor Skanda Gupta, the Huns appeared again. In fact the movement of the Huns which overturned the mighty empire of the Romans and uprooted the civilisations of central Europe failed to destroy India in the same manner only because of the organised power of the Guptas. The Huns pressed continually against the frontiers of India and for over a hundred years there was incessant warfare on the north-west to keep the barbarous hordes out of the fertile plains of Hindustan. Kumara Gupta's later years bore the first shock of the Hun invasion but it was Skanda Gupta, his son and successor, who effectively organised the defence. The Bhitari inscription recounts how in the last years of Kumara Gupta, Skanda spent a night on the bare ground of the battle field. After his succession Skanda Gupta organised the defence of his empire in such a manner that the invading hordes were utterly routed and India was saved from the fate of the Roman empire and Pataliputra that of Rome. The myth of India falling at all times an easy prey to invaders from outside is fully exposed by this single fact.

In truth Skanda Gupta's victory over the Huns has enormous consequences for the world which historians have not realised. At the height of Hun power, by this defeat, its movement was turned west and the continuous pressure on eastern Europe arose in fact from the failure of the Huns to force an entry into India. This may in its results be compared to the failure of the Huns earlier to subdue the Chinese Empire. "After three hundred years of fighting," says McGovern, in his *Early Empires of Central Asia*, "the Huns and their Turanian allies were driven off into the west with the eventual result that the Huns and their successors were destined to destroy not the Chinese but the Roman Empire." When almost a century later, the Huns did enter the Punjab, the momentum of their great move across continents had already weakened and what India had in the shape of Toramana and Mihiragula was no more than an insignificant ground swell which had no serious consequence on national history.

The continuous foreign wars weakened the dynasty and after the death of Skanda Gupta the empire seems to have suffered from wars of succession. After a period of internecine struggle it was again united under Buddha Gupta who was the last great king of the dynasty. After him various branches of the Guptas ruled in different parts of north India, but we know that by about the middle of the sixth century (544 A.D.) the Huns had forced an entry into north India and Toramana was reigning in Malva. The Gupta empire had come to an end.

CHAPTER VI

GUPTA ADMINISTRATION

THE two hundred years of Gupta rule may be said to mark the climax of Hindu imperial tradition. From the point of view of literature, religion, art, architecture, commerce and colonial development, this period is undoubtedly the most important in Indian history. The Guptas inherited the administrative system of the earlier empires. The Mauryan bureaucracy, already converted into a caste, had functioned with impartial loyalty under succeeding empires. Under the Guptas we have direct allusions to viceroys, governors, administrators of provinces, and of course to ministers of the imperial government. The Mahamatras or provincial viceroys go back to the Mauryan period and continue, in fact, up to the twelfth century; these were the highest ranks in official bureaucracy. The position of Kumaramatyas—of whom many are mentioned—is not clear for we see them in posts of varying importance. The gramikas or the village headmen formed the lowest rung in the ladder. Uparikas or governors were also appointed to provinces. In the Damodarpur plates we have the mention of an uparika named Arata Datta who was governing Pundaravardhana or north Bengal. Seals of other officials like police chiefs, controller of military stores, chief justice (Maha Danda Nayaka) leave no doubt about the existence of an organised hierarchy of officials exercising imperial authority in different parts of the country.

The central government was administered directly under the authority of the emperor by a cabinet of ministers with a chief minister at its head. This is of course as laid down in the Arthasastras. Names of a few leading ministers have come down to us—Virasena, who is described as *Anvaya prapta Sacivyo* (minister by hereditary right) was the son of Harishena, minister and poet, and was foreign minister. Shikira Swamin was a governor. Parnadatta, who under the orders of Skanda Gupta repaired the Sudarsana lake built by Chandra Gupta Maurya 600 years before, was a governor of Saurashtra. Obviously during their two hundred years of rule, the Guptas had further perfected the machinery of government which had come down to them.

The Gupta era was one of great prosperity. The acquisition of the Saurashtra province and the ports on the Arabian sea poured into north India for the first time the wealth of the Roman empire. The trading relations of Europe before the annexation of the maritime provinces by Chandra Gupta were with the south. The outlets for the Mauryan empire were the Kalinga ports and their trade was mainly with the east. The Guptas opened up the western trade and this led to unprecedented prosperity. The currency reform of Chandra Gupta II who introduced standard gold and silver coins helped the trade. The Middle East under centuries of Roman peace, had become the centre of world commerce and India under the Guptas benefited by mutual exchange.

Trade between the north and the south also increased. The two land routes most favoured were along the east coast across Jabalpur, and along the west coast via Ujjain, Nasik and Karwar. Armies marched along the same route and the Gupta emperors maintained a highway which pilgrims for many centuries continued to use.

Increased material prosperity was reflected in the art and architecture of the Gupta period. Domestic architecture of the time has not come down to us but some very notable sacred buildings such as the Bhumra temple dedicated to Siva and the Nanchana Kuthara temple in Ajaigarh have been preserved. The famous Dasavatara temple of Deogarh can also be ascribed to the Gupta period. Much more evidence by way of sculpture is available to us to judge the quality of Gupta art. As R. D. Bannerji very rightly remarks:

"Gupta art is really a renaissance due to the transformation of the ideals of the people of northern India in the fourth and fifth centuries A.D. This transformation was based on an assimilation of what was old, an elimination of what was exotic and foreign, and finally a systematic production of something entirely new and essentially Indian. During the inroads of the Kushans and the local power of Greek kings in different parts of north India, 'the Gandharan art,' mainly based on Taxila, a late centre of foreign influence, had become popular. This showed marked Greek influence and scholars like Foucher, basing themselves on these have claimed for Greece a dominant influence in the artistic revival of India. In the unsettled period of the Kushans this tendency was very marked but the essence of the Gupta period in art was the reassertion of Indian traditions notably in plastic art."

The Mathura school of sculpture continued to be influenced for a longer time than the other great artistic centres of the north, Banaras and Pataliputra. In both these places the Hindu traditions reasserted themselves and the movement in due course became universal in India. The sculptures recovered from the Nalanda excavations demonstrate clearly that Kushan and Greek influences were but local and once a stable Hindu empire was re-established the exotic influences of the frontier could not penetrate deeply into Indian tradition. Codrington, in appraising Gupta art generally, says: "Gupta art has been praised for its intellectuality. It would be better to treat it as the natural outcome of ancient Indian art with its vivid appreciation of form and pattern and its love of quick beat and the rhythm of living things and of their poise and balance in repose."

The Gupta era is the classic period of Sanskrit literature. Classical Sanskrit, after five hundred years of evolution from the time of Panini, reached its transcendent glory in the time of Kalidasa about whose date scholars are not agreed, but whom I am inclined to place in the time of Agnimitra. Though this supreme glory, so far allotted to the Guptas by a number of scholars, must be denied to them, the literary greatness of the period is in the mass unequalled. The redaction of the major *Puranas* and the *Mahabharata* itself is a work of colossal magnitude, which alone should give to the Gupta empire a pre-eminent place in the shaping of Hindu civilisation. The story of the *Mahabharata* was undoubtedly known from very early times. The *Puranas* in an earlier form were known to the *Dharma Sastra* writers long before Christ. But undoubtedly the texts of the great epic, as it has come down to us, and of the major *Puranas* were rearranged, added to and edited in the Gupta period in such a manner as to make them complete new literature. The *Mahabharata* is to the Hindus much more than an epic. It is the repository of India's national tradition, a great encyclopaedia of ethics and religion, and of political and moral duties. The *Bhagawad Gita*, the greatest single scripture of the Hindus, is embedded in it.

This great work which dominates the life of the Hindus even today is as the Gupta editors have left it for us. The earlier version has been completely lost and is known to us only from allusions. Similar is the position in regard to the *Puranas*. The *Bhagavata, Skanda, Siva, Matsya, Vayu* and *Brahmanda*, representing the earlier traditions, were rewritten in the Gupta period to serve a national purpose. What was this purpose? It used to be held at one time that this comprehensive rewriting of the entire Hindu popular literature in Sanskrit was meant as a first step towards the eradication of Buddhism from India; that it was an attempt by the Brahmins to create an interest in the popular mind which would enable it to capture the imagination of the public which is presumed to have come under the influence of Buddhist popular literature like the *Jataka* tales. That this interpretation is wholly baseless can be seen from the fact that this period also witnessed the remarkable growth of Sanskrit Buddhism, and the popularisation of Buddhist *Kavyas* like *Buddha Charita* and *Soundarananda* and of Buddhist philosophical schools. It is the period when the University of Nalanda began to exercise its greatest influence. It is also to be remembered that for another four hundred years at least Buddhism flourished in India as an independent and highly respected religion.

The object of the great redactions was therefore something totally different. It was for the purpose of eliminating the foreign and exotic elements which the Kushans, the Greeks and the Parthians had almost imperceptibly introduced into Indian life. From the first century A.D. to the reaffirmation of nationalism by the Guptas there was a noticeable penetration of foreign ideals into Hinduism. The Gandharan art was its visible expression. The danger to Indian social structure was not so much from foreign conquest as from the penetration of barbarian ideals. The comprehensive rewriting of texts introducing into them large sections devoted to popular ethics was essential if these foreign and disrupting elements were to be eliminated and the useful portions assimilated into a vigorous Indian culture.

The success of the Gupta effort in this direction was complete. Till today the books so edited have remained the classics of Hindu literature and the repositories of Indian traditions. As Dr. Sukhtankar, the great *Mahabharata* scholar, has said: "The fact of expurgation and addition and elaboration is only an outward indication of its being a book of inspiration and guidance in life and not merely a book lying unused and forgotten on a dusty bookshelf. These are probably just the touches that have saved the *Mahabharata* from the fate of being consigned to the limbo of oblivion which has bafallen upon its sister epics like the *Gilgamesh*."

The Gupta period also stands out in the history of Indian literature and science. Of the *Kavya* literature it is not possible to speak here, but the first four centuries of the Christian era witnessed an efflorescence of literary effort which has been unequalled. In the sphere of philosophy also, it is generally held that the Sankhya system, which was undoubtedly many centuries older, found new strength in the commentaries of Varsgaganya and Ishwara Krishna of whom we know from Buddhist sources.

In the field of science the fourth and fifth centuries witnessed the highwater mark of early Indian achievement. The formulation of the theory of Zero—surely one of the most revolutionary discoveries in the field of thought—and the consequent evolution of the decimal system are to be credited to the thinkers of this age. In astronomy the progress achieved was remarkable. Aryabhata (born 476 A.D. at Pataliputra), who discovered that the earth rotates round its own axis and who calculated with only a very slight margin of error the duration of the day, is undoubtedly one of the greatest names in astronomy. Aryabhata also stated with unambiguous clarity the reason of the eclipses and was the first mathematician to allude to the decimal system, though its discovery belongs to an earlier period. Varahamihira, the other great scientist of the period, was a man of such a comprehensive mind that there was hardly any branch of natural sciences to which he did not contribute. Truly it could be said that the scholars of the Gupta period were gifted with an insatiable scientific curiosity, a desire to go forward in seeking knowledge and a courage in facing conclusions which is almost modern in its outlook.

Religion was rich, varied and vigorous. The Hindu gods underwent a transformation truly revolutionary and under familiar names and ancient forms assumed dynamic qualities which made their worship more alive to the people. The greatest change came over Vishnu. The God of Preservation in the Hindu trinnity, who was doctrinally immersed in yogic sleep, symbolising the static Vishnu, through the theory of avatars, became a dynamic, faith-giving and hope-inspiring saviour of humanity. The legend of Dasavatara, or the ten incarnations, had been popular long before the Christian era; but the worship of the avatars become popular only after the Christian era. All the ten incarnations never received worship. The earliest which received the honour of being worshipped as a deity in temples seems for some unknown reason to be the Boar Incarnation—the Adivaraha—whose temples are popular even today. The probable reason is that this incarnation is supposed to have redeemed the earth from the control of evil powers. Though other avatars were also worshipped their popularity never equalled that of Krishna. The acceptance of Vishnu's supreme Godhead is connected with Krishna, the last actual incarnation, whose total identification with Vishnu is one of the major developments of Hindu religion. Krishna Vasudeva was known to Panini but his worship as an incarnation of God does not seem to have established itself earlier than the first century B.C. His complete identification with Vishnu is testified by Kalidasa, a Siva worshipper, in two direct statements, one in *Meghaduta* where he uses the phrase "Vishnu in his form of cowherd," and the other in *Kumara Sambhava* where he uses the name of Krishna for Vishnu. While other incarnations including the popular hero Rama—whose name (Ram) was destined later to become the name of God—were never accepted as being anything more than partial manifestations; Krishna's identity with Vishnu and his final transformation as the Saviour and Supreme God took place in the first centuries in the Christian era. In the *Bhagawad Gita,* the first text of which could not be later than the Gupta period, Krishna is the One, Final and Absolute. At least two of the Gupta emperors Samudra Gupta and Chandra Gupta II were Vaishnavas, the second in fact claiming to be a Bhagavata.

It is not to be understood that Siva was less potent or less popular at this period. In fact, one of the outstanding features of Indian religious history is the unvarying influence of Siva—the Ascetic God—and this can only be traced to some aspect of the Hindu mind to which asceticism as a creed has a permanent appeal. Clothed in skin dripping with blood and ornamented with snakes, the Great Ascetic was never a "popular" god. Siva was the God to be worshipped and not loved, not a familiar personal deity like Krishna, or even like the Devi in her pleasanter aspects, but the stern Regulator of the world. Siva has no avatars but as Bhairava, Mahakala, and Ardhanarishwara and above all through his symbol, the Linga, was the object of devoted worship.

Many were the sects of ascetics that wore the marks of the Saivite, and some of them like the Pasupatas and the Kapalikas seem to have followed rites which were inhuman and barbarous. The Barasivas proclaimed their adherence to Siva worship and the Guptas themselves alternated between Siva and Vishnu. Devi worship—the cult of the mother goddess, the oldest of all religions —also seems to have received the imprimatur of orthodoxy at this time. We have the evidence of Gunadhya—as witnessed by all the three abstracts of the *Brihad Katha* now available—that the tantric forms of worship were prevalent in the first century B.C., though discredit attached to the communicants of the left hand path, whose practices then were not different from what they are today. The right hand path, however, had no stigma attached to it and was clearly included within the fold of orthodoxy. Kalidasa himself seems to have been a worshipper of the Devi. His name itself proclaims it, as it is obviously an assumed one which means the servant of Kali. Besides, the benedictory verse in *Raghuvamsa* clearly states the Sakta doctrine of the indivisibility of Siva and Parvati. The God Mahakala of Ujjain, whose worship the poet describes with manifest devotion, was, as we know from Gunadhya's story incorporated in *Kathasarit Sagara*, adored with tantric rites. In fact not only the different modes of Devi worship but the ceremonials of the tantric system in their various forms seem to have been well established in the Gupta period. The idea which once prevailed that the tantric forms of worship arose from the degenerate forms of Buddhism has, in fact, no evidence to support it; on the other hand, the Guhya Samaja doctrines of the Buddhists clearly had their inspiration in the time-old tantric cults of India.

The worship of the Devi penetrated the main bodies of the Saiva and Vaishnava sects. The Siva-Sakti doctrine became the cult of Lakshmi Narayana, and the *Gita* itself alludes to "My Prakriti". It was, therefore, not an independent system but one which was followed by both Vaishnava and Saiva sectarians without distinction.

One point needs special emphasis. The three systems did not constitute three religions for the essential reason that they were different only in the outer forms, characteristics and symbols of the deity, and not in the philosophy, doctrine or formularies of worship. The philosophy on which all these sects were based was the Vedanta. The object which all the three sects had was the same—Moksha. The ritual of worship was also common in essentials, based on the Agamas and not on the Vedas. For the Saivites the symbols were Rudraksha, Bhasma and of course the Linga; for the Vaishnavaites they were different. But apart from claiming for Siva or Vishnu the position of being the One and the Supreme God, there was no essential difference between them. That it was only a question of nomenclature was emphasised in all texts: that all three—Brahma, Vishnu and Siva—were aspects of the same Godhead was taught but the difference was prominent in the mind of the worshipper by the difference in attributes.

India's contacts with China and the penetration of Buddhism into that country also become important factors during this period. With Chang Kun's mission to the Yu-Chi capital (138-125 B.C.) geographical information about India begins to be collected by the Chinese. Indian scholars from Kashmir and elsewhere reached Chang An carrying with them not only Buddhist texts but the artistic and cultural traditions of India.

Buddhism was undoubtedly in a most flourishing condition. We have the evidence of Fa-Hien that monastic life was vigorous, that the religion of the noble eight-fold path was popular with the masses. It also shared very largely in the intellectual revival of the time as most of the great Buddhist classics in Sanskrit were the products of this age. Of the thousands of volumes which the saintly Doctor of Laws, Yuan-Chwang, collected and transported to China two hundred years later, many of the most valuable were the products of this age. Nagarjuna, Vasubandhu, Paramartha and Dinnaga to mention only four names among the most renowned in Buddhist thought lived during this period. Nalanda had already become famous an its fame attracted scholars from all over India and other Buddhist countries.

The general religious revival and the integration of national life following the expulsion of the barbarians give to the Gupta period its unique position in the history of India. That the economic life of the period was generally prosperous owing to increased overseas trade both with the Mediterranean countries and with the colonies in the East, is well established by the large number of inscriptions which have come down to us of endowments by merchant princes, trade guilds and craftsmen's unions. The colonial activity at this period will be separately dealt with, but the changes in habits and social circumstances following the great national expansion may be briefly alluded to. The use of silk had become general. Kalidasa specifically mentions Chinese silk. The use of intoxicants as a luxury by the richer classes was popular and did not involve the least social stigma. The allusions in *Kathasarit Sagara,* which as said before embodies in the main the social conditions of Gunadhya's time, to the use of intoxicants in all classes of society—and also by women—is sufficient proof of the wide prevalence of this habit. Women seem to have enjoyed very considerable freedom and the statement of the young lady in the Ocean of Story about the seclusion of women is worth quoting:

> "I consider," says the heroine Ratnaprabha, "the strict seclusion of women is a mere social custom or rather folly produced by jealousy. It is of no use whatever. Women of good family are guarded by their own virtue as their only chamberlain. Even God Himself can scarcely guard the unchaste."

The absence of any allusion to opium and other narcotic drugs in the literature of the time is also specially illuminating.

CHAPTER VII

SOUTH INDIA

THE evolution of peninsular India in the earlier periods seems to have been unconnected with Aryavarta. Civilisation, it is now recognised, developed independently in the area south of the Vindhyas and pre-history shows definite stages of evolution towards a high type of culture in different centres. Highly organised communities with knowledge of mining and metallurgy seem to have come into existence in different areas of the South long before recorded history begins.

The idea promulgated by some European writers and avidly followed by Indian scholars that the Dravidians were an earlier group of settlers from outside, who brought civilisation to the Deccan, has no evidence of any kind to prove it, and can be explained only by the acceptance of an unstated premise that the people of India cannot develop independent of outside help. In fact all available evidence and the results of investigations into pre-history go to establish that what we call Dravidian civilisation developed independently and without outside influence in the peninsula. The existence of primitive tribes in hill areas only shows that the communities which advanced in civilisation pressed back those who had fallen behind and confined them to inaccessible fastnesses.

The contacts that helped the growth of Dravidian civilisation, at least in the millennium preceding the Christian era, were with countries across the seas, Mesopotamia, Egypt and Palestine. Those contacts are well attested. Maritime intercourse of South India with the countries of the Middle East has been proved to go back at least to 1200 B.C. and a flourishing trade existed between the ports of the Persian Gulf, the Red Sea and the west coast of India. The use of Indian words in Hebrew for commodities in common use and imported into the Middle East from India clearly indicates that commercial relations between India and Judea flourished in the time of David and Solomon when Ophir is mentioned as the great port of commerce. Logs of Indian teak have been found in the temple of the Moon at Mugheir and in the palace of Nebuchadaenezzar. All this can only be said to indicate the development of maritime relations and does not constitute a historical record of importance; but we can legitimately infer from the mass of evidence available of the contact of South India with the west that the Deccan and Peninsular India generally had from the earliest times a civilisation independent of the north and were in close commercial relations with the countries of the Middle East.

So far as the islands of the Pacific are concerned, communications with them began even earlier. As Sylvain Levi very rightly says the sea routes to the East from the ports of South India had come into common use many centuries before the Christian era. Movement which carried Indian civilisation to different parts of the globe about the beginning of the Christian era were far from inaugurating any new route. Large-scale movement of population from South India seems to have taken place in the earlier periods which have had their influence on Austro-Asian peoples and even Madagascar.

It is noteworthy that when South India comes to be known first through the *Ramayana,* specific allusion is made also to Java and to Sumatra. The significant fact that till Rama reaches Kishkindha (modern Bellary) on civilised communities are described is clear enough evidence of the separation of north and south Indian cultures. There was really no common ground between them. Later in the third century B.C., when Asoka issued his rock-edicts, South India was not only known but definitely under the sway of the Neo-Aryan civilisation. Two of the earliest of Asoka's inscriptions are in Chitaldrug in Mysore (Minor Edicts I and II). Deccan up to the Mysore area was within the Mauryan empire The three southern kingdoms, the Chola, Chera and Pandya, were independent States outside the empire, but with them the Mauryan empire maintained the friendliest relations. To Ceylon, as already mentioned, he sent a religious mission.

It is obvious that in the centuries preceding the Mauryan empire the Neo-Aryan civilisation had penetrated the south and established a supremacy which in the time of the Mauryas was converted into a political dominion. The Chola, Pandya and Chera States came to be counted among the recognised monarchies of India, and the difference between the south and the north diminished from the point of view of culture, though South India, as we shall see, continued to be predominantly maritime in interest and in its economic development.

In the first century B.C. the trade of South India with the Roman Empire reached enormous proportions. According to the

Cambridge Ancient History, Italy imported more from India than from any other country except Spain. Pliny computes Rome's annual payment to India at 550 million Sesterii, and the yearly loss to Rome in balance of trade at 100 million (1 sesterce = ½ rupee). The recent excavations at Arikamedu near Pondicherry have established beyond dispute the existence of cosmopolitan maritime towns, depending mainly on their trade with the Roman empire. Muziris on the west coast (in Kerala) and Arikamedu on the east coast were great emporia of Mediterranean trade. The discovery of large collections of Roman coins affords direct evidence of this fact, while the excavations clearly establish the high state of material civilisation which the south had already attained before the Christian era.

The Arikamedu excavations, the results of which have recently been published, are of special importance, as they both confirm the evidence of Tamil literature and establish beyond dispute some of the main features of Dravidian civilisation before the Christian era. An extensive trading centre with large warehouses of foreign merchants has been brought to light, where apart from other interesting things, dated Roman pottery has been discovered. In the Tamil literature of the first century we have the description of Kaveripattanam, a little to the south of the present site. It is stated in a Tamil classic: "The sun shone over the open terraces, over the warehouses near the harbour, and over turrets with windows like the eyes of deer. In different places of Puhar the onlooker's attention was arrested by the sight of the abode of Yavanas whose prosperity never waned. At the harbour were to be seen sailors from distant lands." Roman coins were also in extensive circulation and the trade between Rome and South India seems to have been mainly in spices, cotton cloth, pearls and other traditionally Indian products while Rome seems to have sent pottery, glassware and gold.

The three kingdoms (Trairajya) formed already the traditional polity of the Dravidian system and with the control of oceanic commerce and close relations with both the Mediterranean and the islands of the Pacific, the region evolved peacefully and attained a high state of economic prosperity. Megasthenes had heard of the Pandyas. The country was at that time said to have been ruled by a queen whose army was composed of five hundred elephants, four thousand cavalry and 130,000 infantry. No doubt it is this military strength which prevented the Mauryas from annexing the country.

Patanjali (150 B.C.) speaks of Kanchi (Kanchipuram) and of

Kerala. Patanjali's allusion to Sarasi as being used in the south to denote large lakes indicates the prevalence of Sanskrit in the south as early as the second century B.C. In fact taken with the allusions of Megasthenes and the inscriptions of Asoka, we can definitely assume that the Neo-Aryan culture had established itself firmly in the south at least by the end of the fifth century B.C.

The organisation of the society was however mainly tribal and predominantly non-Aryan. The Dravidian people seem to have been organised under totemic clans, and their worship of totem symbols continued for long. The snake cult among the Nayars is a surviving example. Aryan culture was superimposed on communities which normally lived their own lives. The attack on the indigenous religions seems to have come originally not from Hinduism, but from Jainism and Buddhism. Both these sects obtained an early hold on South India. Asoka's missionaries had a virgin soil in South India, where the thin layer of Aryanism which the earlier influences no doubt established was not strong enough to withstand the activities of zealous and wandering Buddhist monks.

It is with the second century B.C. that South India comes into the full view of Indian History. The Hathigumpha inscription of Kharavela, the Kalinga king, is the first record of a great monarch directly conducting his campaign in the south. The Kalingas were a Dravidian people more Aryanised than the peoples of the South. Under Kharavela, they extended their power to the south and conquered and brought under control practically the whole of South India.

Kharavela speaks of having destroyed a confederacy of Tamil States (165 B.C.). His inscription also boasts that the Kalinga king took away a great quantity of pearls for which the Pandava and Kerala countries were famous. It is clear from these allusions that the Tamil country was already organised as the Trairajya and enjoyed, as reported earlier by Megasthenes, a high degree of civilisation.

The first Chera monarch of whom we have information is Udiyan Jeral (c. A.D. 150) whose son Nedum Jeral Ādan claims to have won a naval victory in which he captured some yavanas. He was evidently a mighty conqueror for he styles himself as the "sovereign who had the Himalayas as his boundary." His son Seran Senguthuvan is one of the great monarchs of South India. A no less important personage was Karikala Chola (A.D. 190) who established his sway over the Tamil country after defeating the Pandyas and the Cheras. He was an enlightened ruler who promoted reclamation of land, built extensive irrigation tanks, and generally looked after the welfare of the people.

The early centuries of the Christian era witnessed also great literary activity in the Tamil country. The first *Sangam* or literary academy is said to have flourished in this period. There is no doubt that some of the greatest classics of Tamil, including the famous epic *Silappadikāaram,* were written during this period.

While the Tamil country was thus prospering under the Trairajya or three kingdoms, northern Deccan was undergoing great changes. The short-lived empire of Kharavela was supplanted in the Deccan region by a more important dynasty which had probably the greatest influence in the integration between the south and north, that of the Satavahanas of Pratistan. This great dynasty, whose first king we know of is Krishna and whose last monarch was Madhaviputra, enjoys a position of unique importance in India's history. Krishnaraja was followed by Sumukha whose successor, Satakarni, enjoyed an imperial position with his authority extending both to the north and to the south of the Vindhyas. The disruption of the northern kingdoms and the consequent inroads of the Sakas and other foreign elements seem to have had their effect on the Pratistan kingdom also, for Gautamiputra Satakarni claims in his inscriptions to have driven out these foreigners and re-established the glory of the Satavahana dynasty. Satavahana power was well established by the beginning of the Christian era and the numerous inscriptional records of the dynasty indicate that in the unsettled period between the fall of the Sungas and the growth of the Vakatakas, Middle India enjoyed settled conditions and prosperity and was hardly troubled by the inroads of foreigners. The Satavahanas held authority for about three centuries from 73 B.C. to A.D. 218 and this period is of supreme importance in the growth of the Neo-Aryan civilisation in the south.

One remarkable feature relating to this dynasty is the maternal names by which the kings are known, Gautamiputra Satakarni, Satakarni the son of Gautami; Vasistiputra Pulumayi, Pulumayi the son of Vasisti; Gautamiputra Sriyajna Satakarni, etc. The same unusual custom will be noticed among some of the matriarchal kings of the far-eastern colonies also.

Placed strategically in the large area which geographically was the laboratory of relations between the Aryan civilisation of the north and the historic Dravidian civilisation of the south, the Pratistan Empire during the three hundred years of its existence can claim to have fulfilled its historical mission of establishing the cultural unity of India. The Mauryan conquest of the South was an extension of northern authority which no doubt was accompanied by a penetration of northern culture and ideas. But the Mauryan hold weakened after Asoka and the influence of the imperial government was too short-lived to have brought the North and the South together in ideas. This was the historic mission of the Satavahanas and the geographical position of the empire, placed as it was in the centre of India, enabled them to fulfil it with success. The South India we see in the fourth century has been Aryanised in thought and ideas. The Pallava power at Kanchi is Sanskritic in its civilisation and even the Pandyas and Cheras have come fully into the composite structure of Hindu civilisation. The credit for this great transformation belongs to the Satavahanas.

Pratistan, their capital, was one of the great centres of civilisation at the time, an imperial city whose glory is fully reflected in literature. It is the Paithana of Ptolemy, the capital of Sri Polemaios (Pulumayi). The great Gunadhya, the author of *Brihadkatha,* lived here and the story of the rivalry between Sankrit and Paisachi (the dialect of the barbarians) on which the story of *Brihadkatha* is itself based is a clear indication of the fight that was then taking place for the predominance of Sanskrit as the vehicle of civilisation and culture.

Under the Satavahanas Hinduism and Buddhism seem to have flourished equally. "In the first centuries of our era," says Grousset, "when northern India was being subjected in art as well as in politics to the domination of foreign peoples—Greeks and Scythians—Andhra has preserved inviolate as well as its political independence the tradition of Indian aesthetics." Amaravati, Goli, Nagarjuna Konda had from the second to the fourth century A.D. become covered with stupas of which the sculpture serves as a link between the primitive Buddhist art of Sanchi and the Gupta workshops of the fourth to the seventh centuries. Religious establishments, temples, monasteries and dharmashalas were built all over the country both by royal bounty and by the munificence of private donors. The foreman of the artisans of Sri Satakarni is recorded in an inscription in Bhilsa tope as having made a grant. In the Nasik inscription, which records the dedication of a great Buddhist cave monastery excavated at his own expense, Ushavadata speaks of his numerous charities to Brahmins also. This Buddhist merchant fed a hundred thousand Brahmins. Gautamiputra Satakarni who declares himself to be the sole protector of the Brahmins records a benefaction for the Buddhists.

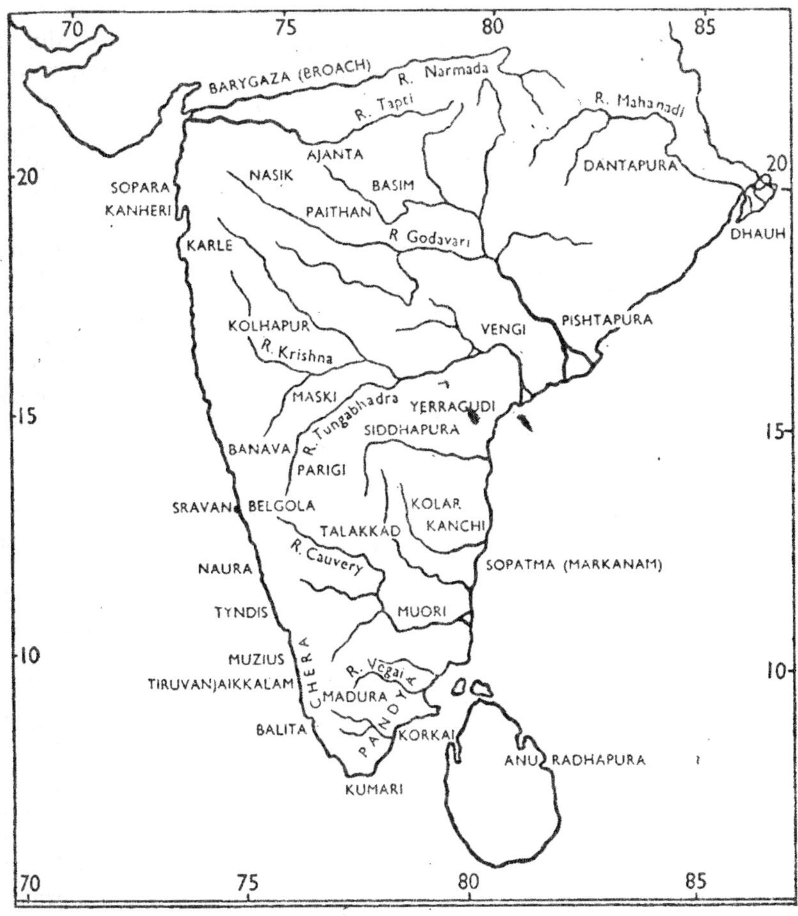

SOUTH INDIA: 300 B.C. — A.D. 500

The Satavahanas were great excavators of cave temples and the magnificent temples of Ellora and Ajanta were the continuation of the Satavahana tradition to which all Middle Indian dynasties in succeeding ages claimed historic relationship. The basic tradition in Middle India is of the Satavahana empire, as in the north it is of the Mauryan. From the point of view of historic continuity it is important to remember this primary fact, as up to quite recent times, the traditions flowing from the Satavahanas were living factors in Indian history, as we shall try to show.

The Satavahana empire extended from sea to sea and virtually included the whole of South India excluding the Trairajya or the Chola, Pandya and Chera kingdoms in the extremity and in the north it included Bhilsa and a great portion of Central India. Orissa was included in the direct domains of the empire. Naturally, with so vast a coastline including many of the more important ports, trade and commerce flourished greatly within the empire. Kalyan was the most important trade centre and we have the names of numerous merchant princes belonging to that place inscribed in the caves of Kanheri and Junnar as having made generous contributions of a philanthropic nature. The extent of individual fortunes of the great merchants of this time may be judged from the fact that the great Karli caves were excavated at the expense of a single pious Seth of Vaijayanti—a commercial town of great importance near Goa.

Another notable fact relating to the conditions within the Satavahana empire was the facility of communications between its different parts. The grants made and recorded in many of the important places are by merchants living in distant parts of the empire. Commerce, which these monarchs specially encouraged, and the influence which the great capitalist class of merchants undoubtedly exercised involved the organisation of easy and peaceful communications, a tradition which a national system of pilgrimages that seems to have come into existence from very early times must have greatly strengthened.

It was the emergence of Vakataka power in the Vindhya area somewhere about the middle of the third century that brought about the downfall of the Satavahanas. But an empire so firmly established in its home domains does not break down with the fall of a dynasty. The Rashtrakutas and the Chalukyas in the Godavari valley and the Pallavas in the south, originally the viceroys of the Satavahanas, claimed succession to the empire within their own territorial limits as the Vakatakas claimed it to the north of the Vindhyas. The Ganges and the Kadambas were also the inheritors of the tradition and as the Vijayanagar emperors claimed in time to be Chalukya Chudamanis, or the crest jewels of the Chalukya dynasty, and as the great kings of Gujerat equally claimed succession from the Chalukyas, the imperial tradition of the Satavahanas may be said to have been carried forward at least to the beginning of the seventeenth century.

The rise of the great dynasty of the Pallavas of Kanchi is shrouded in obscurity. A similarity of names led earlier historians to the hasty conclusion that the Pallavas and the Pahlavas were racially related. This is but another example of the tendency of European historians to believe that anything good in India must have had a foreign origin. Dr. Krishnaswamy Aiyangar, the doyen of Indian historians, after a careful and searching examination of all evidence states:

> "We do not meet with the form Pahlava in connection with the Pallavas of Kanchi in any record of their time. . . . The word as applied to Pallavas in the first instance seems to be a translation of the Tamil word Tondaiyar and Tondaman and this finds confirmation in some of the copperplate charters which do bring in tender twigs of some kind in connection with the eponymous name Pallava. This undoubtedly is a later use of the term but gives the indication that even at that comparatively late period the traditional nation was that they were not foreigners such as the Pahlavas would have been. *In all the material that has been examined there is nothing to indicate either the migration of a people or even of a family that might have ultimately raised itself into a dynasty from the north-west,* so that the assumption of a connection between the one set of people and the other rests upon the mere doubtful ground of a possibility whereas the translation or adaptation of a southern word into Sanskrit is very much more than a possibility as indeed a word like Dravida or Dramida would clearly indicate."

We have in fact in Rajasekhara the distinction between Pahlava and Pallava clearly made and emphasised.

The Pallavas seem to have been the governors of the Satavahanas on the southern marches. With the breakup of the Pratistan empire they assumed their independence and when Samudra Gupta marched to the south they were well established in Kanchi, the ancient capital of Tondamandalam and of the great dynasty of Cholas. Vishnu Gopa, mentioned in Harishena's inscription as having been conquered by Samudra Gupta, was a Pallava king.

But the greatness of the Pallavas was still to come as the Cholas, though driven out of their capital, were still powerful and the Pandyas had maintained their independence and authority even against the Satavahanas.

An equally important succession State to the Satavahanas was that of the Chalukyas, the great bearers of the imperial tradition in north Deccan. The Chalukyas, though claiming descent from the Solar dynasty, were a local family which rose to power gradually and established themselves after a continuous period of fight with the Rastrakutas who seem to have become the rulers of this territory during the declining years of the Satavahanas. In any case the inscriptions definitely establish the fact that Jayasimha, the first important Chalukya king, defeated Indra, the son of Krishna of the Rastrakuta family, and founded his dynasty.

Between them, the Pallavas and the Chalukyas dominated South Indian history for over a period of three hundred years.

CHAPTER VIII

GREATER INDIA

THE expansion of Indian culture and influence both in Central Asia and in the south-east towards the countries and islands of the Pacific is one of the momentous factors of the period immediately preceding the Christian era. Asoka's missionaries travelled far to the west but the result of their work in Antioch and Alexandria and other distant countries must remain a matter of speculation. Their influence on the Greek dynasties of Bactria and the North-West Frontier is however well attested. *Milinda Panho,* or the questions of Milinda or Menander, clearly establishes the increasing hold of Buddhist thought over the Indo-Greek monarchies of the frontier which in due time produced the spectacular efflorescence of Greco-Buddhist art in Gandhara and north-west India.

It is however the Kushan empire of Kanishka, Huviska and Vasudeva which became the carriers of Indian thought into Central Asia. Kanishka was the patron of Mahayana Buddhism, and his empire outside India became a scene of Indian missionary activity. The great Kasyapa Matanga and Dharmaratna were actually employed in missionary work in Indo-Scythian countries when the Chinese ambassadors met them (68 A.D.). From that time there was a continuous and uninterrupted flow of scholars, monks and missionaries to China of whom the most famous was Kumarajiva, who translated into Chinese the works of Asvaghosha, Nagarjuna and Vasubandhu. The Indianisation of Khotan, Kucha and other areas in Central Asia is still evidenced by the great mass of Buddhist literature that has been discovered there by various expeditions.

The influence of India across the land frontier was cultural and religious. Across the sea it was also political. From the first century A.D. we witness the strange fact of Hindu or Hinduised kingdoms in Annam, Cochin-China and the islands of the Pacific. The *Ramayana* knew of Java and Sumatra. Communication by sea between the ports of South India and the islands of the Pacific was well established many centuries before the Christian era. But the earliest evidence we have of actual emigration is in the first century of the Christian era. The route of emigration must have been by land across Malaya and by sea through the Straits of Singapore. Kataha—modern Kedah—is frequently alluded to as the first port of call.

We have numerous instances of stories in the *Kathasarit Sagara*, which embodies the stories of the Satavahana period, of ships sailing direct to Kataha. In the story of Devasmita (pp. 154-5, Penzer's translation) it is stated: "Then Guhasena's (the hero's) father died and he himself was urged by his relations to go to the country of Kataha." Then, after avowing eternal fidelity to his beloved, Guhasena left from Tamralipti, the Kalinga port, for Kataha which country he quickly reached. He engaged in jewel trade there and prospered greatly. Again in the story of Chandraswami it is stated thus: "It is true that a merchant named Kanakavarman did come here with two beautiful Brahmin children whom he found in a wood. But he has gone with him to Kataha-dwipa." The Brahmin followed him to Kataha in a ship with the merchant Danavarman. From there he followed them to Karpanadwipa (the Camphor island) and Suvarna (Sumatra). The recent investigations of Quaritch Wales have also shown that an alternative land route was also used by Indian merchants. The Takola mart, at the mouth of the Takuopa river in the Malayan Peninsula, which was flourishing in the second century A.D., is now proved to have been the great emporium of eastern trade.

The route used by Indian traders must have been both trans-peninsular, along the Malayan coast up to the Mekong Valley, and by sea through the Straits of Malacca, as in the case of Danavarman already alluded to. The discovery and colonisation of Sumatra, Java and Borneo were the results of oceanic navigation. The history of this momentous adventure is what is embodied in the legend of Agastya, the patron saint of navigators and colonists and worshipped even today in Indonesia and Japan. The Puranic story of Agastya drinking up the waters of the ocean is as follows. The peoples of the seacoast of South India were at one time subjected to nightly attacks by rakshasas who arrived by ship and laid waste the coastal villages. They complained to Agastya who, discovering that the rakshasas were the inhabitants of lands under the sea, drank up the water which enabled the population to carry the war against the pirates of the night. This Puranic version, taken with the worship of Agastya in all the colonies, indicates that the earliest Indian voyages to the islands were for the purpose of chasing pirates who had become a source of danger to coastal peoples. The allusions in the *Ramayana* to Java and Ptolemy's mention of Yava-dwipa in the first century A.D. clearly establish the fact that Java had come under Indian influence at least by the beginning of the Christian era.

The earliest evidence of an actually flourishing Hindu community on the Pacific coast comes from Funan, a portion of modern Indo-China, which borders on Tonkin. Chinese records mention the date of the establishment of this kingdom as 192 A.D. and we have also an inscription of a king by the name of Srimara which is also said to be of the same period. The extent of colonisation at this period can be judged from the fact that an inscription in Eastern Borneo tells us of a king by the name of Ashvavarman whose son Mulavarman performed various orthodox Hindu sacrifices under the direction of Brahmins. If Borneo had been colonised in the fourth century A.D. it is obvious that the intervening territories of Malaya, Sumatra and Java should have already come under Indian influence and authority.

The establishment of a Hindu kingdom of Funan (later Kambuja) is alluded to in the history of the southern Thai compiled in the beginning of the fifth century. It is recorded there as an ancient tradition. The story is as follows: "Of old this country had for sovereign a woman of the name of Lieou-ye. Then there was a man of the country of Ki, Hoeun-Tien, who dreamt that God gave him a bow and bade him embark on a junk and go out on the sea. In the morning Hoeun-Tien went to the temple of the God and found a bow. Then he embarked on a junk and sailed towards Funan. Lieou-ye saw the junk and led her troops to resist him. But Houen-Tien raised his bow and shot an arrow which passing through the side of a boat struck somebody within. Lieou-ye was frightened and submitted. Hoeun-Tien married her. He wrapped her in a piece of cloth as she had no clothing."

Hoeun-Tien is a transcription of Kaundinya whose name is revered and often appears in inscriptions as the founder of the Hindu royal families of greater India. For example in a Champa inscription dated A.D. 658 it is stated: "It was there that Kaundinya, the greatest of the Brahmins, planted the javelin which he had received from Aswathama, the son of Drona. There was a daughter of the Naga king. . . . The great Brahmin Kaundinya married her for the accomplishment of the rites."

The Kaundinya tradition is important in three respects. In the first place, the emigrant leader is said to have been a Brahmin; secondly, he arrives by sea; thirdly, his landing is resisted by the local princess whom he overcomes and marries.

The fact that the local population was in a more or less primitive state of civilisation is attested by the fact that the queen was naked and Kaundinya, in accepting her submission, covered her with cloth. The Brahmin conqueror by marrying the Naga princess obtained—as a Pallava inscription describes a similar incident—both a wife and a kingdom. The dynasty so established accepted Hindu rites and codes and became in fact Hindu. Kaundinya's followers also married and settled down in Funan and thus a Hindu community, following as far as possible the traditions of the motherland, was established overseas.

Kaundinya who thus founded a kingdom on the mainland reached there by sea. Did he go from India? We know that before the first century A.D. Java was already a Hindu kingdom. An embassy from a Java king named Devavarman had reached China in 132 A.D. and even before that geographers knew the island by its Sanskrit name of Yava-dwipa—the Barley island. Kang-Tai, the Chinese ambassador who visited Funan in the third century and recorded the story of Kaundinya, mentions the Brahmins as coming from an island in the Archipelago—clear enough evidence that before the third century the islands had been colonised from India.

The kingdom established by Kaundinya flourished greatly, for in the next century some of its vassal kingdoms are alluded to in Chinese annals. Of one such kingdom it is stated: "Merchants come there in great numbers to transact business. . . . The market is the meeting ground of the East and the West." Of another dependency of Funan it is stated: "More than a thousand Brahmins from India reside there. The people follow their doctrines and give them their daughters in marriage."

The kings of Funan also maintained direct relations with India. We have mention of an embassy sent by one of the Funan kings to India in the year 240 A.D. which took four years to complete its mission.

In the fourth century, however, we have another Kaundinya story in a Chinese history which is particularly interesting. Pelliot, the great French scholar who has translated it, gives it as follows: "Kaundinya a Brahmin from India heard a supernatural voice calling to him, 'You must go and reign in Funan'. Kaundinya rejoiced in his heart and reached Pan-Pan which is to the south. The people of Funan heard of him and the whole kingdom was stirred with joy. They came to him and chose him king. *He changed all the rules according to the methods of India.*"

This second arrival is different from the first: for in the fourth century a Hinduised kingdom was already in existence in Funan, as also numerous other principalities in the islands, and in Malaya Pan-Pan mentioned in the extract is specially alluded to in the Chinese chronicles as a small principality under Funan where "they all learn Brahminical writings and pay great reverence to the Buddha's law. There are temples of Buddhist and Brahmin priests. . . . At the king's court one sees many Brahmins come from India in order to profit by his munificence."*

The second Kaundinya arrived from Pan-Pan across the land route from Takola. This is particularly important as a connecting link in the history of the island colonies. During the first three centuries of the Christian era there is ample evidence of Hindu kingdoms in Java, Borneo and the Camphor islands. But they disappear from history till the rise of the Srivijaya Empire in the sixth century, while the continental kingdoms of Funan, Champa and Pan-Pan flourish. The sea route which took Indian emigrants to the islands must have for some reason become dangerous, thereby drying up the stream of emigrants on whom depended the growth of the small principalities established in these outlying areas. These small colonies were assimilated by the local population and the knowledge of Sanskrit which Mulavarman's Borneo inscription shows faded away through lack of contact with the mother country. The principalities in the Mekong Valley were however continuously reinforced across the land route which Quaritch Wales has now traced.

Kaundinya II, who introduced Indian laws and rules in the kingdom of Funan, seems to have reorganised the State and society. We have some records of his descendants, a stone inscription of Gunavarman, described as "the very moon of the Kaundinya dynasty," who consecrated a temple to Vishnu, and of Kaundinya Jayavarman who sent an embassy to China in 484 A.D. to ask for aid against the growing power of Champa. The imperial edict issued by the Son of Heaven states:

> "The king of Funan Kaundinya Jayavarman lives in the extreme limits of the ocean. From generation to generation he and his ancestors have governed the distant countries of the South and their sincerity is manifest even from a distance. It is fit to show in return some favour and to confer on him a glorious title. This can be done by the title of the General of the Pacific South, King of Funan."

*G. H. Luce: *Journal of the Burma Research Society*, Vol. XIV, Part II, pp. 170-2.

We have a description from Chinese sources of the State of Funan under the Kaundinyas. Pelliot gives the following extracts which will be found interesting: "For merchandise they have gold, silver and silks. Persons of high degree dress in brocade, the women wearing also a kind of turban. Poor people wear pieces of cloth. . . . They cut down trees to make dwellings and the king lives in a storied pavilion. They build palisades of wood and people live in houses raised from the ground. They make boats. . . . When the king goes out he rides on an elephant and the women also ride elephants. For amusements they make cocks and pigs fight. . . . " Religious practices are described thus: "Of these divinities they make images of bronze: some of them have two faces, others have four faces and eight arms. In each hand something is held."

Funan was in fact a completely Hinduised kingdom. By the beginning of the fifth century, a new kingdom named Champa came into existence which kept up a continuous war against Funan. It was in fact to solicit the assistance of the Chinese emperor against Champan attacks that Jayavarman sent his first embassy to China.

The States in the islands, though established earlier, do not come into full view at this time, as our sources are limited to Chinese records. The actual colonisation of Java is said to have taken place in 56 A.D. Undoubtedly there were petty Hindu principalities in different parts of the island in the second century A.D., for one of them King Devavarman sent an embassy to China in 132 A.D. We have also the Sanskrit inscriptions of Purnavarman whose father is called Rajadhiraja. Fa Hien, the great Chinese pilgrim who was in India between 399 to 414 A.D., returned to China by sea and stayed for five months in Java. There he found Brahminism flourishing.

The position at the beginning of the fifth century in Further India may be briefly summarised as below. By about the first century A.D. small waves of colonists began to establish themselves on the coastal regions of the Indonesian islands and Indo-China. They established small principalities, married locally and their States became the centres of flourishing trade with India, carried on through the east coast ports from Tamralipti to Negapatam. The entrepot of this great oceanic commerce was the Takola mart in Malaya in which peninsula numerous Hindu kingdoms were in existence of which the most important was Nakhon Sri Dharmmarat (Ligor). Indian colonies which exploited tin and gold mines also existed in Selensing, Panga, Puket, and Takuopa. The region around the Bay of Bandom was the great centre from which Indian influence radiated.

In the third and fourth centuries there is a considerable decline of Indian influence in the islands which can only be explained by the failure of the sea route either by the occupation of the Straits of Malacca by a hostile power or by the growth of piracy. But this decline is undoubted, for the communities planted in Borneo and Celebes fade away and even in Java there is no growth comparable to the development of the kingdoms of Funan and Champa. In the third and fourth centuries the movement of Indian adventurers and merchants to the Far East seems to have been across the peninsula by the land route and the sudden emergence of Funan as a great Hindu kingdom fully justifies this assumption.

The caste system of the Hindus was introduced early enough in these areas: but it could have been by approximation as in South India. Kaundinya, the Brahmin, married the naked princess and his descendants assumed Kshatriyahood and took the names of Varman. We have statements that Brahmins and others from India married the women of the country. In fact the first emigration led to assimilation and when larger numbers began to come as in the case of Kaundinya II the population was already mixed and the transformation of society into a nominally Hindu structure was easy.

Generally speaking Indian colonisation up to the end of the fifth century is one of preparation. It is the establishment of communities and the development of civilised ways of life. The period of achievement and glory associated with Champa, Kamboja, Srivijaya and Java kingdoms is still in the womb of time, but the achievements of the kings of Funan already give us glimpses of the greatness to come.

The reaction of this overseas activity on India was very considerable. An explanation of the immense wealth of the merchants who made such munificent endowments as witnessed by the inscriptions in the temples of the Satavahana period lies in the great overseas trade. This is fully borne out by the constant allusion in the stories of Gunadhya to the frequent voyages of merchants overseas for the purpose of trade. Tamil literature of the first centuries of the Christian era, especially *Silappadikaram* and *Manimekhalai,* also testify to this great interest in overseas trade while in Kalidasa we have the allusion to ships laden with spices from distant islands lying in Kalinga ports.

The Kalingas and the southern kingdoms seem to have been

the pioneers in this activity. The fact that the great navigator (Maha Navika) Budha Gupta's inscribed bell states that he came from the land of red clay, identified with Rangamayi in Midnapur, shows that all parts of maritime India shared in this Great Expansion.

CHAPTER IX

THE PERIOD OF EMPIRE—HARSHA

THOUGH the imperial power of the Guptas broke up by 544 A.D. after Budha Gupta, the Gupta-Vakataka system seems to have continued in different parts of the country for a long time afterwards as we have numerous inscriptions of kings claiming descent from them but enjoying only local authority. The Vakatakas in the Vindhya and Aravali Hills under Pravarasena II and his successors and the disrupted branches of the Gupta dynasty in Magadha continued to rule and to pretend to imperial authority. But north-western India had passed into the hands of Hun Invaders. In 495 A.D. Toramana had already established himself in the Punjab and was attacking Malwa. The hundred years of warfare on the Indian frontier had changed the original character of the Huns. Toramana was no nomadic savage but a Hinduised frontier potentate attacking a decayed empire. He had in fact ceased to be a foreigner. His successor Mihiragula was undoubtedly one of the worst tyrants known to history. Under Baladitya Gupta, the last great monarch of the imperial dynasty, the rulers of North India combined to attack him and overthrow his power in a great battle in 528 A.D. The so-called Hun dynasty which hardly lasted two generations ended with it.

The absence of an imperial authority exercising sway all over North India, together with the known facts of Mihiragula's oppression of Malwa, has led historians easily to assume that the sixth century was a period of political anarchy. It is undoubtedly true that the loss of Malwa involved a withdrawal of Gupta power to the east and a weakening of its authority over the local dynastics. But the period as a whole was one of notable achievements. The Magadha kingdom of what may be called the Later Guptas continued uninterrupted to the end of the seventh century as we know from the dated inscription of Adityasena. It is under the fostering care of this eminently Hindu dynasty that the great university of Nalanda attained its greatness.

The Indo-Gangetic valley was ruled by the Maukharis of Kanauj, who assumed complete political independence in the sixth century. Under a succession of monarchs, who held their own against the pretensions of the Guptas of Magadha, Kanauj attained a glory which equalled that of Ujjain and Pataliputra. Next to Magadha was Karna Suvarna whose ancient dynasty comes to prominence with the breakdown of imperial authority.

The picture of North India during the hundred years that preceded the empire of Harsha is therefore not one of anarchy, but of a few well established kingdoms which in their own territories carried on the traditions of the empire. In the areas surrounding the Vindhyas the Vakatakas ruled with effective authority. In Magadha the diminished but reconstituted empire of the Later Guptas carried on the historic tradition. In the Gangetic Valley the Maukhari kings consolidated their rule. It is in fact a period when the imperial tradition was under an eclipse, but the country as a whole was peaceful and prosperous and not, as usually assumed, subject to anarchical disruption.

This is fully borne out by the achievements of the time. "With a view to seeing Kailasa mountain surpassed, Baladitya erected a great and extraordinary temple of the illustrious son of Suddhodana (Buddha) here at Nalanda," says an inscription. This was the great university which was soon to become internationally famous. The university was well endowed by his successors and flourished greatly in the sixth century. The saintly Sthiramati, under whom the university became renowned, was its head in the middle of the sixth century. Dharmapala who adorned the Rectorship in the later half of the century, was an equally eminent scholar. In fact it can legitimately be said that the period from Vasubandhu (480 A.D.) to Silabhadra in the seventh century was the golden period of Nalanda.

Equally it can be said that the sixth century witnessed the perfection of classical Sanskrit. Bharavi, Kumaradasa (of *Janaki-harana*) and Dandin among the poets and Visakhadatta, and perhaps the author of *Kaumudi Mahotsava,* among the dramatists, lived in the sixth century A.D. European scholarship ascribes to the sixth century the development of Indian mathematics and astronomy. Varahamihira is said to have died in 587 A.D. Aryabhata, born in 476, lived into the sixth century. Indian medicine also saw much development during this period.

Philosophy, logic, mimamsa and exegetics also seem to have received special attention in this century. Prabhakara's Mimamsa was developed during this period and so far as Buddhist and Hindu systems of logic are concerned the sixth century was their golden age. Another notable achievement belonging to this century is the growth of vernacular literature. Prakrit seems to have evolved into a literary language during this time and we have the grammars of Prakritic languages which enabled Rajasekhara and others to make of Prakrit a great classical literature in the next century.

On a careful examination, the old view that the sixth century was a period of anarchy and disruption and the age of Harsha that followed was a last glow has to be definitely abandoned. On the other hand it will be seen that the sixth century was a germinal period, an age which apart from its own very notable achievements in every sphere, sowed the seeds of later development.

The history of Harsha (606-647 A.D.) is known to us in fuller detail because we have both indigenous and external sources relating to his reign. We have the *Harsha Charita* of Bana, a unique biography, which apart from its extraordinary qualities as literature is also a storehouse of earlier historical information. Bana's style was allusive, and spread throughout his great work are allusions to earlier incidents (e.g., Chandra Gupta's rescue of Dhruvaswamini) which are now being corroborated from other sources. But besides *Harsha Charita* we have the unique record left to us by the great Chinese pilgrim, Yuan-Chwang, whose life is one of the romances of world history. Yuan-Chwang was, in matters unconnected with Buddhist miracles, an accurate observer and his travels provide the first complete picture of India that we possess.

The chief events of Harsha's reign can be briefly stated. Harsha's grandfather Adityavardhana was a feudatory ruler of Thanesvar. Under his son Prabhakaravardhana, the principality emerged into a major State which was in constant warfare with the Huns on the frontier and with the rulers of Malwa. Prabhakara was succeeded by his elder son Rajyavardhana who however lost his life in a battle against Sasanka, the king of Gauda. Harsha, his brother, on coming to the throne set himself to bring the whole of Aryavarta under his sway, which he did in some cases by conquest, in some cases by alliance as with Madhava Gupta of Magadha and Kumara of Kamarupa. Nepal and Kashmir were also within his empire.

While his authority north of the Vindhyas was complete Harsha's arms met with a definite setback when he advanced towards the south. The Emperor of Aryavarta was opposed and defeated on the banks of the Tapti by Pulikesena II, the monarch of Chalukyas, who himself assumed the title of Emperor on the basis of his victory over Harsha. Undisputed emperor of the North, Harsha, after the defeat at the hands of Pulikesena, seems to have turned more to the arts of peace. Himself a dramatist and poet of great distinction, Harsha's court attracted the greatest writers of the day, among whom were Bana, Mayura, Hardatta and Jayasena. The Chinese pilgrim lived at his court and we have therefore a trustworthy description of the life of the time.

In his personal religion Harsha was a follower of Buddha; but as in the case of other Indian Buddhist kings he remained a Hindu. In his own books it is to Siva that he prays. Daily he fed five hundred Brahmins along with a thousand Buddhist monks. At all ceremonial festivals of the king, Siva and Vishnu received full honours along with Buddha. The pious Chinese Doctor of Laws himself bears witness to this fact. Though interested in metaphysical discussions and a devotee of liberal arts, Harsha was also zealous in the performance of his kingly duties. He constantly toured his vast empire, as Yuan-Chwang testifies, and kept a watchful eye on the activities of his vassals.

An artificial glow illumines the reign of Harsha, because of the panegyrics of Bana and the interesting details given by the Chinese traveller. But it is important to note that Harsha's empire was one which was composed of powerful independent monarchs, who accepted the suzerainty of Harsha more as a personal homage than as subordination to an empire. The great dynasty of the Maukharis, which was closely allied to that of Harsha, ruled over the eastern portion of their hereditary dominions. Madhava Gupta of Magadha was a powerful monarch. The Maitrekas of Vallabhi and Kumara Bhaskara of Kamarupa were hardly vassals of the empire. All of them recognised the personal greatness of Harsha and accepted him as a suzerain. His dazzling personality alone gave a semblance of unity to the empire which extended from the Indus to the Brahmaputra.

The death of Harsha in 647 after a brilliant reign of 41 years witnessed the end of this artificial unity. The great monarchs who had bowed to his authority recognised no successor to Harsha. During the interregnum that followed in the territories under the direct authority of Harsha, there is one curious incident to which so much importance has been attached by foreign writers as to speak of a Chinese invasion of India. A provincial governor of Tirhut in the Himalayan region insulted a Chinese envoy, Wang-Huen-Tse, who was able to persuade the Nepalese and the Tibetans to take up his cause. The Nepalese and the Tibetans marched into Tirhut, with the assistance of Kumara Bhaskara Varman of Kamarupa and inflicted punishment on the rude governor. This totally insignificant event has been elevated by some historians as a Chinese invasion of India.

From Yuan-Chwang's travels and biography we can have a fairly accurate picture of India in the first half of the seventh century. The Chinese pilgrim entered India from the north-west, visited Kashmir and travelled down by Sialkot and Jullunder to Kanauj. After visiting the holy places of Buddhism in Nepal he journeyed by boat down the Ganges, visited Prayag and Banaras and did his pilgrimage to Buddha Gaya. He stayed twice at Nalanda for considerable periods, visited Bengal and Assam, travelled down south via Orissa, penetrated into the heart of the Deccan, visited Kanchi of the Pallavas, Vatapi of the Chalukyas and proceeded via Malwa to Multan and Sind, returning from there to Nalanda. After completing his studies under the venerable abbot Silabhadra, he spent some time also in the courts of Kumara Bhaskara Varman of Kamarupa (Assam) and of Harsha himself. His travels in India were therefore as complete as could be imagined.

We have in his travel notes detailed descriptions of the more important towns of India in the seventh century. Peshawar and Taxila were then practically in ruins as a result of Mihiragula's ravages. Pravarapura, modern Srinagar, was a flourishing city. Jullunder and Mathura declined. Kanauj, the imperial capital, is described thus: "It has lofty walls and solid trenches; on all sides are seen towers and pavilions. In several places there are also flowery groves and limpid ponds, crystal clear. In this country there are found in plenty the rarest wares of other lands." Prayag (Allahabad) was as important a town as it is today. It was one of the great nerve-centres of Hinduism, second only to Banaras. The number of pilgrims who collected there, and the ascetics who mortified their bodies caused surprise to the Chinese sage. The strange sight of yogis who with one foot on a pole held with one hand, but with the body hanging in air kept looking at the sun in its course during the whole day—which can be seen even to this day—was witnessed by Yuan-Chwang.

Banaras—the eternal city of the Hindus—was in the seventh century much the same as today. The Chinese pilgrim notes the great wealth of the town, and the innumerable temples. "These temples," he says, "which are in several storeys are embellished with a wealth of sculptural decoration and the parts made of wood painted in a variety of dazzling colours. They are situated in leafy parks and surrounded by pools of water." The pilgrim also noted the large number of ascetics of all sects, the predominance of the worship of Siva whose holy place Banaras is, and the yogis who practice mortifications of the flesh. The artistic eye of the Chinese master did not fail to notice the great beauty of the Banaras school of sculpture, which during the Gupta period evolved a purely Hindu style, quite different from the hybrid school of Gandhara and the eclectic school of Mathura. After seeing a colossal statue of Siva (no doubt Kasi Visvanath, destroyed by Aurangzeb) he noted that it was full of grandeur and majesty—"at sight of it one is overcome by awe, as though one were in the presence of God."

Vaisali, the great capital of the Lichhavis, was, alas, a dead city. The great republic had met its end at the hands of Samudra Gupta who had proudly proclaimed himself to be the grandson of Lichchavis. Pataliputra was already in decay. It was already so in Kalidasa's time, as the poet mentions it rarely, and then along with the capitals of all other countries. Of Nalanda it is necessary to speak separately.

Is the picture of North India as left by Yuan-Chwang essentially different today so far as it relates to the Hindus? We see the same life lived in the main cities. The life in the villages has probably changed even less. Hinduism which had never lost its hold even during what was known as the Buddhist period was as vigorous in its strange and varied forms as today. Caste, which Yuan-Chwang describes with great insight, ruled the social structure.

The university of Nalanda which reached its high-water mark at this period was an educational centre of international fame comparable in the universalism of its thought, the wide range of its studies, the international character of its community to the greatest universities of modern times like Oxford, Cambridge, Paris and Harvard. Founded in the fifth century by one of the later Gupta emperors as a Buddhist Sangharama, it was endowed munificently by monarchs and rich men from all parts of India and the Hindu colonies overseas so that in course of time it became a truly international centre of learning. Apart from the detailed descriptions of Yuan-Chwang and his no less famous successor I Tsing we have now sufficient epigraphical and archaeological records to draw upon for the history of this great institution.

Universities have existed in India from the earliest times. Two traditional universities for imparting instruction in all branches of Vedic knowledge have their modest existence even today in the ancient State of Kerala. Apart from such theological schools which must have existed in different parts, there were also well known universities in the more technical sense of which we have information in ancient literature. Such were the great centres of Taxila and Ujjain, the former renowned for its medical school, the latter for its secular learning including mathematics and astronomy. Kanchi in the south, Vallabhi, established by Dudda, the niece of Dhruva I, which I Tsing declared was as great and famous as Nalanda, Vikramasila, a neighbour to Nalanda, were other renowned seats of learning which existed at the same time as Nalanda.

Endowed by successive monarchs, Nalanda was a city of imposing buildings. There were at least eight colleges, built by different patrons including one by Balaputradeva, King of Srivijaya (Sumatra). From the excavations we can see that these colleges were built in rows, enclosing fine quadrangles, at least one of which was four storeys high as definitely stated by Yuan-Chwang. The stone inscription of Yasovarmadeva at Nalanda praises the grandeur of the buildings and the results of archaeology fully bear this out.

The university area was enclosed by a brick wall. Yuan-Chwang's description may well be quoted: "The whole establishment is surrounded by a brick wall. One gate opens into the great college from which are separated eight other halls standing in the middle. The richly adorned towers and fairy-like turrets like the pointed hill tops are congregated together. The observatory seems to be lost (in mist) and the upper rooms tower above the sky. . . . All the outside courts in which are the priests' chambers are of four stages. The stages have dragon projections and coloured eaves, pearl-red pillars carved and ornamented, richly adorned balustrades, and roofs covered with tiles that reflect the light in a thousand shades."

It is not bricks and mortar that constitute a university, though its noble housing is by no means unimportant. Every facility existed in the university for studies of different kinds. There were three great libraries, as we know from Tibetan records, called appropriately Ratna Sagara (sea of gems), Ratnodadhi (the ocean of gems) and Ratna Ranjaka (collection of gems). Over ten thousand students including teachers of all kinds studied at the university. They came from all parts of India, from Further India, from Central Asia, China and Korea—in fact from all parts of the Buddhist world. We know the names of many Korean scholars, for example, Huih-Nieh, Aryavarman (Sanskritised name). Huih-Nieh's presence at Nalanda is attested to by the fact that I Tsing discovered on a manuscript the statement: "Whilst dwelling under the toothbrush tree, the Korean priest Huih-Nieh wrote this record."

Though Buddhist in atmosphere Nalanda, like other Indian

universities, was essentially catholic. A candidate for admission was required to be familiar with "old and new books." Apart from Buddist texts, religious and secular, the studies at the university included the great body of Hindu scriptures, philosophy (Sankhya etc.), grammar and medicine, and it would appear from the biography of Yuan-Chwang that scholars were expected to familiarise themselves with miscellaneous works. Logic and exegetics were of course pre-eminently important, because the scholars of the university were expected to enter into dispute with visiting doctors of all schools. This practice of public disputations with learned men from all over India made it necessary both for professors and students to be familiar with all systems of thought much in the same way as Jesuit doctors try to understand the metaphysics of other religions. An accurate summary of the Sankhya system is, for example, included in Yuan-Chwang's biography to indicate how he worsted in debate a Sankhya disputant. The Chinese pilgrim himself says: "Learned men from different cities who desire quickly to acquire a renown in discussion come here in multitudes." This tradition is still widely prevalent in India and the most notable examples in recent times are the famous disputations held at different centres by Swami Dayanand, the founder of the Arya Samaj.

The cosmopolitan and catholic character of the university was fully reflected in the succession of great teachers of whom we have record. Dharmapala, who was the predecessor of Silabhadra as the Head Abbot, was a Tamil noble from Kanchi in the south, Jinamitra, another renowned master, came from the Andhra country; Silabhadra, the saintly guru of Yuan-Chwang, came from the eastern districts, probably Assam, and was a converted Bhramin. In fact the university was truly the centre of Indian intellectual life attracting scholars and professors from all parts of India.

Another notable fact which is worthy of mention is that Nalanda also trained the missionaries who continuously revivified Buddhism in far-off countries. Tibetan records leave no doubt that Nalanda sent to that country a succession of learned monks and the works of some of the great scholars of the university are preserved in Tibet. We also know of Subhakara Simha, a Pandit of Nalanda early in the eighth century, who went to China and worked there on the translations of Buddhist texts. Of those who went to Java, Srivijaya and other Indian colonies it is unnecessary to speak as the Srivijaya emperor had himself endowed the university and was one of its patrons. Indian culture in the seventh and eighth centuries radiated from Nalanda to all over Buddhist Asia.

The re-fashioning of Buddhist philosophy was the main achievement of the great patriarchs, Vasubandhu, Asanga, Nagarjuna and others, and it was their tradition that Nalanda perfected and maintained. Buddhist thought from the third century became metaphysical and scholastic and the transition was well indicated by the use of Sanskrit as the language of theological studies. With Dinnaga a great school of logic began to develop and theories of knowledge and doctrines of metaphysics, of which the Yogacara school was the most important representative, became the characteristics of Sanskrit Buddhism. This was an approximation to Hinduism and in fact the difference between the Madhyamikas and the Vedantins is hardly perceptible except to philosophers. It is Nalanda that was pre-eminently responsible for this re-fashioning of Buddhism, which made it possible for the religion of the Sakya to be assimilated wholesale in the body of Hinduism in the period that followed.

The disappearance of Harsha from the scene blurred the picture of North India from the point of view of imperial unity. Kanauj after a short interregnum, however, claimed its primacy under Yasovarman whose reign falls in the first half of the eighth century. This king re-established a shadowy imperial authority in northern India but his ambitions were restrained by the defeat he sustained at the hands of Lalitapida Muktaditya of Kashmir in 733 A.D. The Kanauj monarch seems however to have retained his kingdom, for we have the statement of Ou-Kong that the Kashmir ruler was in alliance with the ruler of central India. Yasovarman has another and better title to greatness. He was the patron of the great dramatist Bhavabhuti and of Vakpatiraja, the Prakrit epic poet.

The successors of Yasovarman maintained their authority in the Indo-Gangetic valley till Dhruva the Rastrakuta king, whose authority was primarily based on his homelands in western India, invaded the Doab (785) and "taking from his enemies the Ganga and the Yamuna . . . acquired at the same time the supreme position of Lordship in the form of a visible sign." The emblem of the Ganges and the Yamuna was the insignia of imperial authority and is stated by Dhruva to have been assumed as such.

The Rastrakuta monarch claims to have also defeated the king of eastern India.

An important shift of political power had taken place in the eighth century. The establishment of Muslim authority in Sind and its annexation to the Empire of the Khalifs created a new threat to India from an unaccustomed side. In 726 under Junaid Muslim forces based on the mouth of the Indus led expeditions into India and reached as far as Marwar and Malwa. The coast of Gujerat was subjected to their constant attacks. This menace shifted the emphasis of India's defence to Gujerat. Under a great leader, Nagabhata I, effective resistance was organised and the Muslim invader was driven back to the sea. Freeing the parts of India which had temporarily fallen under foreign sway, Nagabhata I established his authority in the area stretching from Gujerat to Gwalior. The Pratiharas, as this dynasty is called, seem to have stepped into monarchical dignity from the position of court dignitaries to a previous dynasty. Whatever their origin, the Pratiharas have claims to national gratitude as having at a critical time assumed leadership against invasion.

The growth of the Pratihara power also witnessed the rise of the rival dynasty of Rastrakutas. Dantidurga Rastrakuta and his successors moved to the Doab, as stated earlier, after an indecisive fight in western India leaving the Pratiharas in undisputed authority in Gujerat. The successors of Nagabhata consolidated their power in the Gujerat, Malwa and Rajputana areas. From Jain records we know that in 788 A.D Vatsaraja Pratihara, known as Ranahastin, was the master of this area, and performed the sacred Hiranyagarbha at Ujjain. Vatsaraja defeated the ruler of Kanauj and carried his arms as far as Bengal (783). He may be described as the founder of the Gurjara empire.

Nagabhata II who succeeded his father is described as Paramabhattaraka Maharajadhiraja Parameswara—in fact by full imperial dignities. With Dharmapala of Bengal he shared the mastery of North India, the eastern half being under the effective authority of the Pala king whose dynasty in Bengal had risen to imperial dignity and had in the first half of the eighth century brought the feeble successors of the Guptas in Magadha under its control. He was able to move his capital to Kanauj after defeating Chakrayudha who was the ruler of the imperial city. This Chakrayudha had been elevated to the throne by Dharmapala of Bengal and the two imperial rulers of North India met to fight out the issue at Monghyr. The division of North India into an Eastern Empire and Western Empire was the result.

The Pratiharas, now fully established at Kanauj after the expulsion of the Gauda vassal, exercised imperial authority over an area which included the Punjab, Rajputana, Malwa, Gujerat, the Indo-Gangetic valley up to Magadha and to the south up to the Vindhyas. Nagabhata II died in 833. His achievements were really notable. Though he did not bring under a shadowy suzerainty, as Harsha did, the whole of Aryavarta, the Gurjara empire he left to his son was more integrated, more effectively organised, and based on a tradition of national greatness in resisting the invasion of foreigners. The Gurjara Pratiharas of Kanauj have thus an indefeasible claim to be in the direct tradition of the Mauryas, Vakatakas and Guptas of an earlier period.

Ramabhadra, the successor of Nagabhata, reigned only for two years. The newly consolidated empire of Kanauj had in his time to resist the attack of Devapala of Bengal in the east and the rebellion of feudatories in Gujerat. His son Mihira Bhopa who took over the imperial authority in 835 and reigned for fifty years not only revived the glories of Kanauj but established firmly the claim of imperial authority over the whole of his vast dominions. At this time North India was divided into three great States. The kingdom of Bengal was under the Pala dynasty, founded by Gopala in about 765, whose son Dharmapala was Nagabhata's opponent. Dharmapala's son Devapala was the master of eastern India and Magadha. Hindustan proper was under the Kanauj emperors and the Vindhya country was under the Rastrakutas whose dynasty held sway in that strategic area since the fall of the Satavahanas and had gradually, with the weakening of the Chalukya power, assumed imperial authority. Amoghavarsha, who was a contemporary of Mihira Bhopa, was a ruler of great ability and the inherited prestige of his dynasty was such as to give him a dominant position in the middle region.

In successive campaigns Mihira Bhoja reduced the power of Devapala. Amoghavarsha was kept in check and the whole of Hindustan may be said to have accepted the Pratihara sovereignty. This was important, for Imran Ibn Musa, th Muslim Governor of Sind, decided at this time on a policy of expansion and seems to have even occupied Kutch, and attempted to extend his authority over the mainland. Mihira's power rendered such a policy impossible and before he died Islam in Sind had been reduced to two petty principalities.

Mihira was not merely an overlord as Harsha had been. He annexed kingdoms, administered them directly and maintained large garrisons in important frontier towns. He may well be said to have organised India for defence against Islamic attack, an organisation which lasted for over a century and a half. Mihira's son Mahendrapala worthily maintained the imperial tradition but after him the empire began to decline.

The Gurjara political organisation consisted of a confederacy of five kingdoms: the Pratiharas, the Parmaras, the Chahamanas, the Chalukyas and the Guihilots—the ancestors of some of the major clans of Rajputs at the present time. When the Pratihara power declined the Paramaras of Dhar took over the imperial dignity. Islam in the meantime had organised itself on the north-west frontier and a great conflict was impending.

CHAPTER X

SOUTH INDIA (*continued*)

The history of South India has certain special characteristics which clearly differentiate it from the story of the rest of India. They are the continuity and stability of its social organisation and the unity of its culture. The Chera, Chola and Pandya kingdoms of the earliest days continued unbroken in tradition through ages up to quite recent times. Changes in dynasty did not affect the political entity of these units any more than England ceased to be England because the Stuarts were displaced by the Hanoverians or France ceased to be France when the Napoleonic dynasty held court in Tuileries. The Pandyamandalam, Tondamandalam and Kerala were in fact geographical units which had an established and continued political existence, the individuality of which is still very strongly felt. In North India, on the other hand, history was to a large extent based on dynasties, though at one time Magadha attained its individuality and in the later period, Gujerat and Bengal became differentiated.

By the beginning of the fifth century the Tondamandalam of which the capital was Kanchi was, as stated before, under a dynasty which is known in their inscriptions as Pallavas. They were the Tondaiman kings and were known as such in Tamil literature. Kanchi was at all times a very important city and a great centre of learning and the seat of a famous university. With the growth of Pallava power which extended up to the Krishna in the north and to the outskirts of Madurai of the Pandyas, Kanchi became the metropolis of the south.

The Pallavas, who have left us a voluminous record of inscriptions, maintained originally the tradition of the Satavahanas in encouraging Prakrit. Their Prakrit inscriptions are specially interesting as they show the gradual Aryanisation of the south and disprove the view of Jayaswal that the Pallavas were the representatives in the south of the Sanskrit culture of the Guptas.

By the beginning of the sixth century however the Pallavas had become great advocates of Sanskrit and their inscriptions were invariably in that language. Perhaps the university of Kanchi came under Acharyas who were great masters of Sanskrit learning.

The growth of Pallava power was gradual but by about 550 A.D. the rulers of Kanchi had attained primacy in the south and were continuously at war with the equally great dynasty of Chalukyas whose capital was at Vatapi. The Chalukyas had taken over from the Rastrakutas power over the Maharashtra country, and had under Pulikesena I established a monarchy whose imperial glory was to live long in Indian history. These two rivals to the mastery of the Deccan were in a perpetual state of conflict. That the conflict was not dynastic but geographical may be seen from the fact that the organised monarchy of the South continued to meet the powers of the Maharashtra country on the banks of the Krishna right down to the battle of Talikotta in 1565.

The Pallavas were not a single dynasty. Four separate dynasties were known under this name. The earlier dynasties which used Prakrit were no doubt feudatories of the Satavahanas who had assumed independence and were anterior to Samudra Gupta. No less than thirty-six Pallava kings are known from inscriptions, a record of continuous reign which is really remarkable. Their dynastic history matters little, but the eminence which the Pallava empire achieved by the middle of the fifth century and continued to the middle of the eighth century is a matter of supreme importance to India. Under Narasimhavarman, known as Mahamalla, who ruled from 625 to 645, the Pallava empire reached the zenith of its power. In 642 he attacked the Chalukya capital itself, occupied Vatapi and the great Pulikesena II, victor over Harsha, was himself defeated and killed. But Chalukya power did not end with it. One of Pulikesena's successors, Vikramaditya II, even occupied the Pallava capital for a short time in 740. After the fall of Chalukyas, the Rastrakutas who occupied the Maratha country were forced by the inescapable facts of geography to press southwards and the struggle continued this time with greater success. The revival of the Pandyas in the extreme south helped Rastrakuta aggression and Krishna of the Rastrakutas finally destroyed Pallava power in the latter half of the ninth century.

The Pallava contribution to Indian culture is in every sense unique. As Grousset very rightly says: "From an early date they created an architecture of their own which was to be the basis of all the styles of the south and at the time of Yuan-Chwang's visit their metropolis, Mavalipuram, began to be filled with those admirable works of art that have made it one of the chief centres of Indian art . . . monolith temples which cover the whole shore, challenging their replicas of Cham or the Malay Archipelago, rocks sculptured in the shapes of animals with a wonderfully broad and powerful naturalism, whole cliffs worked in stone frescoes, immense pictures which were unparalleled at the time in all India in their order, movement and lyrical value."

The great builder of the dynasty was Mahamalla himself from whom Mavalipuram takes its name. The Descent of the Ganges, the unique masterpiece of Pallava art and surely one of the most remarkable compositions of all time, in which is portrayed the Ganges coming down to earth, with gods, animals, men and all creation in adoration, was the work of his time.

Many of the Pallava kings were also poets and patrons of literature, and Mahendravarman, the author of *Matta Vilasa Prahasana,* a social comedy, was the father of the greater Narasimha Pallava. Dr. Krishnaswami Aiyangar, the historian, has also adduced evidence to prove that Bharavi and Dandin lived in the Pallava court.

It was also at the Pallava court that the great religious reform which was to sweep India in the eighth century first originated. The Vaishnava and Saiva literature of the Tamils, a great, and to the rest of India a still unknown, mine of the highest expression of religious thought and devotion, developed mainly during this period. Both the Siva and Vishnu cults in South India are forms of Bhakti. In fact the Saiva and Vaishnava saints, whose lives and works still dominate the religion of the south, seem all to have lived during the Pallava period. Sundaramoorti, the last of the Saiva saints, lived in the closing years of Pallava authority, while the greatest in that succession were contemporaries of Narasimha. The Jain and Buddhist teachers of the earlier period slowly lost ground, as Yuan-Chwang himself noted during his vist to Kanchi, though there is evidence to believe that at one time the religious tradition of South India was dominated more by the Jains. The Pallavas were orthodox Hindus, sometimes Saiva but generally Vaishnava, and it is they who thus laid the foundation of the Great Reformation in the eighth century.

The "Aryanisation" of South India was completed during the period of the Pallavas. Their grants show that the Aryan structure of society had gained firm hold on the South by the sixth century. Grants to Apathambhiya and Baudhayana Brahmins are specifically mentioned which show that the North Indian Dharma Sastras had acquired authority in the Pallava kingdom. Sanskrit had established its sway. The university of Kanchi played no doubt a great part in this, and we know from Yuan-Chwang that it was the greatest centre of education in the south. Vatsyayana, the logician, the author of *Nyaya Bhashya,* who lived in the fourth century A.D., seems to have been a Pandit of Kanchi. Dinnaga is also said to have had his training in the southern capital. In the fifth century we have epigraphic record of Mayuravarma of the Kadamba family going for higher studies to Kanchi. In fact it can legitimately be claimed that Kanchi of the Pallavas was the great centre from which the Sanskritisation of the south as well as the Indian colonies in the Far East proceeded.

Allusion has already been made to the Chalukya dynasty which shared with the Pallavas the imperial dignity of the south and the succession of the Satavahanas till the destruction of their power in 642 by Narasimha Pallava. The Chalukyas came into prominence in the beginning of the sixth century when Jayasimha, by destroying the growing power of the Rastrakutas, established his authority in what is now the Maharashtra country. Jayasimha's son, Pulikesena I, performed an Aswamedha which would clearly indicate that in his own region he had assumed imperial dignities. In their attempt to expand towards the south the Chalukyas encountered the power of the Pallavas and towards the north that of the Vakatakas who were still in occupation of the Vindhyan area. But the present Maharashtra country was organised by them into a powerful State; Harsha after conquering North India attempted to move south but found his way barred by Pulikesena II.

The defeat of Pulikesena II by Narasimha Pallava was a great blow to the Chalukya power. But Vikramaditya II, "resolved to uproot the Pallava foe who had robbed of splendour the former kings of his line," carried the war into the enemy territory, occupied Kanchi itself and put a rival Pallava claimant on the throne. It is interesting to note that the Chalukya king brought back with him some of the great architects of Kanchi—the Sarvasidhi Acharyas, one of whom constructed the Lokeshwara temple at the command of Vikramaditya's queen.

Both the Pallavas and the Chalukyas were great maritime powers. The activities of the Pallavas on the sea were mainly directed towards maintaining friendly contacts with the Indian states in Further India, Malaya and Indonesia. Of Chalukya naval power we have inscriptional evidence that Pulikesena with a hundred ships attacked and reduced the capital of a hostile state to submission. Yuan-Chwang, who visited the Chalukya king, has left us a description of the country. He testifies to Pulikesena's broadmindedness and generosity and notes that the country was organised on a military basis.

The history of the Maharashtra country like that of the states of the South is continuous and the fall of dynasty, however glorious in its achievement, does not break the continuity of its annals. The Rastrakutas, whom the Chalukyas had displaced two centuries before, stepped into the vacant imperial authority. The weakened princes of the Chalukya dynasty continued to rule for a century until Dantidurga of Malkhed finally broke their power. His son Krishnaraja, "who churned the ocean of the Chalukya race," has other and more important achievements to his credit, for it was he who built the great Kailasa temple of Ellora of which he was justly proud as may be seen from his Baroada grant where it is stated that he "caused to be constructed a temple of wonderful form on the mountain", seeing which the gods said: "This temple of Siva is self created for such beauty is not to be found in a work of art." Krishna's successors were also powerful monarchs, especially Govinda III and Amoghavarsha, and the dynasty held authority till 973 when they were again ousted by the Chalukyas whose restored line assumes a glory which continues down centuries to the end of the Vijayanagar empire, while the fame of the Rastrakutas is still upheld by the great Rathod families of Rajputana and Central India.

Something may also be said of the extreme south, alluded to generally as Chera or Kerala. The strip of country that lies to the west of the Ghats and down to Cape Comorin was from the earliest times the seat of trade and communication with the West. Its ports, Muzuris and Kollam, were famous from the earliest times. The two significant events in the history of this area before Sri Sankara emerged from there to reform Hinduism are the arrival of St. Thomas the Apostle and of the Jewish exiles. Though no definite proof exists regarding the ministry of St. Thomas the tradition is of very considerable antiquity and cannot be discounted easily. Since we know now from the Arikamedu excavations that the Greco-Roman world was in constant communication with South India, the probability of the tradition being true has very greatly increased. In any case we have the very high authority of Eusebius that Pantaenus, the first Principal of the Alexandrine school among whose disciples are numbered Origen and Clement of Alexandria, visited India and found a flourishing Christian community which had preserved the writings of St. Matthew. It is therefore difficult to deny the tradition of the apostolic origin of the Christian church in Malabar. Also a Syrian merchant by the name of Thomas of Kana visited Malabar in the fifth century and established a community which, though confined to the Malabar area, gives to Christianity an indigenous authenticity which at least is not later than that of St. Augustine in England.

Education in the Deccan and South India during this period seems to have reached a high level. We have already alluded to the great university of Kanchi which dominated the intellectual life of the south as Nalanda did of the north. But apart from this great centre of learning, South India was well endowed with colleges and schools for higher studies. The Salogti College, built and endowed by the foreign minister of Krishna III of the Rastrakuta dynasty, is a notable example of such institutions. It had twenty-seven houses for the free lodging of students and the college was staffed by well-paid professors. The support that the public gave to this institution is also interesting. A graded system of payment at important ceremonies towards the funds of the college was accepted by every householder in the town. The Ennayiram Temple College, which accommodated 340 students, had ten different departments, and the students were educated completely free. In fact colleges seem to have been attached to the more important temples where free education was given in religious and secular subjects. The colleges in South India at least after the time of the Pallavas were predominantly Hindu in character.

It was seen in an earlier chapter that at the end of the fifth century the area of Mekong valley, Malaya and the Indonesian islands were dotted with Hindu principalities some of which, like the kingdom of Funan, had attained considerable importance and prosperity. This was the formative period. Hindu culture and organisation had been established on a firm basis, and the local population—at least the higher strata—assimilated with the Indian emigrants and colonists. The next five centuries witness a great flowering of Indian culture in these areas which properly belong to Indian history, because at least till the twelfth century these people considered themselves as integrally belonging to the Indian world.

When the sixth century opens in Further India, three important kingdoms—Kambuja (still known by that name though in English called Cambodia), Champa (modern Siam) and Srivijaya, a great maritime empire which included the Malay Peninsula and

Sumatra—dominate the scene. Java was still an island of small principalities, while Borneo seems to have reverted to barbarism.

Kambuja which started as a vassal state of Funan became, according to Chinese annals, its master during the middle of the sixth century. The founder of the dynasty bore the name of Stiravarman, for all later inscriptions trace the genealogy of Kambuja kings to him. A long line of kings, the details of whose reign have come down to us through inscriptions, increased the glory and wealth of Kambuja and made it a centre of Sanskrit culture. The early inscriptions are in classical Sanskrit, full of allusions to ancient India, indicating a nostalgia which is characteristic of the period. The Kambuja kings were Hindus, mainly Saivite, for we have numerous allusions to the consecration of Sivalingas. The following inscription shows both the orthodoxy of the kings and the pains they took to make their countries the centres of Hindu culture.

> "There was the daughter of Sri Viravarman, the sister of Sri Bhavavarman, who, devoted to her husband and to her religion, was like a second Arundhati the Puranic model of the perfect wife, performing the austerities of religion by the side of her husband). He (Sri Somasarman took for wife this lady) and the foremost of those who were versed in Samaveda consecrated this Tribhuveneswara (Siva together with an image of the sun) . . . with the Ramayana and the Purana he gave the complete Bharata and arranged for a daily recitation without interruption."

Even more interesting from the point of view of Indian civilisation is the *Prasasti* of Bhavavarman written in Kavya style and closely imitating the *Raghuvamsa* of Kalidasa. As it was this Bhavavarman's son who annihilated Funan power in the middle of the sixth century the popularity of the kavya style and especially of Kalidasa's great epic in Further India at that time demonstrates clearly the close connection between the motherland and the colonies. Kambuja was ardently Hindu till the middle of the seventh century when Buddhism is first alluded to. The two religions co-existed as in India, though till the very end Hinduism continued predominant.

Till the eighth century Pallava influence is predominant in Kambuja. It is the southern doctrine of Saivism that is the official cult. It is in Pallava characters that the inscriptions are written and even names of royal personages like Mahendravarman closely follow those of the Pallavas. Kambuja architecture bears the undoubted marks of Pallava tradition as Parmentier has clearly established. The greatest builder among the Kambuja kings was Yasovarman whose father Mahipativarman, it would appear, married a Brahmin lady, Indra Devi, the descendant of a Brahmin from Aryadesa. So close were the cultural relations between India and Kambuja.

The intensive study of Sanskrit in Kambuja is well illustrated in an inscription of this Yasovarman, which speaks of him as a greater one than Pravarasena for his Setubandha (Pravarasena of the Vakatakas), a Gunadhya who does not like Prakrit, a Vishalaksha who is opposed to Niti, a Sura who humiliated Bhimaka, etc. He also alludes to the poet Mayura of Harsha's time. "The sun has been satisfied with the Stotra of Mayura but the king to rival the sun is worshipped by swans" (a pun on Mayura which also means a peacock).

Champa (or modern Siam) was a equally ancient kingdom. Before the sixth century it seems to have been a vassal state of Funan. The first important Champa king that comes to view is Rudravarman who claims descent from Gangaraja. Many dynasties, all strongly Hindu, ruled over Champa. They were also Saivites, though some among them professed the cult of Vishnu and a few of a combined form of Sankara Narayana.

Like Kambuja, Champa was also a great centre of Hindu culture. Of King Indravarman III of the Bhrigu dynasty, it is said that he mastered the six systems of Hindus philosophy, the Buddhist philosophical system, the grammar of Panini and the commentary Kasika, besides the sacred texts of the Saivites. Sanskrit was the official language and more than a hundred inscriptions in that language have so far been discovered. The Vedas and the Dharma Sastras were carefully studied and one of the kings, Sri Jaya Indravarman VII, claimed to be an expert on Naradiya and Bhargaviya Dharma Sastras. Ramayana and Mahabharata were widely studied. Architecture was predominantly of the southern type and we have the authority of a noted Bengali scholar for the statement that "on the whole it seems impossible not to connect the style of Champa with the early Dravidian style." In fact it is demonstrably clear that the cultural influences working in both Champa and Kambuja had their origin in South India.

Champa disappeared from history after an epic fight of many centuries with the kingdom of Annam which was the advanced post of Chinese culture. In fact both Kambuja and Champa have exceptional claims to the gratitude of Indian people. If the ever expanding empire of China did not extend its authority to Singapore and if the Indian Ocean remains today what its name indicates, it is due to the resistance which Kambuja and Champa put up against the continuous pressure of China. Kambuja is now but a small kingdom. Champa's glorious tradition is represented by Siam but between them they still mark the boundary of Chinese culture and expansion.

If the land route of Chinese expansion was barred for a thousand years by the kingdoms in Further India, the glory of guarding the sea route fell to the great dynasty of Sailendras whose empire included the kingdom of Srivijaya. Established originally at Srivijaya (Palampong in Sumatra) the Sailendras consolidated their authority over the island, conquered the neighbouring island groups and established their hegemony over the Straits of Malacca by the beginning of the seventh century. In the eighth century they extended their power to the Malay Peninsula. Thus with one foot on the continent and the other on the great island of Sumatra they bestrode the Straits and retained the mastery of both seas for over five hundred years.

Their authority in the Bay of Bengal was challenged by the Cholas in the eleventh century. Rajendra Chola, as we shall have occasion to discuss later, entered on a hundred years' war with the Sailendras, and though the Chola empire was for a time established on the Malay Peninsula, the Sailendras remained masters of the sea at the end of the war. Chinese accounts of the twelfth century attest the fact that the Sailendras controlled the maritime traffic through the Straits. For full seven hundred years they had held sovereignty over the seas surrounding the islands and upheld Indian culture in the Archipelago.

The Sailendra monarchs were Buddhists and we know that their interest in the propagation of the faith was such as to move them to establish Viharas in far-off Nalanda as well as in Negapatam in the south. They were in close communication with the southern kingdoms, Chola and Pandya, and we have records of the visits of scholars from South India to the Sailendra capital. In many of their inscriptions the South Indian grantha character is used. Also many of the clan names in Sumatra are the same as in South India, e.g. Cholas and Pandyas.

The great naval activity which was the basis of this long chapter of colonisation was carried on by public corporations, the best known of which are the Manigramam and the Nanadesis. Of the Manigramam corporation which traded with the whole world as known then, we have authentic record in grants and inscriptions.

They had monopoly rights of trading and special privileges like the chartered companies of later days and enjoyed the "sword of sovereign merchantship." The Nanadesis (men from all parts), the Valangai and the Etangai are described in a Mysore inscription as "brave men born to wander over many countries . . . penetrating lands of the six continents by land and water routes and dealing in various articles such as horses and elephants, precious stones, perfumes and drugs either wholesale or in retail." Such was indeed the adventurous nature of these corporations which guided for centuries the commerce and politics of Further India.

CHAPTER XI

HINDU REFORMATION

THE redaction of the texts which may be said to have ended in the Gupta period and its great importance to national development have already been alluded to. From the point of view of religion the movement was even more significant. The re-written *Puranas* and the *Mahabharata* provided the people of India with a mythology, a corpus of unexampled heroic poetry, a rich system of popular ethics and a religious literature for the masses, catholic enough to include the worship of all creeds inside Hinduism. In fact by the sixth century Buddha himself had been included among the avataras of Vishnu and proclaimed an orthodox god entitled to worship by Hindus. The *Matsya Purana* includes Buddha among the avataras and the passage is quoted by early writers. In the *Bhagavata Purana* also Buddha is mentioned as an avatara of Vishnu and the *Brahmanda* prescribes a festival for the anniversary of Buddha where it is declared that the image of Buddha should be worshipped in a particular manner on that day. From an inscription of the seventh century we know that even in South India Buddha was counted as an avatara.

In fact one of the great contributions of the Gupta religious revival is this emphasis on the doctrine of avataras. The theory of avataras goes back to pre-Buddhist times. Some of the avataras were known and worshipped as such in the time of Panini, but it is in Patanjali (circa 150 B.C.) we have a definite allusion to Krishna being an avatara of God and not merely a deified human being. The doctrine of avatara is simple enough and is stated with the greatest clarity in the *Gita* itself. "When religion declines and evil-doers are to be destroyed, I shall be born, at different periods," says Krishna. According to the now universally accepted doctrine of the Hindus, whenever the state of human society requires to be regenerated, divinely inspired men are born for the purpose. They are avataras but only part avataras, not the Godhead himself in human form, but only men with such part of divine powers as is required for the purpose in hand. Vishnu as the protector is the God of avatars and of his incarnations only Krishna is identified with him, while his other human forms like

Rama Dasarathi, Bhargava Rama and Balarama, though entitled to worship, are not equated with God himself.

The doctrine of incarnation was interpreted elastically from the very beginning. Thus the *Puranas* include such Rishis as Kapila, Dattatreya, and Vyasa as avataras of Vishnu; also others who worked for the re-establishment of Dharma are often locally elevated to semi-divine dignity on the same score. The avatara doctrine had also the advantage of providing the worshipper with personal gods, without his having in any way to break with the general body of Hindu thought which emphasised the impersonal aspect of Godhead and insisted on the doctrine of Neti (not like this). The unknowable nirguna God becomes knowable when it takes human forms and the compromise between the rigidity of Hindu philosophic thought and the popular demand for devotion to personal gods was easily effected by the doctrine of avataras.

If the Puranic and *Mahabharata* redactions provided Hinduism with a magnificent religious literature for the common people, it also brought to prominence a sacred text, the *Bhagavad Gita,* which was soon to become the scripture *par excellence* of the intelligentsia. The *Gita* is embedded as a dialogue in the first battle parva of the Mahabharata and is an essential part of the great epic. Even Rudolf Otto, who set out to find the "original *Gita,*" comes to the conclusion that "the *Gita* in its entirety was not dovetailed into the epic at some late period: rather was the original *Gita* a genuine constituent of the epic when it became Krishnaized. . . . The remainder of the material . . . consists of individual doctrinal treatises." The *Gita* with the doctrinal treatises which is the Upanishad is what matters from the religious point of view and this is the great book which comes to prominence as a scripture of Bhakti, Action and Knowledge in the fifth century.

The importance of *Gita* in the doctrinal reorganisation of Hinduism cannot be overestimated. There it was in a single compendious book which could be learnt by heart, the entire doctrine of the great Upanishads discussed and stated in the clearest terms. Since its formulation there is no book which has exercised so great an effect on Hindu thought, which is proved by the fact that the great Sankara commented upon it in the eighth century as an authoritative text to establish his doctrine of Advaita and others who followed him had equally to depend on the authority of the *Gita* to prove their doctrines. By the time of Alberuni the authority of the *Gita* was pre-eminent, for the Muslim author not only quotes the text at different places but places his reliance mainly on Krishna's sayings when he discourses on the Hindu view of God. The importance of the *Gita* through ages can be judged from the numerous commentaries produced in every part of India and, what is equally significant, the voluminous literature that is published annually in India as modern interpretation of the text.*

The reorganisation of Hinduism was on a popular basis. But the Brahmanical mind which was ritualistic in regard to religion elaborated at the same time the great doctrines of Mimamsa. The Sutras of Sabara and Jaimini's commentaries on them are no doubt anterior to the Gupta redactions but the popularity of the system as a school of religious thought dates only with Prabhakara at the end of the sixth century. Kumarila who probably belongs to the seventh century was the other great figure of this school. As a system of philosophy Mimamsa, both according to Prabhakara and Kumarila, deals more with the technique of thought than with thought itself. It is the unique case of a system interested in the methods of ascertaining validity and the rules of interpretation without attempting to search for ultimate knowledge. As a religion it is only concerned with rituals. The Mimamsaka lives in a world of self-revealed Vedas, and he is concerned only with the correct performance of the rites as laid down. This is the reason why Jaimini was himself attacked as an atheist, an accusation against which Kumarila defends him with vigour. But even Kumarila's defence only leads us to the conclusion that God does not matter as the results of Vedic rites correctly performed are automatic and not dependent on any Divine will.

The Mimamsa doctrine which under its exponents, Prabhakara and Kumarila, gained great ascendancy among the thinkers of Hinduism in the seventh and eighth centuries was in fact a protest against the Puranic religion of the people and was opposed both to Buddhist and Upanishadic thought. It excluded not only a personal deity to be realised either through Bhakti or through Yoga, but also fundamentally clashed with the teachings of Buddha. It was Sankara—the protagonist of Advaita—who prevented this barren ritualism from becoming a national religion and provided Hinduism with a corpus of philosophic doctrines, which has endured against the attacks of Islam and Christianity.

* Among the innumerable commentators of modern times may be mentioned Tilak, the father of nationalism, Aurobindo, the saint of Pondicherry, Mahatma Gandhi and Shri C. Rajagopalachari.

Sankara is generally placed in the eighth century. Born of a Nambudiri family on the west coast of South India at Kaladi in Kerala, Sankara came to northern India after his education and propounded in different places his doctrine of Advaita Vedanta which he traced to ancient Upanishadic teachings, especially to Badarayana's Brahma Sutras. He buttressed his views further by a commentary on the *Bhagavad Gita,* extracting from its teachings the essence of his Advaita. Armed with a philosophy which claimed to be in the true tradition of Upanishadic teaching and a body of religious beliefs which gave a higher vision of religious reality, Sankara met the scholastic teachers of the age, both the doctors of Mimamsa and the acharyas of Buddhism. His contest with Mandana Misra, who was the leading exponent of the school of ritualism, is famous in Indian tradition. The accusation hurled against Sankara by the Mimamsakas was that he was a concealed Buddhist. This is undoubtedly true to the extent that like the Buddhist he was opposed to the system of mechanical rituals which, claiming Vedic authority, usurped the position of religion. Equally he was considered the strongest opponent of their creed by the Buddhists and the decline of Buddhist philosophical schools in India is attributed rightly to his influence.

It is appropriate that the great movement which provided Hinduism with a catholic philosophy and a conception of God which was acceptable to the highest thought of every sect should have had its origin in South India. From very early periods, powerful theistic schools following Siva and Vishnu, both philosophical and devotional, existed in South India. Tamil Saivism especially was a theological doctrine of great importance. The literature of this school assumed great spiritual authority between the third and the seventh century A.D. The *Tiruvachakam,* or the holy writ of Manikka Vachakar, may be considered the most characteristic classic of the Tamil Saivites but its importance to Indian religion has not been fully recognised. While it is undoubtedly devotional, its philosophic forms have close affinity with the orthodox doctrines of Hindu philosophy.

The Vaishnava movement of the Alvar saints which is contemporaneous was also devotional. The *Nalayiram* or the Four Thousand which contains the hymns of the saints is accepted as a cannonical scripture by the Tamil Vaishnavites. In fact the period immediately preceding the arrival of Sankara on the scene was one of notable spiritual and philosophical activity in the south. It is obvious that Sankara's thought was greatly influenced by his upbringing in the south. His own devotional hymns in Sanskrit, addressed to Siva, Vishnu and the Devi, which are still the most popular of all the devotional literature in Sanskrit, clearly indicate that the Philosopher of the Absolute also recognised the great value of devotion in religion.

Sankara was not merely a philosophical thinker reconciling a bold and original system with the doctrines and traditions of the past, thereby providing Hinduism with a philosophical background, but also a practical reformer. He purged the worship of the Devi of objectionable features which had crept into it from the practices of the tantrics. The samayachara form of worship of the goddess claims Sankara as its originator and the most famous hymn of this form of worship, the *Soundarya Lahari* or the waves of beauty, is his composition. It may however be added that the followers of left-handed marga of the worship of Devi also claim *Soundarya Lahari* as their text and are able to find interpretations suitable to their creed in it.

The main organisational work that Sankara undertook was the establishment of the four great Mutts, at Badari in the north, high up in the Himalayas, at Puri in the east, at Dwarka on the west coast, off Jamnagar and at Sringeri in the south. These pontifical seats were to be occupied by Sankaracharyas, who were to maintain unpolluted the teaching of Advaita and to uphold the ascendancy of Upanishadic thought. It is undeniable that these great monasteries together with their subsidiary institutions, also under religious teachers sometimes assuming the title of Sankaracharya, have helped to maintain the orthodoxy of Sankara's teachings and the hold of Hinduism on the people.

Connected with the establishment of these pontifical seats is the reorganisation of the monastic orders which is also associated with Sankara's name. The Dasanami Sanyasis claim their spiritual descent from him. A body of trained missionaries who would carry far and wide the teachings of the Master was necessary if the movement initiated by Sankara was to succeed. India always had its wandering religious teachers, but apart from the monks of Buddhism and Jainism, these Sanyasis do not seem, in earlier times, to have been attached to any monastic order. They were the disciples of individual Gurus. Sankara organised them into a regular body, and it is permissible to argue that the wide acceptance of his creed all over India was in a measure due to this reform.

The doctrines of the new school were popularised by the very large number of temple colleges which came into existence at this time about which allusion has already been made. These colleges which gave free higher education on a large scale were predominantly religious and from inscriptional evidence it is clear that Buddhist thought was rigidly excluded from them. While in Nalanda and other Buddhist universities Hindu systems were freely studied and discussed, in the temple colleges of the Hindus a more narrow view was upheld and the curricula made no provision for the understanding of the doctrines which had for so long a time held sway in India. In the reorganisation of Hinduism these colleges played a great part.

The "disappearance" of Buddhism from the Indian scene is one of the facts of Indian history which have puzzled European thinkers. It is undoubtedly true that by the ninth century Buddhism had ceased to be a vital religion in India. No doubt in isolated centres like Nalanda it existed as philosophical schools up to a much later time, but actually as a religion of the people it disappeared by the beginning of the ninth century. The movement had in fact started much earlier for early in the seventh century Yuan-Chwang had noted its decay in many important centres. But its virtual disappearance after having so profoundly influenced Indian thought for over thirteen centuries requires explanation. The reason is that gradually Buddhism and Hinduism became indistinguishable. Those who accused Sankara of being a Prachanna Buddha or a concealed Buddhist were in a measure right. Not only did the philosophical concepts of the Madhyamika school find echoes in Advaita, but Sankara by his fight against the Mimamsakas broke down the barriers between the Buddhist laity and Hinduism. Buddhist temples like the famous Jagannath temple of Puri became Hindu temples and with the laity accepting Hinduism recruitment to the monasteries became more and more difficult. As Elliot, the historian of Buddhism, says: "The line dividing Buddhist laymen from ordinary Hindus became less and less marked, distinctive teaching found only in the monasteries: these became poorly recruited. . . . Even in the monasteries the doctrine taught bore a closer resemblance to Hinduism than the preaching of Gotama and it is the absence of the protestant spirit, this pliant adaptability to the ideas of each age which caused Indian Buddhism to lose its individuality and separate existence."

In short it may be said that by the end of the tenth century Hinduism had asserted its universal supremacy in India, reorganised its popular doctrines, provided itself with a higher philosophy which found general acceptance among the intellectual classes and absorbed into its fold the religion of Buddha. From

Kashmir to Cape Comorin, the worship of Shiva, Vishnu and the Devi prevailed and the background of philosophy accepted without question the main doctrines of Paramatma, Jivatma, Maya and re-incarnation in a society organised on the basis of caste and the Dharmasastras.

CHAPTER XII

INDIA ON THE EVE OF MUSLIM CONTACT

THE most remarkable fact which has escaped the notice of historians is that for over five hundred years, that is, from Toramana to Mahmud of Ghazni, India was free from the threat of external aggression. Except for Sind, which was occupied by the Khalifs of Baghdad whose authority was confined to that inhospitable desert land, India enjoyed unbroken immunity from external troubles. No part of the known world has for so long a period been free from threats of invasion. The miseries to which the north-western areas and occasionally the Gangetic valley had been subjected by the Kushans, Sakas and Huns were not only forgotten, but people lived under a facile feeling that there was no question of their country being ever invaded. Eternal vigilance which is the price of freedom had weakened to a vanishing point and the Hindus of the seventh to the eleventh centuries had, as a result, lost completely the sense of patriotism and national honour which grows up only under the stimulus of danger from outside. The author of *Vishnu Purana* sang the glory of Bharata Varsha because at that time Bharata Varsha was something to be defended and fought for. To the authors of the period that followed Bana it meant but little for even the themes of literature had become parochial instead of the birth of the war-god, or the fight of Arjuna with Siva.

Another consequence of the absence of any external threat was the consuming arrogance of the Indian people. As Alberuni, surely the most observant scholar who studied Indian things, notes: "The Hindus believe that there is no country but theirs, no nation like theirs, no kings like theirs, no religion like theirs, no science like theirs." . . . "If they travelled and mixed with other nations they would soon change their mind," he adds, "for their ancestors were not so narrow-minded as the present generations." And he quotes from Varahamihira who says that Yavanas, though impure, should be honoured. Varahamihira wrote at a time when there was a wholesome fear of foreigners but the five centuries of security had destroyed it. Alberuni also alludes to the extremes reserve of

Indian scholars who refused to discuss science or literature. Surely much must have changed in the Indian of the eleventh century from the time when Yuan-Chwang, I Tsing and thousands of scholars wandered all over the country and were received with open arms. The foreigner was not looked down upon in the seventh century, and the arrogance of the Indian literati is not commented upon by any Chinese student.

A further comment of Alberuni is also worth noting. He observes that the Hindus did "not desire that a thing which has once been polluted should be purified and thus recovered." Obviously this is very different from the time when even Huns could become Hindus and Greeks could be accepted into the Hindu fold as Heliodorus was, as worshippers of Vishnu. Hinduism had, through lack of contact which shook its system, crystallised a leaden outer crust which enveloped its gold.

There is nothing more dangerous for a country than the feeling that it was ordained by God to remain safe: that no foreigner could reach it. Such a feeling of peace will necessarily weaken the springs of national greatness, the rigidity of discipline, the desire to work together for upholding what is of value, the subordination of material interests to the idea of general good. This is what seems to have happened during the long period between the Huns and Mahmud of Ghazni.

Also it is important to realise that during this period India was isolated from the rest of the world. The overland contact with China had dried up as a result of changed political conditions in Central Asia. The sea route was controlled by the naval power of the Sailendra monarchs whose position astride the Straits of Malacca, while it gave them mastery of the seas, made free communications with China dependent on their good will. No known country was isolated from the rest of the world for so long a time as India was for three hundred years.

Completely insular in ideas, without any knowledge of what was happening in the rest of the world, the Indian people ceased to grow. Civilisation became decadent and inbred for lack of fertilising contacts with dissimilar cultures. Society became static and the systematizations of previous ages, which were more academic than real at the time of their conception like Chaturvarna —the four castes—and food and drink taboos came to be accepted as divine regulations and conformed to with a rigidity which would have surprised Manu and Yajnavalkya.

This decadence was visible in every sphere. In literature even Bana evidences a decay of taste which in later authors like Magha and Harsha became more marked. The kavya style degenerated into a vain parade of futile learning, while the restraint, poise and delicacy of Kalidasa gave place to extravagance in conceit and artificialities in language which make the later kavya literature a unique creation of futility like Chinese puzzles and crossword competitions. The moral tone also degenerated so that long and sensuous descriptions of debaucheries were considered necessary even in the kavyas of poets of known personal purity. The position is no better in architecture. After the great impetus which created the Ellora, Khajuraho and Bhuvaneshwar temples in northern India, the taste seems to have degenerated and in place of the magnificent sculptures of the earlier temples we have the representation on stone of moral perversities which can only be accounted for by the utter demoralisation of the higher classes. In religion also, this degeneration was apparent. The great reforms of Sankara provided the moral strength which enabled Hinduism to survive as it provided the Hindus with a higher thought and Hinduism with a common philosophical background. He provided Hinduism with an enduring body of philosophic doctrines but he was unable to reform the grave evils which had crept into the practice of religion. The Left-hand Marga had taken deep roots and a nursery for it existed at Vikramasila, Kashmir and Bengal. The following incident which took place in the Vikramasila university will show how deep was the canker that had eaten into the vitals of national life. A priest studying at the university was discovered with a bottle of wine. When asked, he stated that it was given to him by a nun whom he used to meet. The authorities of the university decided to take disciplinary action but on this the members of the university split into two factions and great troubles followed.

It was in fact the age of the Guhya Samaja—the secret congregation—which is claimed to be one of the most sacred books of the Buddhist Tantrics. In this amazing book Buddha is represented in acts of continuous debauchery with angels. The descipline of the Vinaya was deliberately set at nought in this book which is held to be canonical by the practitioners of tantra. Everything was permitted in this worship, flesh, fish, wine and women. Even human sacrifice was allowed. One passage would seem even to indicate that human flesh was also used in worship and consumed as Mahaprasada. Blood of men along with wine was also used.

The establishment of the great Mutts was one of the achievements of Sankara. The reorganisation of the Sanyasai Orders was also undertaken by the great reformer. The Dasanamis, or the Ten Orders, trace their succession to him. The objects of both these reforms were excellent. The four great Mutts were founded with the object of providing learned teachers of religion who would watch over orthodoxy. The Sanyasis were no doubt meant to carry the message to the homes of all. For a short time the tradition of the great Master inspired these organisations. Soon, however, especially after the disappearance of Buddhism, the Mutts became centres of luxury like the great abbeys and the Sankaracharyas who presided over them assumed pontifical dignities. The heads of the smaller Mutts became even grossly licentious as in works like Kshemendra's *Narmamala* they are held up to ridicule for their conduct. The Sanyasis became a burden on society. Their numbers increased; superstition fed them; common people paid them reverence. With the majority it became an easy method of life. This of course does not mean that there were not many genuinely holy men among the Sanyasis, then or at any other time in India. But the great majority of them were worthless men who concealed their preference for an indolent life under ochre-coloured robes.

The growth of the Devadasi system which can also be traced to this period shows the degradation to which even religion had fallen. In fact, side by side with the highest religious speculation Hinduism had always given shelter to the strangest practices. They existed in the time of Buddha; they flourished in the time of Sankara. The Pasupatas, the Kapalikas and the worshippers of every form of religion had their temples, all equally orthodox and the social validity of practices attaching to them was never called into question or taken into consideration.

The development of what has been called temple prostitution had the effect of loosening moral codes. Books like *Samaya Matrka* and the *Kuttini Matam,* both written by men of the highest social position and known for their pure life, dealing with the lives of prostitutes, give a clear picture of this dissolution of morals. *Samaya Matrka* of Kshemendra may be described as the autobiography of a prostitute. Kshemendra was perhaps the greatest educator of his day, a writer of popular abstracts of *Ramayana, Brihadkatha,* etc., and a person of encyclopaedic knowledge. In the *Samaya Matrka,* the heroine describes her adventures in every sphere of society, as a courtesan, as the mistress of a noble, as a street walker, as a go-between, as a false nun, as a corruptor of youth, and as a frequenter of religious places. The picture conveyed is one which would show that society generally had lost the sense of moral rectitude. Nor is this to be dismissed merely as imaginary. *Kuttini Matam*, or the opinions of a go-between, by Damodara Gupta who was a minister to one of the Kashmir kings and itself a poet of extraordinary merit, corroborates the picture. The extreme obscenity of some of the tantric literature of the time as of the sculpture in many temples, perfections of modelling and execution though they be, tell the same tale. Ibn Batuta even makes the cautious remark that prostitution is not held in discredit in India.

In other words social life had crystallised. The rigours of widowhood were enforced strictly in higher class families. We hear no more about widowed princesses like Rajasri taking part in public discussions; on the other hand literary evidence in the eighth and ninth centuries show a hardening of attitude. It is of course to be remembered that among large classes of ordinary people like the Jat cultivators widow remarriage was permitted by custom, but the more orthodox and certainly the higher classes held firmly to the prohibition.

There was great disparity of wealth. We have recorded evidence of two hundred crores of rupees being spent by the brothers Vastupala and Tejapala in charity, of the immense fortune of Bimal Shah who built the marble temple of Abu, of the wealth of the Manigramam corporation which traded with the Indies, etc. But the ordinary villager was poor, though his poverty was probably less than what it is today as the pressure on land was not so great. The wealth of the rich was generally spent in charities, but it is noteworthy that charity had become limited in scope. The generosity of the merchants was displayed in the building of temples, in the adornment of places of pilgrimage, in grants to religious institutions.

Another noteworthy aspect of this generosity was the establishment of hospitals, well stocked with medicines and with a trained staff of doctors and nurses. In the *Bodhi stavāvadana kalpalata* there is an interesting description of such a hospital. The king Punyabala, who established hospitals in every town laid special emphasis on providing trained nurses in these institutions, for, says the author, "Is not the trained nurse the first element in treatment. Rare indeed is a nurse, who has love, efficiency, patience and obedience to the doctor's orders." The author also makes the king exhort the nurses thus: "I have appointed good doctors and stored the hospitals with medicine. Now it is for you to restore the health of sick people, by applying appropriate remedies, strengthening the patients with suitable diet, removing their gloom by pleasant conversation and their *ennui* by recreation."

Kshemendra in his *Narmamala* and *Desopadesa* has left us a description of the state of society which is particularly interesting. The bureaucracy in all its stages is described by him and this is particularly valuable as from other sources we have but little information about the structure of government. From *Narmamala* which is a satire on officialdom we see that the lowest rung of the official ladder was the village Divira (or what is known now as Patwari). Asthana Diviras or clerks of the court are also described. Next higher than the Divira was the Niyogi whose function was to supervise a district, check the accounts and generally see to the administration. The Niyogi's tours in the districts with their attendant troubles for the villagers are carefully described and the description is as true today as in the time of Kshemendra. Above the district officers were Paripalakas or governors who were assisted by superintendents of finances. Paripalakas were very important officers with extensive powers. They had control over the entire administration of the provinces. A governor's chief assistant was Lekhakopadhyaya who was in charge of all government records, and responsible for the issue of all orders. The Ganga Diviras or superintendents of finance were also provincial officers. The summit of the official structure was of course the ministry and the central secretariat.

The detailed description by one who was himself descended from Nagindra, the prime minister of Kashmir, and was in his lifetime (990-1065) associated with the highest in the land is of particular value as clearly proving the existence of a regular bureaucracy, a hierarchy of officials in which promotion was according to ability. Kshemendra in fact describes mainly the methods by which the officials rose to high dignities. The existence of an official hierarchy is corroborated from other sources also. The Vishnu Dharmasastra in defining a public document says that it should be written in a public office by a Kayastha (a clerical official) and attested by the superintendent of the office.

The generic term used for officials was Kayastha, and up to the eleventh century the Kayasthas were an official class though in the works of Kshemendra and in *Rajatarangini* the word is used as signifying officialdom: for example, in *Rajatarangini* the Brahmin Sivaratha is described as a Kayastha. In numerous inscriptions dating from the middle of the eighth century we have mention of Kayasthas as officials.

The official classes were mainly recruited from among the Brahmins and certain castes included among the Sudras who had a tradition of education. The educated castes among the Sudras assumed naturally a higher social status especially in areas where Buddhist ideas were widely prevalent and the upward movement was clearly marked in the numerous castes outside the first three Varnas who had achieved high social position. They formed in fact the basis of all officialdom in India at least from the time of the Mauryas, though the higher officers at court, governors of provinces and judges and magistrates belonged to the Brahmins and the higher castes.

A bureaucracy with so long-established a tradition was bound to create its own forms and formulae, especially in a country where literary precision was so highly esteemed as in India. We know from the Hathigumpha inscription of the first century B.C. that Kharavela underwent training in the drafting of documents. We have in fact a Lekhapadhati or standard form of writing of official documents in Sanskrit which has come down to us and which shows us the elaborate nature of the forms in use by the bureaucrats of ancient India. The Lekhapadhati of the Gujerat kings gives us fifty-four different forms in use; and the abstract of *Sukraniti,* a late work on politics, contains what may be described as a secretarial manual.

All Indian kingdoms were organised on a semi-military basis, with large though inefficient armies, with fortifications in important places, with reasonable methods of transport and an inherited system of storage of grains. But except under warlike rulers, bent on conquest, their actual military strength seems to have been little, as even in case of defeat by a ruler claiming imperial authority, it was very seldom that a king was dispossessed or a State annexed.

The general picture we have of India at the end of the tenth century when it first came into collision with an organised Islamic kingdom may be summarised as follows. The Hindu social structure was firm and had undergone a reorganisation which made it capable of resisting external pressure. The Hindu religion had received a new and vigorous impetus with the gradual absorption of Buddhism, with new popular forms which satisfied the religious aspiration of the masses, and with a philosophic background which satisfied the more intelligent minds and united the different sects into one faith. Economic life was prosperous, with the accumulated wealth of five centuries of peace, commerce and colonisation. As against this, the political structure was weak. There was no sense of India. The ideal of Bharata Varsha as one country which dominated Hindu mind in the days of foreign invasion had been forgotten. Patriotism was wholly absent an even the idea of unity to resist the foreigner was non-existent. The political structure of the states was based on a corrupt bureaucracy and united only by a dynastic interest. In itself often weak it was not strong enough when India had to meet the first shock of Mahmud's invasions. Southern India was in a measure different, for there the monarchies were national from the beginning and the State represented a people who felt pride in their kingdom. The Cholas, the Pandyas and earlier the Pallavas were, as stated before, national monarchies and received a loyalty and obedience which the fleeting empires of later times in North India were unable to enforce. Thus the area open to foreign attack was unprepared for a struggle for national independence.

CHAPTER XIII

ISLAM AND INDIA

THE Arab conquest of half the known world within a period of fifty years (670: conquest of Persia—711: conquest of Spain) is one of the most remarkable chapters in the history of the world. In 711, ninety years after the Prophet left Mecca for Medina, the empire of Islam extended from the frontiers of China to the shores of the Atlantic. A military power such as the world had not witnessed ruled, with its capital at Baghdad, territories which were even larger than those of Rome at the height of its power and possessed a military strength which not only destroyed the empire of Persia but with one sweep annexed the north of Africa, conquered Spain and took the arms of the Khalif into the heart of France. The only country which was able to resist the attack of Islam during this great period was India. In 712, Mohammed Bin Kassim gained for the Khalif a foothold in Sind. The desert kingdom in the hands of minor local potentates was annexed and converted into a base. By slow degrees the Muslim power was extended to Multan, a great centre of trade and industry. There it remained.

With a sufficiently large advance base, and with absolute mastery of the sea, why the Khalifs—at the height of their power, when all over the known world their name was causing terror—were unable to push forward their advantage requires examination. The old idea that it was for lack of effort can no longer be sustained. We know that the governors of Sind made continuous efforts to extend their territory. In 725, we know that Junaid, who had followed Bin Kassim as Governor of Sind, made a great effort to conquer Broach, Gujerat and Malwa. The expedition, though successful to start with, failed to achieve its object. In 731, Junaid's successor Tamim decided to enter the Deccan as the attack on Malwa had proved too difficult. He landed with a large army but met with disaster at the hands of Pulikesena Chalukya at Navasari in 738. These reverses in no way affected the imperial power of the Khalifs and a new and greater effort was made when their armies reached as far as Ujjain. There the Gurjara king Nagabhata defeated them, as stated earlier, and the invader was driven back. As Baladitya, the contemporary poet, says, "he crushed the mighty hosts of the Mlechhas, those foes of godly deeds."

This victory saved India for over 275 years. There was no further attempt to conquer India in the days of the Khalifs when Islamic power was at its height, though one of the Governors of Sind, Imran Bin Musa, attempted the conquest of Kutch in 883 and was driven out by Mihira Bhoja. Actually, after Nagabhata's victory, the danger from Islam disappeared till new conditions arose on the north-west frontier.

As a result of nearly three centuries of peace the menace of Islam was forgotten even in Gurjara country. The warring Hindu kings of the ninth and tenth centuries of North India had no realisation of the cloud that was gathering. To all outside appearance the period was one of prosperity under the Gurjara emperors of Kanauj. From them the empire of the Gurjara Desa had passed to the Parmaras of Dhar, of which dynasty Bhoja was the most magnificent and the most illustrious. It is unfortunate that the homelands of his empire were in the middle of India and his own territories were organised around Malwa, for the threat which the Hindu kings had not foreseen had arisen on the north-west, and no state of equal power was there on the Indian side to fight the hosts of Mahmud of Ghazni.

The area now known as Afghanistan had for long been one of the outlying provinces of the Khalif's empire. But it was a neglected area. During the break-up of the Khalif's power in Baghdad, Alaptijin who had been an officer of the Governor of Khorassan, Abdul Malik, established himself at Ghazni and governed the area as an autonomous State defying the authority of the centre. Ghazni however became an organised and important power only in the time of Sabaktijin who assumed authority in 977. A portion of modern Afghanistan was then under the rule of a Brahmin dynasty, known as the Shahi dynasty. For centuries this State had flourished on the frontier and its territories at this time extended well into the Punjab. Sabaktijin's policy of uniting the whole of Afghanistan under this rule brought the new State of Ghazni into conflict with the Hindu Shah Jayapal who accepted, after a half-hearted resistance, the suzerainty of the Ghazni monarch.

Once again in history a revolutionary situation had arisen on the frontier. As long as the Afghan area is disorganised or weak, there is no question of any invasion of India. But when a great power controls Afghanistan, the Punjab is not only threatened but the inevitable pressure of political power will be towards it. Indian history provides ample illustrations of this thesis. The Punjab became a part of the Persian empire when the territories of the Great Kings included the valley of Kabul. It was the Persian province of India that Alexander attacked. Again when the Kushans had established their authority over this area and had behind them the resources of the rich lands of Khiv and Bokhara, the Punjab passed into their hands. Similar was the case with regard to the short-lived Hun monarchy. What had happened under Sabaktijin and to a much larger extent under Mahmud was something similar. A great military state which included Khorassan and parts of Central Asia had come into being in this vital area of India's frontier and unless the Indian side was equally well organised the fate of the Punjab was sealed.

There was hardly any realisation in India of the tremendous change in the situation that had taken place across the frontier. The sense of isolation, which India's geography enforced, gave the Indian rulers no continental views and no appreciation of the dynamics of power in the international world. She had had ample warnings. The abortive efforts of the Khalifs should have indicated to them the danger, but the ease with which those attempts were defeated and the great interval of over two hundred and fifty years made them forget and ignore or underestimate the anger that was now gathering.

Jayapal, the Shahi monarch, after his first encounter realised the danger that his dynasty and Hinduism faced. He organised a confederacy of the more powerful princes near him, the Chahamans of Ajmer and the rulers of Kanauj and raised an army and marched to meet the menace in person in 991. The battle ended disastrously for Jayapal. Peshawar was occupied by Sabaktijin's son and successor, Sultan Mahmud, one of the great figures of Islamic history. A just and wise monarch to his own subjects, a great patron of science and arts whose fame spread to all Islamic lands, a champion of orthodoxy and a pious Muslim, he was the pattern of Islamic kingship. It was a military state that he inherited, with a trained and powerful army accustomed to the rigours of warfare in mountainous Afghanistan and in the deserts of Khorassan. With Peshawar in his possession the routes to the plains of the Punjab lay open to him. Mahmud led a number of expeditions originally for plunder and with every successful raid his appetite for the accumulated riches of the states and temples of Hindustan increased. The Punjab was annexed to the Empire and converted into a base for further raids. Far into the Gangetic valley, down south to Anihilapatan and Somnath in Gujerat, he led his warriors incited alike by the prospect of plunder and the fanaticism of destroying the temples of the idolators. Much destruction he inflicted on the prosperous towns of the Gangetic valley, on Thanesvar, Kanauj, the imperial city, Mathura, the city sacred to Krishna and for over a thousand years the centre of an unparalleled artistic culture. The description of the temples of Mathura left by Utbi, the contemporary historian, is worth quoting:

> "In that place there was a place of worship of the Indian people: and when he came to that place he saw a city of wonderful fabric and conception, so that one might say this is a building of paradise. . . . They had brought immense stones and had laid a level foundation upon high stairs. Around it and at its sides they had placed one thousand castles built of stone. . . . And in the midst of the city they had built a temple higher than all to delineate the beauty and decoration of which the pens of all writers and the pencils of all painters would be powerless. . . . In his memoirs which the Sultan (Mahmud) wrote of this journey he thus declares that if anyone should undertake to build a fabric like that he would expend thereon a hundred thousand packets of a thousand dinars and would not complete it in two hundred years with the assistance of the most ingenious masters. . . . "

The cities of India were laid waste. The glories of India's architecture which called forth such reluctant admiration from the Sultan himself were razed to the ground, and an incalculable amount of wealth carried away. But Mahmud, apart from the annexation of the Punjab (1018), made no attempt to conquer any portion of India. His were merely raids of devastation, looked upon by the Hindus of the time as acts of God, like plague, before which they fled. It had but little effect on Indian history, except as a forerunner of the more ambitious and more successful efforts, hundred and fifty years later of Mohammed Ghori who displaced the successors of Mahmud of Ghazni.

The resistance which the Hindu monarchs offered is not alluded to by the court panegyrists of Ghazni. But at least in one case Mahmud met with such determined opposition that he had to retreat in haste suffering, even according to Muslim historians of the time, great hardships on the way. Mahmud descended on Somnath, the great pilgrimage centre in Kathiawad, in January 1026 marching across the deserts of Rajputana. He attacked the town of Somnath, captured it and plundered the temple, but according to the official historian he turned away in haste.

"From that place" says Ibn-ul-Athir, the Sultan's admiring historian, "Mahmud turned back and the reason was that Paramdeo who was the King of the Hindus was in the way and Amir Mahmud feared lest this great victory may be spoiled. He did not come back by the direct way but took a guide . . . and went towards Multan. His soldiers suffered heavily on the way. . . . Many animals and a large number of men of the Muslim army perished on the way. . . . " The Hindu king who opposed Mahmud in Kathiawad was none other than Bhoja, the Parmara king of Dhar whose dominions at the time extended to Kathiawad. Bhoja of Dhar had come to the throne in 999, two years after Mahmud ascended the throne of Ghazni. As a great ruler and even as a greater scholar and potron of arts Bhoja's name is still cherished all over India. Of his greatness as a writer and patron of letters nothing need be said here. As a ruler he revived the glory of the Gurjara empire. At the time that Mahmud was raiding the Gangetic valley, Bhoja was consolidating his authority over central India, Gujerat and Kathiawad. It is this great ruler that Mahmud challenged by his raid on Somnath. Bhoja marched into Kathiawad and barred Mahmud's way of retreat. The Sultan of Ghazni fled in haste through the waterless regions and reached safely "at last after suffering great distress and hardship," as Ibn-ul-Athir himself states.

No encounter between the opposing forces is mentioned in Muslim histories but the Udaipur prasasti of Bhoja claims that he defeated the Turks. And it is hard to believe that merely because Mahmud felt that "his great victory will be spoiled" he would have chosen a route through a waterless desert. Clearly Mahmud was unable to force his way, was either defeated or checked and in any case the great victory became an ignominous rout.

Mahmud's successors held to their Indian province, but it is noteworthy that in the time of Masud, his son, it was a Hindu general, Tilak, who was entrusted with the duty of restoring order in the Punjab which had risen in revolt under the Muslim governors.

From the death of Mahmud to Mohammed Ghori's invasion in 1191 for a period of hundred and sixty years India, apart from the Punjab, was undisturbed by Muslim invasions. With a foreign power established at Sirhind and holding the land of the five rivers the danger to the Gangetic plain was indeed obvious, but the Hindu monarchs of the time did not seem to have realised the danger. Indeed, powerful states capable of offering firm resistance had come into existence. Jaya Simha Sidharaja had revived the glories of the Gurjara empire, the northern portion of which based on Sakambhari (or Sambhar) was under the powerful Chahamana kings who were united in alliance with the Gurjara rulers. Visala Deva Chauhan, the earliest of the dynasty of whom we have authentic record and whose inscription on the great iron pillar of Delhi records his achievements, was well established in Sambhar and his territories extended up to the boundaries of the Ghaznavid province of the Punjab. His son Someswar, in alliance with Sidharaja, strengthened the position of the Chauhans in the north and claimed semi-imperial sway over the rulers of Delhi and the northern territories. Someswar's son was Prithviraj under whom the Chauhan power reached its zenith. A valiant and impetuous monarch capable of great acts of heroism, he was hardly the leader to organise a systematic defence against a determined enemy.

Apart from the Chauhan monarch of Ajmer, the most important monarch of North India was Jayachandra, the ruler of Kanauj. As the master of the imperial city and as the sovereign of the Gangetic valley, Jayachandra's prestige was immense and was acknowledged by the princes of Hindustan. His power was also great. To an outside observer Hindustan was not ill-organised to meet the attack of the Muslims from the Punjab.

Mohammed Ghori displaced the dynasty of Sabaktijin in 1186. After re-establishing order in the Punjab he marched into India in 1191 and met the forces of Prithviraj in battle. The Muslim forces were defeated and Mohammed himself had to flee for his life. But he returned next year with an army better organised and superior in numbers and the rival armies met again in the same field. This time disaster overtook Prithviraj. The Hindu army was broken, Prithviraj himself captured and killed and the confederacy of Rajput rulers who had come to the support of the ruler of Ajmer scattered to the winds. The Sultan occupied Ajmer but he handed it over to a son of Prithviraj who accepted the suzerainty of the Sultan.

The history of the conquest of the Gangetic valley after this historic success can be summarised in a few sentences. Kutubuddin Aibak, whom the Sultan left behind as his governor, occupied Delhi which he made the seat of his government. Delhi, which had been founded by a local king in 993 A.D., was but a small provincial town but Kutubuddin by making it his capital, made it the centre of Mussalman power in India for the future. In 1194, Jayachandra was defeated and Kanauj conquered by the Sultan himself. By this victory the rich plains from Meerut to Banaras came under the Ghori king. With his power thus established in the heart of Hindustan, expansion was easy. Bakhtiar Khilji with a small force reduced Bihar and among his achievements may be noted the wanton destruction of the university of Nalanda and its great and unique library which contained the acquisition of many centuries (1197). Two years later the same commander conquered Bengal whose ruler Lakshman Sen, a poet and scholar of distinction, escaped on hearing of Bakhtiar's arrival. The Chandela Prince of Bundelkhand was reduced by Kutubuddin himself in 1202. Thus in a period of five years Mohammed Ghori, through his Governor Kutubuddin, ruled over an empire in India which included the Punjab, the Gangetic plains and Bengal. Mohammed died in 1206.

Kutubuddin was elected Sultan by the Turkish Amirs in the capital and became the first of a succession of kings, known very inappropriately in history as the "Slave Dynasty." The succession of the first few Sultans of Delhi was by election by the Amirs and Generals, and, as in many cases the highest posts in the court, in administration and the army were held by the slaves of the monarch, the elected ruler had often started his life as a slave. Kutubuddin himself had been purchased in his youth. The new Sultan who had actually been responsible for the main conquests, consolidated the empire and established it on a firm basis.

The dynastic history of the Delhi Sultans from Kutubuddin's death in 1210 to Babar's conquest of Delhi in 1525 is one of dull monotony, of wars, of succession, murders of nobles and leading men and a few able men succeeded by weak and licentious potentates. The first or the so-called Slave Dynasty produced two rulers of remarkable ability, Iltamish (1210-1235) and Balban. Iltamish carried the Muslim rule up to Ujjain in Central India and also reduced the Khilji Maliks of Bengal who never actually accepted the authority of Delhi and were continuously in revolt. He is also credited with having built the Kutub Minar. Apart from the romantic figure of Rezia Begam, whose one weakness was, it was said, that she was a woman, his successors proved themselves incompetent and the Turkish Amirs again selected a soldier, Balban (1266), to succeed to the throne. He was able for a time to put down the recurrent revolt of the Khiljis of Bengal and to restore order; but the Sultanate had lost the momentum of invasion and was confined to the territories left by Iltamish. The successors of Balban were unable to hold the provinces together and the Hindus of the hardly conquered areas of Bundelkhand and Central India asserted their independence.

A new and more vigorous dynasty now stepped in. The Khiljis produced one remarkable ruler who, though a megalomaniac, was able to carry the Muslim arms down to the extreme south of India. Allauddin reduced the great and historic kingdoms of the Yadavas of Deogir and the Chalukyas of Gujerat. The main opposition to his imperial pretentions came from the Ranas of Ranthambor who under Rana Hammir had now assumed the leadership of Hindu resistance, a position which they maintained up to the time of the Moghuls and, so far at least as heraldry goes, handed over to Sivaji who claimed descent from the rulers of Mewar. From the *Hammira Mahakavya* we know that the mission of Hindu renaissance was fully realised by the kings of Mewar who put themselves forward as the champions of Hinduism. The fight with the Rana was a victory for Allauddin who occupied Ranthambor, and he even captured the great fortress of Chitor. But Mewar was not conquered and the Sultan had to find his laurels elsewhere.

He turned his attention to the Deccan and his general Malik Kafur carried out a bold raid which took him as far as Rameshwaram. This sharp reminder of the existence of a great military state in northern India, which was powerful enough to overflow long established dynasties in a lightning-like campaign, had a remarkable effect on the people of South India. It led to the immediate reorganisation of the political system and we see, within the short period of twenty-five years, the establishment of a state powerful enough to withstand invasions from the north. Far otherwise was the case of Gujerat. The great kingdom which had thrown back the invasions of Islam four hundred years earlier fell at the first onslaught of Allauddin's generals. It never rose again though Gujerati nationalism, the product of centuries of independence, asserted itself vigorously later under its Muslim Sultans.

The history of the Khiljis told the same wearisome tale as that of the Slaves. The death of Allauddin was followed by civil wars in which the successful party put to violent death the princes and leading men of the last reign. Naturally conspiracies and revolts followed and the distant provinces threw off the yoke of Delhi. The imperial court became the scene of disgraceful orgies and in the case of one ruler, Kutubuddin Mubarak, it is said that "he often dressed himself in female attire and with his body dressed with trinkets he went out in the city in the company of harlots and danced at the houses of nobles." As a result, a new dynasty, the Tughlaq, was elevated to the throne, the third in the course of hundred years. Ghiasuddin Tughlaq (1320-25) was able to restore order in some of the provinces. His successor Mohammed Tughlaq, at whose court Ibn Batuta, the famous traveller, lived for a time, is one of those strange characters in history whose schemes were perfect on paper but led to absurd results and untold misery in execution. He succeeded to an extensive empire which was reasonably prosperous and left it utterly in ruin. It is vain to argue that the fault was none of his as his ideas which produced these results were excellent. One of his schemes was to issue stamped leather in place of coins, an idea which in the form of currency notes today dominates the whole trade, commerce and banking of the world. But in his case it led to the bankruptcy of the state treasury. Another of his ventures was to remove the capital to Daulatabad, the former Devagiri. He built a road for the purpose, arranged for the free feeding and accommodation of the population of Delhi on the march, but also ordered the compulsory evacuation of every man, woman and child from Delhi. Ibn Batuta says that the mad king even instituted a search to find out whether anyone still lurked in Delhi. The thorough search is said to have resulted in the discovery of two men, one lame and the other blind! Whether the story is an exaggeration or not, it is characteristic of the mad despotism of Mohammed Tuglaq.

Mohammed's reign is important as it enabled the surviving Hindu kingdoms to organise themselves. Chitor and Ranthambor were retaken by Mewar which state under a succession of able Ranas consolidated its power over Rajputana. In 1336, Vijayanagar was founded on the banks of the Tungabhadra and this mighty empire organised the Hindus of the South. Elsewhere also the revival of Hinduism was marked. In fact it may well be said that the anarchy of Mohammed Tughlaq's reign marks the re-birth of Hindu India, its rise from the ashes and its re-establishment as a political force in Hindustan.

The more settled portions of the Sultanate also did not survive the Tughlaq monarch's mad eccentricities. Bengal, never too serious in its dependence on Delhi, finally threw off the yoke in 1336. In the territories of Maharashtra, a new and independent kingdom was founded by Hassan Gangu, which under the name of the Bahmani monarchy achieved fame in Indian history. Gujerat continued in a doubtful vassalage. Imperial authority had broken down even in what may be called the home domains in the Gangetic valley.

Mohammed's successor Firoz was a weak and irresolute ruler, bigoted in his religion and unwarlike in his pursuits. But he is honourably remembered as the only Muslim monarch of Delhi before Sher Shah who undertook any work of public utility. Firoz undertook extensive irrigation works which harnessed the waters of the Ghaggar and the Jumna for cultivation. His work is the predecessor of the great irrigation systems of the Punjab and is a most notable achievement, a worthy monument to the liberality and farsightedness of the Tughlaq king. Firoz's administration was weak and under his successors the Delhi Sultanate gradually broke up. A new and powerful kingdom was established at Jaunpur which exercised authority in Bihar. In Malwa, a Khilji Amir established a new dynasty and Gujerat which had so long been loyal also proclaimed its independence. By the end of the century the Sultanate of Delhi was confined to the Punjab and to the immediate appendages of the capital. When in 1398 Timur crossed the Indus, there was no opposition to speak of till he reached the very gates of Delhi. Delhi was occupied after a battle outside its walls and Timur with unusual ferocity allowed the soldiery to plunder the city and massacre a large number of its inhabitants.

Timur's invasion gave the *coup de grace* to the Sultanate of Delhi. After claiming imperial dignity for nearly two hundred years Delhi sank to the position of a provincial capital. The Sayyad and Lodi kings who ruled from Delhi exercised no imperial sway and though the Lodi dynasty produced one remarkable personality in Sikander, who founded the city of Agra which was soon to rival the glories of Delhi for over a hundred and fifty years, his time was mostly spent in reducing the rebellious nobles. But the disintegration had gone too far and the imperial sway of Delhi could not be re-established. Thus when Babar, the descendant of Timur, invaded India (1525) the opposition which the Afghan king of Delhi was able to offer was insignificant. The real opposition which the Moghul invaders met with came from the Rajput confederacy which during the hundred and fifty years following the misrule of Mohammed Tughlaq had attained power and authority over the vast area lying between Gujerat and Delhi.

In fact, after the decay of Turkish power under the Tughlaqs, the representative Muslim dynasties of India were no longer in Delhi. Muslim civilisation was represented not by the weak and dissipated kings who followed Firoz Tughlaq, but by the Sultans of Bengal, Jaunpur, Gujerat and Malwa. Indian Islam in the fifteen century in the courts of the rulers of these states began to disclose characteristics which evidenced the synthesis of culture that was going on beneath the surface. The Delhi Sultanate, dominated as it was by Turkish Amirs and new arrivals from across the border, maintained its foreign character while the Muslim kingdoms of Bengal, Jaunpur, Gujerat and in a lesser degree Malwa developed tendencies which were to find their supreme consummation later under the Moghuls.

Gujerat had been conquered by Allauddin Khilji in 1297. After a hundred years of subordination Zafar Khan in 1401 formally assumed the title of Shah and proclaimed his independence. For the next century and a half Gujerat was one of the leading states of India, a centre of civilisation, culture and learning. The ports of the coast poured wealth into the country and the monarchy, dependent for its separate existence on the loyalty of the people and for its wealth on the merchants, both predominantly Hindu, followed a policy of reconciliation. Under Ahmed Shah (1411-1441) the city of Ahmedabad was founded and the king adorned it with beautiful structures which show marked influences of Hindu architecture. His successor Mohammed Shah was also a liberal patron of arts.

Characteristic of the changed times was the fact that the Hindu rulers of intervening territories were taking sides in the wars between the Sultans of Malwa and Gujerat. More, the territory of the Rajput princes lay between the two Muslim powers and under the leadership of the Ranas of Mewar the policy followed by them was to prevent a union between the Muslim powers. Gujerat, therefore, was constantly at war with the Ranas of Mewar whose power extended up to the Abu Pass and whose fortress at Achalgarh on the Abu hills marked the limit of Muslim authority.

The kingdom of Malwa which also assumed importance under its Khilji monarchs became independent in 1401. Husung Shah, its first monarch, transferred his capital to the historic city of Mandu built by Bhoja. Husung was a great builder and the architectural beauties of Mandu also bear witness to the interpenetration of Hindu and Muslim culture. It was however under Sultan Mahmud that Malwa became a really important state. Mahmud was an ambitious prince and led seven campaigns against Rana Kumbha of Mewar who in one campaign occupied Mandu and in another carried off the Sultan as prisoner and kept him for a short time at Chitor. Under Sultan Mahmud, Feristha says, "his subjects, Mohammedans as well as Hindus, were happy, and maintained friendly intercourse with each other." The relations between the two communities in the Malwa Sultanate were so cordial that in the reign of Mahmud II the Sultan requested the assistance of Hindu rulers to put down the turbulence of his own nobility. His own prime minister was a Hindu, Medina Rao.

The Sultanate of Jaunpur, short-lived though it was, has claims to remembrance. Under the successors of Malik-us-Sharq—or the Lord of the East—this kingdom became not only a great seat of learning but a centre of architectural revival. Under Ibrahim, eminent Muslim scholars from all over India flocked to Jaunpur especially as conditions in Delhi following the invasion of Timur and the breakdown of central authority had become altogether chaotic. Jaunpur architecture was perhaps the noblest combination of Hindu and Muslim ideas prior to the great days of the Moghuls.

Bengal, the other independent Muslim kingdom in Hindustan, had, even from the time of its first conquest under Bakhtiar Khilji, yielded but a shadowy allegiance to the Sultans of Delhi. Practically every one of the Delhi Sultans had to lead an expedition to the great province of the east to reduce it to submission. The final separation of the province came under Firoz Tughlaq. The glory of the independent kings of Bengal began however only with Hussein Shah whose dynasty continued in authority till Bengal was conquered by Akbar and annexed to the Moghul territories in 1576.

Examined in the light of what has been briefly sketched above, it will be seen that the period between 1210 and 1525 separates itself into two equal halves; the period of conquest when the theory of empire was still in the air, and the period of dissolution when the great national monarchies came into existence. The period of conquest was also a period of destruction and loot. In fact the public finance of the Turkish Sultans of Delhi seems to have been based on the assumption that its expenditure should be met from the accumulated treasures of other kingdoms. Allauddin's instructions to Malik Kafur when the latter attacked Telingana are significant. "If the Rai consented to surrender his treasure, his jewels, his elephants and his horses and also to send treasures and elephants in the following year" he was to be let off lightly. Kafur sent the booty on "a thousand camels groaning under the weight of treasure." In the latter period, when Delhi shrunk into a local sovereignty, though still possessing the rich province of the Punjab, the monarchies which were established in Gujerat Malwa, Jaunpur and Bengal became settled governments interested in the arts of peace and in the welfare of the people. The real greatness of Islam during this period is not in Delhi, but in Ahmedabad, Mandu, Jaunpur and Laknauti. For an appreciation of Islamic contribution to India at this period this distinction should be carefully borne in mind.

The pre-Moghul contribution to Indo-Muslim architecture has not receive adequate and general recognition. The glory of the Taj Mahal and other Moghul masterpieces has eclipsed the greatness of the architecture of the first period and yet it is clear that Indo-Islamic building art originated and developed and produced some of its masterpieces in the fifteenth century. The Jami Musjid of Jaunpur, the mosques and palaces in Mandu and Ahmedabad demonstrate the truth of this observation. The Indo-Muslim architecture which these kingdoms developed was a harmonising of Hindu and Muslim traditions. As Sir John Marshall has pointed out "when the Muslim architect, who had inherited a vast wealth of rich and varied designs particularly from the Sassanian and Byzantine empires, saw the great buildings in India, a new vision was opened to him and he at once gauged their vast possibilities and set about taking the fullest advantage of them." The Indo-Muslim style is a complete harmonisation of the artistic spirit of Hinduism and Islam and nowhere does it become more clear than in the mosques at Ahmedabad and Jaunpur. The architects were no doubt Muslims but the master-builders and craftsmen continued to be Hindus. The fame of Hindu craftsmanship was such that, according to the *Zafarnama,* Timur assembled several thousand craftsmen in Delhi and reserving the best for himself distributed the rest to his Amirs. He had formed the design of building a great mosque in Samarkand and "he now gave orders that all the stone masons should be reserved for this pious work."

If in architecture and building early Islam made a noble contribution to India, the same cannot be said in the field of learning, sciences or poetry. During these three hundred years Indian Islam produced no outstanding divine, scholar or scientist. No Averroes or Avicenna, no Tabari or Masudi is there to illumine the pages of Islam in India. In fact the period between 1200-1525 is one of general barrenness in Islamic history when the great cultural traditions of earlier Islam were overborne by the barbarian invasions of Turks and Seljuks. The college at Jaunpur, which Hassan Shah endowed, might have in time led to notable contributions but it existed for too short a time. In the field of literature the only outstanding Muslim name is that of Amir Khusru whose Persian poems shed glory on the period. Probably the reason is that Indian Islam had not evolved a language of its own and was tied to the thought and literature of Persia. Muslim rulers however seem to have encouraged local talent for we know Maladhar Vasu's translation of the *Bhagavata* was undertaken by order of Nusrat Shah and Kavindra Parameswar's translation of the *Mahabharata* was undertaken at the command of Parangal Khan, a general of Hussein Shah. If Islam's direct contribution to literature at the time is negligible, its encouragement of poets and writers deserves special appreciation.

Indo-Muslim achitecture, glorious in its harmony of Indian and Islamic traditions, did not at this period materially affect Hindu architecture. The great Hindu temples and buildings of this period even in northern India continue to be in the orthodox style of Hindus Silpasastra. The Konarak temple of Surya (1285) is an outstanding monument of the time. Chitorgarh in Udaipur designed by Mandana is perhaps the supreme example of Hindu architectural achievement in northern India after the Muslim invasions: but it bears no trace of Islamic influence. Fergusson describes it as a pillar of victory like that of Trojan at Rome but in infinitely better taste as an architectural object than the Roman example. Of the temple architecture of the period Rampur is perhaps the most notable. The magnificence of its conception, the beauty of its execution and the "endless variety of perspective and play of light and shade which results from the disposition of the pillars and the domes" make it one of the great masterpieces of Hindu architecture.

Naturally at a time of war and strife much of the building work was concentrated on fortresses. The Rajput revival in the thirteenth and fourteenth centuries covered the hilltops of Rajasthan with forts which are themselves monuments of the military architecture of the period. These show no influence of Islam. Thus Indo-Muslim and Hindu architecture developed side by side during this period.

We shall get a very inaccurate and altogether false view of the situation of the Hindus during the first period of Islamic Empire in Hinduism (1210-1370) if we depend on the court chroniclers and annalists of Delhi. Historians like Barani were primarily anxious to picture their heroes as the patterns of Islamic orthodoxy and virtue. The stories of temples desecrated, idols demolished and Hindus converted or massacred which they relate must therefore be read in the light of their desire to show to an orthodox Islamic world, for which they wrote, the glory of these monarchs and their zeal in dealing with the kafir. In the period of conquest the Hindus had no doubt to undergo great miseries. They were deprived at one stroke of all political power in large areas. Their religion was held in contempt and their places of worship were constantly being destroyed. But all the same after the first enthusiasm, the structure of economic life in the country forced even the most zealous and fanatical of kings to moderate this policy. The Muslim invaders brought no cultivators with them. It was an army that occupied Delhi and destroyed the Hindu monarchies in the Gangetic valley. It was impossible for the Muslim kings, had they even desired it, to have the lands cultivated by the soldiers. Lands could only be given in jagir to the great Amirs, but the cultivating classes remained Hindu. Nor was conversion on such a scale as would displace the Hindu Zamindar and cultivator ever carried out or even attempted as is demonstrated by the fact that even today in the Doab which was continuously under Muslim rule for seven hundred years the Hindu population is in an overwhelming majority. The land system in fact did not change and therefore the Hindus in general in the countryside led fairly the same life as they had led before.

Nor is it to be understood that commerce and trade changed hands to any considerable extent. The Muslim invaders were military adventurers who looked down upon trade and to whom the elaborate system of Hundi and credit on which Indian business was based was a mystery. The commercial classes were no doubt mulcted heavily both by the imperial government and by its local officials but the Hindu bania remained then, as now, a necessary element in the structure of society.

Even in regard to religion the idea that Hinduism was always held in contempt by the early Muslim rulers would not bear examination. In fact we have ample evidence that even under the most bigoted kings, like Allauddin Khilji and Firoz Tughlaq, the Hindu religious leaders received honour and recognition. From Jain sources we know that Allauddin held religious discourses with Acharya Mahasena who had to be brought from the Karnataka country for the purpose. It is also said that the Digambara Jain, Purna Chandra of Delhi, and the Swetambara ascetic Ramachandra Suri were in favour with the same Sultan. Ghiasuddin Tughlaq had two Jain officers who exercised great influence over him, while Firoz held in high honour the poet Ratnasekhara.

A more important factor which helped to keep Hindu society intact was the undoubted fact that the lower ranks of the bureaucracy had of necessity to be Hindus. India had, as emphasised in an earlier chapter, an ancient and elaborate bureaucracy with its own forms and procedure. While the higher officials were all Muslims the lower rungs of officialdom had of necessity to be

Hindus. The *patwaris*, the accountants, the treasurers and others in the districts were invariably Hindu while the governors and even district officials were Muslim. Only judicial administration was taken over by the Islamic rulers and the Qazis administered Muslim law. It is the existence of this bureaucracy which enabled Iltamish and Allauddin Khilji to restore order in a short time and to build up an imperial structure. Again it is the same bureaucracy which gave opportunities to provincial governors to establish states with but a small Muslim army at their command, as in the case of Bakhtiar Khilji who when he invaded Bengal had but a small raiding party with him.

The despotism of the Sultans fell mainly on the Amirs and nobles of the court. The activities of the rulers so minutely chronicled by the annalists will be seen, if examined closely, to relate to party factions among the nobility, when they did not deal with campaigns against other states. These party factions led to massacres and atrocities which were gruesome enough. But they were against Muslim nobles themselves. Then again the continuous revolts of governors which were put down with a heavy hand, as for example by Ghiasuddin Tughlaq in Bengal, were campaigns against Muslim nobles and armies. The despotism of a court affects in the first place the courtiers and the terrible deeds of the later Tughlaqs hardly affected the general public, except in the sense that the central government weakened and as a result the rural population was left a great deal more to themselves.

The Hindus in the conquered areas were no doubt depressed. Political power which gives a people dignity and self-respect had gone from them. They were excluded from high offices, were treated as being not in the same as the rulers, were subjected to differential taxation; but there is no reason to believe that their life was too hard. As Barani says, humility and obedience were to be expected from them. A Qazi when asked about the true position of Hindus replied—as quoted by Barani—"they are called Khiraj Guzars (payers of tribute) and when a revenue officer demands silver from them, they should without question and with all humility and respect tender gold. If the tax collector chooses to spit into the mouth the latter must open his mouth without hesitation. The meaning of doing such a thing is that the Hindu in acting this wise shows his meekness and humility and obedience and respect." This was no doubt the theological position and the exposition of the doctrine in this picturesque form might have pleased Allauddin. But from the annalists themselves we know that the big landholders of the Doab were often in revolt and the theological doctrine could hardly be enforced without a much larger army of civilian officials which the Sultans of Delhi could not create except on the basis of the employment of the old Hindu bureaucracy.

The surprising fact which emerges from the history of the first hundred and fifty years of Islam's conquest of North India is the strength of the Hindu religion. Everything was open to a Hindu who changed his religion and accepted Islam. There was no post or dignity which was not open to a Hindu who accepted Islam. Khusrau, an outcaste slave from Kathiawad, even ascended the Delhi Throne for a short time under the title of Nasiruddin. With the short-cut to prosperity and power so clearly marked out for them, it is remarkable that Muslims today number only 14 per cent in Uttar Pradesh which was continuously under Muslim rule for six hundred years. Hindu religion withstood the shock, and the evidence is incontestable that forcible conversions were few and the lot of Hindus could not have been exceptionally hard.

The depression of Hindus did not last very long. It is the undying glory of the Rajputs and their main claim to India's gratitude that the resistance to foreign invasion during the days of conquest was organised by them and kept up with continuous heroism for a period of four hundred years. When the Chauhan arms met with disaster in the battle against Mohammed Ghori, the Rajput States lay disorganised and helpless for a short time. But a new family claimed the leadership and this was the Guihilot dynasty of Mewar. The area between Abu and Ranthambor was organised into military confederacy and even Allauddin at the height of his power found it hard, as Akbar was to find at a later time, to humiliate the pride or break the spirit of the Mewar rulers. The great Hammira whose glory is sung in *Hammiravijaya* was able for a long time to stand up to the might of Delhi. Kheta, his son, even occupied Ajmer and by the end of the fourteenth century the Mewar rulers had risen to the position of one of the major powers of North India, constantly at war with Malwa and Gujerat. Under Lakha Singh the Mewar army even invaded the Gangetic valley. But it was under Maharana Kumbha, one of the most notable figures of medieval India (1433-68), that the Mewar kingdom attained the height of its power. The Sultans of Gujerat and Malwa were defeated and held in check and Hindu power was established over large areas of North India. The glory of Kumbha and his successors was that they were the champions of a Hindu revival which, apart from saving large areas from Muslim conquest, also put heart into the Hindu people of other areas of North India. The claim to be Hinduan Suraj or the Sun of the Hindus was fully sustained by the descendants of Bappa Rawal from Hammira to Pratap.

Nor was Hindu resistance only in Rajputana. Elsewhere also Hindu influence began to assert itself and by the fourteenth century even in the Gangetic valley the great landholders had come to have sufficient influence and authority to rebel against the centre when it became weak. We hear continuously of the revolt of Zamindars which the rulers in Delhi had to put down with a strong hand.

The great culture of Islam could hardly be represented by the Turks and Afghans who entered India in the wake of Mohammed Ghori. They no doubt represented the religion of Islam, but the civilisation associated with the Muslim empires of Baghdad or Cairo or Cordova found no echo in the hearts of the Turkish Maliks in whose hands political power was vested. The religion of Islam was itself the main contribution of these dynasties of Delhi. Apart from its doctrinal aspects, Islam also introduced into India a conception of human equality, a pride in one's religion, a legal system which in many ways was an advance on the codes of the time. In the fields of culture the Turkish Sultans introduced new styles of architecture and buildings of which the Tughlaq monuments with their Central Asian domes and glazed tiles are perhaps the best examples. The strongly egalitarian character of Islam and the pride of the Muslim in his religion had their repercussions which we shall notice later. It is sufficient to emphasise here that the new spirit which the Hindu monarchs of Rajputana and of the Vijayanagar dynasty displayed as champions of Dharma and the upholders of religion was a direct result of the contact with Islam. Even the most orthodox kings of ancient times, the Bharasivas and the Guptas in the north, and the Pallavas and the Cholas in the south never claimed to be the champions of a creed or the upholders of a society. While they were orthodox believers, the idea that it was their duty actively to support and protect religion was foreign to them. To Hammira and to Kumbha, no less than to Krishnadeva Raya and to Rama Raya this was the main function of the state. Religious faith became an active factor of policy with Hindu kings as a result of Islam.

The main social result of the introduction of Islam as a religion into India was the division of society on a vertical basis. Before the thirteenth century, Hindu society was divided horizontally, and neither Buddhism nor Jainism affected this division. They were not unassimilable elements and fitted in easily with the existing divisions. Islam, on the other hand, split Indian society into two sections from top to bottom and what has now come to be known in the phraseology of today as two separate nations came into being from the beginning. Two parallel societies were established on the same soil. At all stages they were different and hardly any social communication or intermingling of life existed between them. There was of course a continuous process of conversion from Hinduism to Islam; as against it there was also a continuous strengthening of the Hindu social body, both by the rise of new doctrines and sects as well as by defensive feeling of security. In fact one of the most remarkable factors in the India of this period is the revival movements in Hinduism. The Vaishnava movement with its great devotional figures from Jayadeva to Mirabai, Ramananda and Kabir in the north, Namadeva and Jnaneswara in Maharashtra and Gujerat, the rise of the Lingayats in the Karnataka, all these vital movements belong to this period. *Gita Govinda,* written at Puri, attained such wide popularity that its standard commentary even today is the one by Maharana Kumbha, the hero of Rajputana. Ramananda's great movement, which is related to the earlier religious doctrines of the Tamil country, had its centre in Banaras and to his influence can be traced the eclectic teachings of Kabir, and the pietic mysticism of Nanak, and the devotional ecstasies of Chaitanya.

Generally speaking it will be noticed that the religious movements of the period were non-ritualistic and based on Bhakti. The doctrines of the Bhakti school are undoubtedly ancient in India, based on the teachings of Pancharatra and Bhagavata schools, but their sudden popularity at this period can be explained only by the feeling of escapism which dominated the Hindu mind as a result of the conquest of its sacred places by Islam. Bhakti yoga is preached in the *Gita* and its final message is the abandonment of all to the Supreme, but the doctrine of the *Gita* is not one of mysticism of devotion in the way that Mira and Chaitanya understood it. The vigorous and strenuous life preached by the *Gita* finds no echo in the Krishna and Radha worship which became the symbol of the Bhakti cult in the fourteenth and fifteenth centuries.

One thing is clear. Islam had a profound effect on Hinduism during this period. Medieval Hindu theism is in some ways a reply to the attack of Islam; and the doctrines of medieval teachers, by whatever name their gods are known, are essentially theistic. It is the one supreme God that is the object of the devotee's adoration and it is to His grace that we are asked to look for redemption. All Bhakti cults are therefore essentially monotheistic, not in the exclusive sense that other devotees cannot worship the same supreme being under other names, but in the affirmative belief that whether known as Siva, Krishna or Devi, they all symbolise the One and Eternal. This is of course most noticeable in the songs of Kabir, the influence of which was very great among the common folk.

The development of the Virasaiva sect in Karnataka is also an important feature of this period. Karnataka, like the Tamilnad, had a long tradition of vigorous Saivism. In the 12th century a great leader arose among them who emphasised the twin principles of this sect, a strict monotheism, based on an exclusive worship, of Siva and a denial of caste and consequently the primacy of the Brahmins. Basava, who is acclaimed by the Virasaivas as the Reviver of the Faith, is a notable figure among the medieval saints of Hinduism.

In another and no less important manner Islam influenced Hinduism. It gave an immediate fillip to the vernacular languages which were in the course of evolution. True, Hindi under Chand Bardoi had clearly attained high literary status but, carefully examined, it will be seen that the development of the major North Indian languages can be traced to this period. Sanskrit could no longer be the language even of official documents and as a result, the common *patois* was elevated to a position of greater importance. Amir Khusru (fourteenth century), the one great Muslim poet whom this age produced, in comparing Hindi with Persian and Arabic, declares that the Indian vernacular was in some ways richer and more flexible than Persian. Bengali, Gujerati and Marathi were also coming into prominence, for Vidyapati's songs in Maithili, Chandidas's in Bengali, Mira's poems in Rajasthani and Nathaswami's in Marathi were not merely popular but were recognised as great literature. The translation of Sanskrit classics into the vernacular languages sometimes under the direct patronage of Muslim rulers as in Bengal was also the work of this period. In fact due to the crisis brought about by Islam, religion and literature tended to become less the monopoly of the learned, and more and more a cause of the common people.

It would, however, be untrue to say that Sanskrit literature ceased to be cultivated. We have in Gujerat the great resurgence of Sanskrit associated with Hemachandra Suri and the magnificent and learned court of Viradhavala whose minister, Vastupala himself a poet of eminence, revived the traditions of Bhoja in the west. Nor was Sanskrit less patronised in Rajputana. Apart from

Prithviraja Vijaya of Jonaraja and *Hammiravijaya* of Allauddin's time, we have the outstanding figure of Kumbha whose court was a centre of learning and culture. Kumbha himself was the commentator of *Gita Govinda,* author of *Sangitaraja,* an encyclopaedic work on music, and numerous other poems in Sanskrit. What presumably happened was that with the conquest of the Gangetic valley, scholars and poets took refuge in the courts of Hindu rulers in distant areas and this would perhaps explain the sudden efflorescence of Sanskrit literature in places like Mewar, Khalinjar and Gujerat.

Unconnected with the influence of Islam but contemporaneous with it is the great revival of Jainism. The religion of Vardhamana had been eclipsed for long by the success of Buddhism. But from the Hathigumpha inscription of Kharavela we know that the Kalinga monarch was a follower of the Tirthankaras. It seems to have had also a considerable vogue in the south in the first six centuries of the Christian era, as we know from Pallava records and South Indian literature. In Gujerat it had at all times a vigorous, if restricted, life. In the twelfth century however when Kumarapala comes to power it suddenly rises into prominence. An Acharya of outstanding ability, scholarship and wide vision, comparable only to Sankara, arose among them. Hemachandra Suri, ascetic, lexicographer, epic poet and teacher is indeed a unique personality, one of the greatest that India has produced. His main contribution to Jainism may be generally described as a very successful attempt to combine the Aryan culture with Jain thought. In his Lives of Great Men—the *Purusha Charita* —an epic in many volumes—Hemachandra popularised in a Jain garb the entire mythology of the Hindus. The stories of the Mahabharata and Ramayana and the great traditions of the past were all embodied in this monumental work which earned for its author the title of Kalikala Vyasa. Hemachandra is one of the makers of modern Indian mind and takes his place with Valmiki, Vyasa and Sankara.

Hemachandra wrote in Sanskrit and the impetus he gave to the language was no doubt responsible for the great amount of Sanskrit literature produced at this time in Gujerat. Balachandra Suri (*Vasanta Vilas,* 1296), Yasapala (author of *Maha Moha Vijaya*), Ramachandra Suri (*Nala Vilasa*), Vastupala himself (*Naranarayaniya*), to mention but few, are among the prominent Jain authors of the thirteenth century who contributed to the richness of Sanskrit. Jainism after Hemachandra took its place as a great vehicle of Sanskrit culture.

Nor was the Hindu mind of the time in North India limited to the cultivation of literature and arts. Social reconstruction which Islamic invasions necessiated could only be based on Smritis. Devala, writing in Sind, and Medhadhiti, writing at the time of the Muslim invasions, had both of them to deal with the problem of social adjustment. Devala was faced with the problem of conversions, of higher castes who had been made slaves, etc. The Prayaschitta section of the Smritis assumed more and more importance. Defensively, the Smritis were strengthened in order to make apostasy difficult: at the same time provision had also to be made for taking back into society those forcibly removed from it. Consequently in the social thought of the time there is a double and apparently contradictory process. There is the tendency of all societies on the defensive to be more rigid in their rules, to be more violent in their reactions towards non-conformity, in fact to be more reactionary. On the other hand, there is the tendency to find solutions for problems which the original lawgivers did not have in mind.

The number of commentaries and nibandhas (or digests) produced by Hindu India during the period between 1200-1500 is indeed voluminous. The great Mitakshara of Vijnaneswara cannot be placed earlier than the twelfth century. Kalluka, the most famous commentator of *Manusmriti,* lived early in the fourteenth century in Bengal. Chandeswara, who belonged to Bihar and who wrote numerous digests of Smritis, claims that he was a minister and had himself weighed in gold in 1314 A.D. (in the time of Allauddin Khilji). It is also noteworthy that *Dānaratnakara* mentions him as having rescued the earth from the flood of Mlechhas. In fact this period was the heyday of writers on Smriti for the reason that the adjustment of social relationships had become an important problem.

From what has been stated above it will be seen that there was no domination of the Hindu mind by Islam. Such influences as became apparent in the field of thought were in religion and here the ancient Bhakti philosophy merged harmoniously with the Sufi doctrines of Islam. It is difficult to recognise much difference between the mystic songs of Ramananda, Kabir and Mirabai and the Sufi saints of Islam and the influence of the one on the other cannot be definitely claimed or established.

The growth of vernacular literature as evidencing the resilience of Hindu mind and the influence of Islam has already been alluded to. A comparison between the Sanskrit and vernacular productions of this period would show that while Sanskrit under the weight of its immense literature was becoming more and more unreal, ornate, technical and unrelated to life and the aspirations, spiritual or social, of the people, vernacular poetry was showing a naturalness and beauty which reflected a living faith. It is not only in the devotional songs of Vidyapati, Kabir and Mira that we find these. The love-songs in the vernacular have a freshness which the erotic poetry of the Sanskrit stylists lack. But the importance of Sanskrit did not decline. It alone united the Hindus. From Travancore to Kashmir the language of scholarship and thought of the Hindus continued to be Sanskrit. Without the continued cultivation of Sanskrit the Hindu people would have lost all sense of unity. But at the same time Sanskrit had become totally divorced from the life of the common man. It was only by tying the vernaculars to the thought-forms and traditions of Sanskrit that this dilemma was overcome and this is also an achievement of the period under survey.

CHAPTER XIV

SOUTH INDIA AND ISLAM

THE reaction of South India to Islam has a different story to tell. After the fall of the Pallavas, the Cholas assumed power at Kanchi and exercised imperial sway for over three hundred years. The glory of the Cholas, their colonial empire in Malaya and their hundred years' war on the sea with the Sailendra kings of Sumatra can only be briefly alluded to here. Gradually extending their kingdom to the ancient boundaries of the Pallavas, the Cholas in the tenth century established primacy in the south. Rajaraja, who succeeded to the Kanchi throne in 969, extended his territory up to the confines of Orissa and to Tungabhadra on the side of the Deccan. His policy of expansion brought him into conflict with the Chalukyas of Maharashtra. His son Rajendra, or Gangaikonda Chola, carried on the same policy of expansion and also conquered and annexed Ceylon. He it was who crossed the seas, attacked and annexed the Nicobar islands and occupied Kadaram in Malaya. Rajendra's name is associated not only with these conquests and the war against the Sailendra monarchs across the seas, but with magnificent irrigation works, which continued to supply water to the fields till the nineteenth century.

The historic struggle with the Chalukyas, inherited from the Pallavas, continued in each succeeding generation. Thus, having to equip fleets, transport armies and carry on a war in distant Malaya against Sailendra power and at the same time to fight against the Chalukyas, the Chola monarchs had to exert their whole might to keep together the empire of the south. They seem to have been on the whole successful in this warfare on two fronts for Vira Rajendra not only conquered the Chalukyas in a great battle but was able to uphold and extend his power on the Malayan Peninsula. Kulothunga, one of the greatest of the Chola monarchs, added the victories of peace to the victories of war and made a detailed survey of his territories. The dynasty under his successors maintained its power without any serious disturbance till the middle of the thirteenth century, but vanished from history in the period between 1250 and 1300 from a weakening of central authority which enabled the Pandyas from the south and the Hoysalas from the north to expand their territories at the expense of the descendants of Rajaraja the Great.

The four hundred years of Chola authority in the south constitute a period of extraordinary political, literary and artistic achievement. The Cholas were the first Indian rulers to appreciate the value of naval power and to undertake an oceanic policy. They not only controlled the Bay of Bengal effectively but for nearly a hundred years maintained their imperial authority in Malaya, thus making the Bay of Bengal a Chola lake. The continuous warfare with the Sailendras which drained the resources of the empire was no doubt in part responsible for the final breakdown of Chola power, but it is interesting to note that the South Indian empire successfully carried on an oceanic policy and maintained its conquests across the seas and over the island of Ceylon for a considerable period.

Of the artistic achievements of the Cholas we have ample records not only in their great temples but in that special genre of Indian plastic art known as the Chola bronzes. The Nataraja figures of the period and the images and portraits of the saints have now been recognised as coming among the masterpieces of the world. Their temple architecture of which the best examples are in Tanjore and some of the temples in Chidambaram have also received appreciation for the purity of artistic traditions which they preserved.

The Cholas however were not merely builders of magnificent architectural masterpieces. Their claim to greatness is based on works of public utility. Great works of irrigation were undertaken by successive kings which made the Kaveri delta a granary of the empire. Madras can claim, states a modern authority, to have introduced, if not originated, a style of construction which has been widely adopted within and without the (British) Empire, and to have established a plan of dealing with deltaic lands which has not been improved upon. A portion of the credit for these achievements belongs to the native engineers preceding the British advent. This in fact was the work of the Cholas who conceived the idea "of controlling a river at the head of its delta and thus securing the regular watering of lands."

By the end of the thirteenth century this great empire had broken up. South India was facing an interregnum when Malik Kafur at the orders of his master made his great raid. His success was immediate. There was no power strong enough to withstand his authority.

After the fall of the Rastrakutas, their empire had been inherited by three dynasties, the Yadavas at Devagiri, the Kakateyas at Warangal in Middle Deccan, and the Hoysalas in the Karnataka territory. The Yadavas of Devagiri were powerful monarchs under whom learning and arts flourished. The country, as it had a fair share of maritime trade, was extremely rich but militarily it was not strong enough to meet the organised forces of the Khilji Sultans. Warangal under the Kakateyas was equally notable, and its queen Rudramamba was considered by Marco Polo a lady of great ability and wisdom. Under Prataparudra it attained considerable literary fame but again its might was insufficient to meet the onslaught of Islam. The Hoysalas of Dwarasamudra under Vira Ballala II had attained great power. Their artistic monuments attest to their glory.

Singly none of these were in a position to resist Malik Kafur. The Yadavas had already been conquered and the Kakateyas had become tributaries.

The fall of Hoysalas of Dwarasamudra is an important fact in South Indian history. They had profited most by the decline of the Cholas with whom they had carried on an intermittent war for a long time. Under Vira Ballala II Dwarasamudra attained a position of supremacy in the south claiming authority as far as the Madurai country. Ballala's own mother was a Pandya princess as he himself proudly proclaims and during his long reign of nearly fifty years (1173-1220) he extended his authority up to Mangalore on the Malabar coast, asserted suzerainty over the later Chola monarchs and consolidated the sovereignty of the Hoysalas on what is now the territory of Mysore. His successor Vira Narasimha was also a monarch of ability. In fact at the time of Malik Kafur's invasion the Hoysalas were the dominant power in the south. The fall of Dwarasamudra opened the way to the southern capitals.

As the Cholas had ceased to exist there was no power in South India to resist the Muslim commander. The Pandyas were engaged in a war of succession and Malik Kafur after conquering the intervening countries attacked Madurai itself in 1311, conquered it and returned with booty to Delhi.

The chaotic conditions following Malik Kafur's raid brought to the fore Vira Ravivarman Kulasekhara, the ruler of Quilon country, who expelled the Muslim garrisons and had himself crowned at Kanchi in 1312. The Muslims thus got no chance to establish themselves in the south and the achievements of Ravivarman is important for Indian history, for it enabled Hindu resistance to be organised on the Tungabhadra twenty-five years later.

The withdrawal of Muslims left South India north of Kanchi

without any settled authority. The great Kakateya dynasty of Warangal had been destroyed and the Yadavas of Devagiri existed no more. But soon a widespread movement of resistance began to show itself. Under Prolaya Nayaka the people of the Kakateya country around Warangal organised a great movement of liberation, which led to the foundation of the Reddi kingdoms of Addanki and Kondavidu. Somadeva, a descendant of imperial Chalukyas, freed the western Telugu country in 1331. In fact the Tungabhadra region threw off the Muslim yoke, as a result of popular insurrection. The unity of South India began to assert itself and under two great leaders, Harihara and Bukka, originally said to be officers of the Kakateyas or, according to Heras, of Hoysalas, a new state was organised which came to be known to history as Vijayanagar (1336). By 1340 Vijayanagar had assumed importance but its ruler had not assumed royal dignity for Ballala III of the Hoysalas was still reigning nominally at Dwarasamudra. When Virupaksha Ballala died in 1346 Bukka stepped forward as the legitimate emperor of the South, the successor to the traditions alike of the Chalukyas, Hoysalas, Pallavas and Cholas. The empire that he founded continued for over three hundred years, a mighty and impregnable bulwark against Muslim invasions and disappeared from history only by the middle of the seventeenth century after Sivaji had taken up the cause of Hinduism.

The essential condition of a successful defence of the Tungabhadra line is the consolidation of the South. It is to this important work that the successors of Bukka immediately applied themselves. Under Kamparaya, whose conquest of Madurai is the subject of a remarkable Sanskrit poem by his queen Gangadevi, the empire was consolidated and the whole area from Rameswaram to the Krishna was brought under one authority. The northern expansion of the dynasty was checked by the rise of the Bahmani kingdom in 1347 under Hassan Gangu who united under his authority the territory to the north of Krishna and established a Muslim state in the historic region between the Narbada and the Krishna. The stabilisation of Muslim power in the Deccan plateau was an event fraught with great consequences as the circumstances of the birth of the Bahmani State led to its continuous fight with Vijayanagar in the south and with the monarchies in the north, forcing it in time to become more and more dependent on its Hindu population. The unending struggle between the Bahmani Sultanate and the Vijayanagar empire kept both in a state of military preparedness and the Vijayanagar emperors were not allowed to forget for a single moment the historic mission of their state to defend South

India and Hinduism from Muslim conquest. The wars of Firoz and Devaraya and of Ahmad Shah and Devaraya II show how determined this fight was and how, but for the strength of Vijayanagar, the South would have been trampled under foot as the Gangetic valley had been.

We have a description of Vijayanagar by Nicolo Conti at this period. "The great city of Vijayanagar," he says, "is situated near very steep mountains. The circumference of the city is sixty miles, its walls are carried up to the mountains and enclose the valleys at their foot so that its extent is thereby increased. In this city there are estimated to be 90,000 men fit to bear arms." The king of the city, he adds, is more powerful than all kings of India, which was undoubtedly true in 1420. Abdur Razzak, who visited Vijayanagar as an ambassador of Persia and who was familiar with the cities of the Middle East, declares: "The city of Vijayanagar is such that eye has not seen or ear heard of any place resembling it on earth. It is so built that it has seven fortified walls, one within the other. Beyond the circuit of the outer wall there is an esplanade extending to about fifty yards, in which stones are fixed near one another to the height of a man, one half buried firmly in the earth and the other half rises above it, so that neither foot nor horse however bold can advance with facility near the outer wall."

The greatest monarch of the Vijayanagar dynasty was Krishnadeva Raya (1509-1550) under whom the power of Vijayanagar reached its zenith. He conquered Orissa and extended his kingdom along the coast up to Cuttack. The disruption of the Bahmani kingdom and the rise of the Deccan Sultanates gave him an opportunity to carry the war into the territory of Islam. Bijapur was defeated in a pitched battle and the Muslim Sultans made no serious attempts against Vijayanagar for two generations.

Krishnadeva Raya was a great emperor in the tradition of Asoka, Chandra Gupta Vikramaditya, Harsha and Bhoja. Himself a scholar, poet and author of no mean merit he consciously lived up to the tradition of Hindu kingship. He administered the country directly, commanded his armies in person, toured incessantly over his wide territories, built and endowed magnificent temples and gave liberally to charity. He maintained the most cordial relations with the Portuguese, received friendly embassies from Persia and other foreign countries and enjoyed a prestige which few medieval kings before Akbar enjoyed.

After Krishnadeva Raya the prestige of the empire continued undiminished, but the Muslim rulers, who realised the danger to their authority from the growing power of Vijayanagar and their own disunity, formed an alliance and the army of Vijayanagar was defeated at Talikotta in 1565. The defeat was a crushing one and the great city itself was sacked. But the old view that the Vijayanagar empire perished on the battlefield of Talikotta has now been found to be untrue. The strength and greatness of Vijayanagar were not based on dynasties but on the national feeling of the Hindus of South India and their determination to resist the Muslims. A great military disaster may spell the end of a dynasty and demoralise for a short time the resistance of a people, but it cannot extinguish the national spirit of an old and powerful empire. Under a new dynasty Vijayanagar soon reorganised itself and this reorganisation was the work of Tirumala. Under Venkata II the empire retrieved a great deal of its pestige and some of its glory and for more than fifty years after the battle of Talikotta, Vijayanagar continued to be the centre of Hindu culture and civilisation. With time however the central power weakened and the great viceroyalties assumed independence. One of these, Mysore ceased to exist as a princely state only after India attained independence in 1947.

Vijayanagar was essentially a military state. Its organisation reflected the primary purpose of maintaining a successful resistance against the Muslims. And yet it was also the centre of a Hindu revival, of the rejuvenation of Sanskrit and the vernacular languages, the proclaimed successor of the orthodox doctrine of Hindu empire. Madhava Vidyaranya is traditionally associated with the founding of the empire itself. The growth of later Vaishnavism is closely connected with the Vijayanagar kings and the temples they built and endowed over the length and breadth of the country are evidence of the great religious feeling that animated the people at this time.

So far as Sanskrit was concerned, Sayana who was the minister of Bukka and younger brother of Madhavacharya is the last great commentator on the Vedas and his work is still considered authoritative. Madhavacharya, the great jurist whose *Parasara Madhaviya* is considered even now a work of authority, was also associated with the Vijayanagar court. In fact he describes himself in his books as a mantri of Bukka. Successive queens of the Vijayanagar dynasty figure as poets and Gangadevi, the authoress of *Madhura Vijayam,* and Tirumalamba Devi, the authoress of *Varadambika Parinayam,* deserve special mention. Krishnadeva Raya, as stated before, was himself a scholar and writer. Telugu and Kanarese also developed greatly under the patronage of the

Vijayanagar emperors. In Krishnadeva Raya's court were the Astadig Gajas or "the eight supports of the world" of Telugu literature. The Raya himself was a writer of distinction in Telugu and his *Amuktamalayadei* is considered a classic, while his laureate Pedana is recognised as one of the fathers of Telugu.

The Vijayanagar emperors were fully alive to and consciously cultivated the idea of being the emperors of orthodox India in the tradition of the great kings of old. In an inscription in the Madana Gopalaswamy Temple at Madurai, the Vijayanagar monarch is described as the gem of the Chalukyas. Hampi is called Hampi-Hastinavati, thereby claiming spiritual descent from the imperial capital of *Mahabharata*. And the emperor is described as seated, "on his throne ruling the whole kingdom extending from Setu to Sumeru and from the hill of sunrise in the east to the end of the western mountains, eclipsing the fame and righteousness" of epic kings. In fact the claim of Vijayanagar emperors was that though the rest of India was under the Mussalmans, the tradition of Hindu empire was lodged with them.

South India under the Vijayanagar emperors attained a remarkable state of prosperity, as may be seen from the records of Portuguese and Muslim writers. There were no less than three hundred ports carrying on maritime commerce, and regular trade was maintained with Persia and the countries in the West. In fact much of the prosperity of the Portuguese depended on their commerce with the empire. The provincial capitals were themselves centres of great commercial activity and with the arrival of the Portuguese, as the carriers of world trade, the markets of Europe also were opened to the products of India and the produce of the West flowed into Indian ports continuously. This great prosperity which amazed foreign observers was reflected in the style and splendour not only of the monarchs but of the nobility. The architectural glories have now vanished though from their ruins one can imagine their greatness; but the magnificent temples which the great emperors and their officials built, with which the whole of South India is studded, bear witness to the greatness of a civilisation which successfully maintained in art the traditions of its predecessors.

The simultaneous growth of the Bahmani kingdom has already been alluded to. Founded by Hassan Gangu in 1347 the dynasty consolidated the Muslim hold in the area north of the Krishna river and carried on continuous war with fluctuating success against Vijayanagar The policy of the Bahmani kings was to encourage able men from Persia to take up service with them and this led to a rivalry between the local amirs and the foreign nobles. The policy was successful in so far as it maintained the Islamic character of the state but the rivalry it engendered was also the cause of its downfall. For over a hundred and forty years the Sultanate maintained its unity but by the end of the fifteenth century the kingdom broke up into five States (Berar, Ahmadnagar, Bijapur, Golkonda and Bidar) which united only for the purpose of opposing the power of Vijayanagar.

The historical importance of the Bahmani kingdom lies in the fact that like the Satavahanas, the Vakatakas and the Chalukyas of old it held the central position which bridged the North and the South. Though religiously devout the Bahmani kings were not oppressive or intolerant towards their Hindu subjects. Great works of irrigation were undertaken; art and letters were encouraged and endowments for education were common in the case of most rulers. Mohammed Gawan, the great minister, even founded a fine college with a library containing over three thousand volumes. Both Jainism and Hinduism flourished as numerous temples of the period bear witness. No doubt there were persecutions but life in the Deccan villages seems to have followed a course of normal activity, without fear of invasions.

CHAPTER XV

MEDIEVAL RELIGION

THE development of religious feeling in India during the three centuries of Hindu-Muslim conflict is a subject of special interest. The reorganisation of Hinduism in the previous periods under the Guptas and in the time of Sankara was in relation either to social conditions or to heresies. The penetration of barbarian social elements and ideas was the main problem that the Vakataka-Gupta period had to deal with. What Sankara was mainly concerned with was the ritualism of the Mimamsakas and the heresies of the Buddhists. In the thirteenth century the problem was a fundamentally different one. Hinduism stood face to face with a dynamic religion which challenged its philosophic basis, attacked its social structure and denied its pantheistic doctrines. The reaction of the Hindu mind to the challenge of a monotheistic religion, essentially democratic in its organisation, which did not accept any of the characteristic doctrines of Hinduism, purusha, prakriti, gunas, transmigration, etc., is what produced the great devotional sects of medieval Hinduism.

It is noteworthy that the main trend of all medieval Hindu thought is theistic. Equally remarkable is the fact that most of them deny by implication, if not by direct teaching, the validity of caste distinctions. The emphasis is on the personal God, a unique, supreme and merciful God, surrender to Whom and living in Whose grace is the one way of attaining the Life Divine. Such a development within the fold of Hinduism would have been difficult if the impersonal philosophy of Sankara had remained unquestioned. An alternative philosophy on which the later theistic cults were able to draw was provided by an equally eminent thinker and reformer, Ramanuja, whose influence dominates the religious thought of this period.

Ramanuja was in the direct line of succession to the great Vaishnava pontiffs of the South whose headquarters were at Sri Rangam. The Sri Vaishnavas never fully accepted the unemotional and abstract thought of Sankara, and under a succession of Acharyas, most notably Yamuna, developed an opposition to the theories of Maya and Avidya. Ramanuja (born 1017) succeeded to the pontificate by the middle of the century and the whole work of his historic apostolate was devoted to the elaboration of a philosophic theory which could contend against the monism of Sankara. The commentary on Brahma Sutras known as the *Sri Bhashya* was his main work. He also wrote a commentary on the *Gita* in order to contest Sankara's interpretation of that scripture. Ramanuja while accepting the oneness and reality of the Absolute, emphasised that though Chit and Achit (soul and matter) were included in the Absolute they were separate and equally eternal. This is what came to be called qualified monism. It is not the philosophic distinction that is important. It is the religious aspect of Ramanuja's teaching that was more fundamental. To him Karma can be overcome by Divine Grace. The idea of a loving and just God—in contrast to the abstraction to which Godhead was reduced in Sankara's philosophy—was Ramanuja's main contribution to Indian spiritual revival. As Prof. K. V. Rangaswamy Aiyangar has stated: "To the comprehensive philosophy which vindicated the rights and obligations of the free soul Ramanuja attached a religious side which gave wide scope for spiritual emotion. . . . The idea of God as immanent in all high thought and endeavour by whomsoever the effect was made unfolds a limitless tolerance which overrides the barriers of caste and creed. By demonstrating the compatibility and his views of redemption with the old tradition he assured its defenders."

It was this doctrine of Bhakti or grace through devotion that provided balm to the bleeding soul of Hinduism in Northern India during the period of Muslim occupation. Ramananda, a Vaishnava Sanyasi born in Allahabad, preached the gospel of Bhakti. He wandered from place to place calling on all to put their trust in a merciful God and to surrender themselves to Him. To the Hindus of Aryavarta this gospel with its other-worldliness, its escape from the miseries they were then subject to, its great assertion of equality of all before God and especially its conception of God as a loving father made a powerful appeal. Ramananda settled in Banaras where he gained numerous followers, the most remarkable of whom was a Muslim weaver by the name of Kabir (1398).

Kabir's influence on the thought of the Hindus in the fifteenth century is something more remarkable. A Muslim by birth, he was fundamentally monotheistic—

> He is one: there is no second,
> Ram, Khuda, Sakhi, Siva are one,

By the one name I hold fast.
Kabir proclaims this aloud.

On my tongue Vishnu,
In my eyes Narayan,
In my heart Govind dwells,
My meditation with Hari.

The doctrines that Ramananda preached and Kabir popularised were a strong monotheism, an absolute surrender to God and a direct realisation of God through devotion. To such a religion caste rules did not matter. Essentially, therefore, the Bhakti movement was a new interpretation of Hinduism in terms of Islam's monotheism and egalitarianism: but its religious doctrine was that of the *Bhagavad Gita* whose summons to surrender all and take refuge in God, came to have a special significance in the circumstances of the time.

Kabir permeated the thought of most of the religious leaders after him, especially Nanak, for the *Adi Granth* not only recognises him as a Mahatma but contains many of his songs. The Order which his disciples established carried these doctrines through wandering minstrels all over India. It is noteworthy that among the disciples of Ramananda were Sona, a barber, Dhanna, a Sudra peasant, and Rai Das, a shoemaker. In the cult of Bhakti, even when preached by a Brahmin Sanyasi, caste did not count—

Jat pante puche na koi
Hariko bhaje so Harika hoi

"Who asks of caste and birth of people who worship Hari and belong to him." This was the view of Bhaktas.

The doctrine of Bhakti was expounded by a thousand tongues. Vidyapati in Mithila was its first great poet. His lyrical songs, full of surrender and abandonment to God and of love for Krishna, popularised the cult in Bengal. Mirabai, the princess of Chitor, whose spiritual inspiration is still a source of light to the peasants of Rajputana and Gujerat, lost herself in her holy love of God. Commentaries on the *Gita* emphasising the Bhakti part of the doctrine, the most important of which is Jnaneshwari, which has become canonical for the Bhaktas of Gujerat, became popular.

Medieval religion was therefore escapist in its devotionalism and eclectic in its combination of Hindu and Muslim ideas. Of course it was not necessary for the orthodox Hindu to go to Islam for a rigid monotheism, or for believing in the equality of man before God. All such doctrines could be found in the *Upanishads*: but it could not be denied that the emphasis that the medieval teachers attached to them had its inspiration from the teaching of Islam.

A more significant point is its escapist character. All this sudden desire to surrender everything and seek refuge in God, normal as it is in mystics and religious men, found universal acceptance among the Hindus of the day, because of the terrible misery in which the mass of Hindus in North India lived at the time. The religion of mysticism is the religion of the elect: it becomes popular only when the masses have lost all and can look for nothing of value in this world. The ordinary man turns to heaven for his refuge when he has nothing to look forward to in this world. Healthy materialism is the normal outlook of even religious people when things go well. When on the other hand a country is enslaved and its spirit weakened, it finds solace in a doctrine of other-worldliness. The saints and teachers of Bhakti, themselves mystics and men of God, found the people waiting for their message. The Bhakti cult became the new Gospel of the fifteenth century—a religion of escape and essentially of worldly pessimism. It is Tulsidas who interpreted the doctrine again as a dynamic conception of active life. Mystic though he was, his *Ramayana*, singing the glory of the active hero-God Rama, turned men's mind again to the glory of action as against the glory of surrender. A similar service was rendered by the later Gurus from Arjun to Gobind, when the pietist Bhakti cult of Nanak was turned into the vigorous and dynamic religion of Sikhism.

It is remarkable that in South India, the original home of the Bhakti movement, devotionalism never achieved the same vogue as in North India. Vaishnava mysticism remained the religion of the elect, entitled to the greatest reverence and respect, but certainly not the popular cult of the masses. There was no ground for the psychology of national escapism during the great days of Vijayanagar, which it will be noted, coincided with the period of the Bhakti movement. Under these champions of Hinduism, religion was the inspiration of great human endeavour and not a refuge of the defeated. The magnificent temple architecture of the Vijayanagar kings finds no echo in the North, no doubt due partly to Muslim rule, but mainly, at least in Hindu areas, to other-worldliness of the religious movement itself.

Though devotionalism was the chief feature of the religion of North India during the pre-Moghul period, it is not to be assumed that other forms of worship had gone into the background. Saiva doctrines flourished in Kashmir, and though we have no great teachers of this sect in this period, it is obvious that, as at all times, Siva found his worshippers in all ranks of society. If anything, the Sakta doctrines, because of their secrecy, had become even more widely prevalent than ever before, since many of the Tantric texts we have, can be traced to this period. The absurd extremes to which the Tantrics pushed their symbolism and their practice were perhaps a reaction to the misery of ordinary life. Tantricism became a kind of freemasonry and as there was no difference of caste or rank within the mandala, its popularity even when the practices and the forms of worship degenerated, as it did in some cases, into gross obscenities, found favour with those who had but little outlet in normal life for the enjoyment of human pleasures.

Allusion may also be made here to the Vaishnavite movement in Assam of which the leader was Sankara Deva. Assam in the medieval period had, as a result of its conquest by Ahom kings from the Shan area, become non-Indian in its culture. Its early affiliations with India in the time of Kumara Bhaskara had been practically forgotten. It is to the credit of Sankara Deva that he re-integrated Assam into the cultural and religious life of India.

Sankara Deva (born 1449) was a Kayastha by caste, but early in his life he became a devotee of Krishna. As a Vaishnavite he preached the doctrine—

Ek déu ek séu, ek viné nai kayo

"There is only one God, there is only one devotion and there is none but one." As a pilgrim he wandered all over India and the unity of Hindu culture became a deep conviction with him. He travelled everywhere in Assam preaching his new gospel, converting even the Kotch king to his creed. He was the father of the religious revival of Assam, where his influence is very widespread even today.

The religious literature produced during the period in North India was in many cases of the highest quality. Vidyapati, Kabir, Umapati, Nanak and Mirabai are among the inspired singers of all time. Kesavadas and Surdas may also be fairly included in the list of religious poets of this period. But it is noteworthy that the great works of philosophic Hinduism during the fourteenth century, the most important of which are Madhavacharya's commentaries and Sayana's commentary on the Vedas, were written in the South.

CHAPTER XVI

TOWARDS A NATIONAL MONARCHY

THE king who rode to Delhi and assumed for himself the title of Padshah-i-Hind was a very different person from the Afghan and Turkish adventurers, the Khiljis, Tughlaqs and Lodis who had succeeded Mohammed Ghori to the throne of Delhi. Descended in the direct line from Timur and from his mother's side from Genghiz, Babar united in his person the two main streams of Central Asian sovereignty. His ancestors had conquered and ruled the world. To him every country in Asia was his by hereditary right if only he could gain possession of it. To the Delhi Sultanate, as having been conquered and occupied by Timur, he even put forward a hereditary claim, flimsy enough but no doubt valid in his own view. Whether at Fergana or at Kabul, or in Delhi, Babar therefore claimed that he was in his own domains, temporarily lost to him before, but regained by his valour. He was therefore a king by profession and this feeling was never absent from his mind.

After the invasion of Mohammed Ghori, but for the interlude of Timur's occupation, India had not been invaded from beyond her frontiers. The hordes of Genghiz Khan mercifully left India to herself on the advice of his Chinese prime minister and Timur's invasion, though pregnant with great things, passed off at the time, as merely a calamitous episode. The reason for this long period of freedom from external aggression was the condition to which the Afghan uplands had been reduced. The great Khwarizmian empire ruled from Central Asia and the valleys of Kabul, Herat and Kandahar were only neglected and outlying provinces. After Genghiz had reduced that empire to ashes and the forces of Islam were destroyed on the banks of the Indus by the Mongols, the areas of the frontier fell back into anarchy and chaos. The later eruption of Timur did not help to improve matters and the seat of dynamic power in Central Asia was shifted to Samarkand with the intervening area in a state of political breakdown.

Babar succeeded to the kingdom of Samarkand in 1500 A.D. but was driven out by the Uzbegs in the following year. Three years later he obtained possession of Kabul which was organised once again as a base for the conquest of Delhi. In April 1526, the Sultanate of Delhi succumbed to the onslaught of Babar, and the Timurids sat on the imperial throne. The fall of Delhi gave him the province of the Punjab and for the rest only a vain title as he or his successors had to conquer the territories themselves. Indeed the most noticeable fact which historians often forget is that except in the Gangetic valley the opposition that Babar met and had the greatest difficulty in overcoming was from the Hindus. Gwalior itself was under the occupation of a Hindu ruler, Vikramajit, whom Humayun, then Crown Prince, was sent to attack. But the most effective opposition to the conquest came from the Rajputs under the leadership of Mewar which under the successors of the great Kumbha had organised the Hindu princes of the old Gurjara country into a confederacy. They had found a valiant leader in Rana Sanga. It is also significant to note that Mahmud Lodi had made an alliance with Sanga to resist Babar. The change in Hindu-Muslim relations which this alliance indicated is an index to the revival of Hindu power and of the growth of friendly relations between the two religions. At Biyana the Hindu forces met the army of Babar. Babar won a notable victory which, if it did not break the power of the Rajputs, at least enabled the Moghul to consolidate his hold on Delhi and on the possessions of the Lodis.

Babar died in 1530 and was succeeded by his son Humayun who set himself to the task of bringing the provinces of the empire under control and again we have evidence that the Delhi Sultanate in spite of its claim of empire never exercised effective authority outside the Doab. Humayun's first campaign was against Kalinjar, a historic State which had existed under its Hindu rulers for over eight hundred years. The Kalinjar ruler had fought against Mahmud of Ghazni in 978 and 1008. Kutubuddin and Iltamish and others claimed to have conquered and annexed the territory but strangely enough we see in 1530 Humayun leading a great expedition to reduce the same Hindu State. Humayun found the conquest of Kalinjar difficult and a treaty was made with the Hindu ruler by which he was made a grandee of the Moghul kingdom.

Here we have the beginning of the policy of the Moghul emperors which was to bear such remarkable fruits in the reigns of Humayun's successors. The Hindu ruler of Kalinjar as a grandee of an Islamic kingdom is a political idea, which neither the Turks nor the Afghans could have conceived. In fact it is not from Islam the conception originates, but from the Mongols, who under the successors of Genghiz had evolved a world policy which was strictly political and not based on religion. It is well to remember that Genghiz's own prime minister and that of his son was Ye Liu-Chutsai, a Khitan from China and to the Moghul mind there was nothing strange or unreasonable in a Hindu ruler being a grandee of the empire. Babar's successors, like himself, were kings by profession and looked mainly to the benefit of the State.

Humayun's authority over the eastern provinces was shaky. Bengal of course was independent and if the infant State of the Moghuls was to survive, the Gangetic valley had to be reduced. The Afghan governors were in no mood to yield to the Moghul: and they found a leader of great ability in Sher Khan, who defeated Humayun in a carefully planned campaign. The descendant of Timur was again an exile and he fled through the deserts of Rajputana encountering great hardships. On the way at Amarkot was born Akbar. Humayun spent fifteen years in exile but in 1555, two years after Sher Shah's death, he returned in triumph to Delhi carrying with him his young son aged fifteen.

These fifteen years of exile are of some importance to Moghul and Indian history. The fact that the Mongols had, after Timur, become Iranian in culture has been noticed by historians. As Pradwin states: "He, Timur, believed that with the help of Turanians he would definitely suppress Iran: but the Iranian culture which he was determined to preserve marched over him, for he was no more than a semi-nomad. What he diffused through Central Asia by his campaigns of conquest was after all Iranian culture, Iranian civilisation." Babar was indeed in a measure the representative of that civilisation. A writer and a man of refined sensibility, a lover of gardens, this king by profession was the ambassador of a culture: but Humayun was even more than that. His years of stay in the Persian empire gave to the empire of his successors a definitely Persian character. Apart from the nobles who accompanied him to Persia and the Iranians who came back with him, who formed a nucleus for a policy of Persianisation, there was also the continuous flow of Persian adventurers of merit who attained the highest position in court. To a large extent the character of the empire for the next hundred years was coloured by this long exile.

Akbar succeeded to the throne of Delhi in 1556. The State which he inherited in India was less in area, resources and strength than the Vijayanagar empire in the South and was certainly less populous than the Sultanates of Bengal and Gujerat. The new ruler was only a boy and the Moghuls in the time of Humayun had already demonstrated how strong their internal jealousies were. Few could have foreseen for the infant State and the boy-king the future that awaited them. The conquest of the provinces, the organisation of the empire, the building up of new loyalties, the complex and remarkable personality of the emperor who left his impress on India for ever, can only be briefly alluded to here.

For the first four years of his reign Akbar was served loyalty by a capable regent, Bairam Khan, who had played a notable part in the restoration. But in 1560, he dropped the pilot. Bairam Khan had brought under control Gwalior and had annexed Jaunpur. When Akbar assumed direct charge his territories included the Punjab and the Gangetic valley up to the frontiers of the Bengal Sultanate. To the south it hardly extended beyond Gwalior. In a series of campaigns Malwa and the territory to the south were brought under control. Gondwana was conquered, Ranthambor and Chitor were captured after epic fights with Rana Pratap and Gujerat with the great sea-port of Surat was occupied in 1573. Two years later the Sultanate of Bengal was conquered and annexed. Thus twenty years after his accession, when Akbar was barely thirty-five, he was the master of an empire which extended from the borders of Central Asia to Assam in the east and to the Vindhya mountains in the south. The great ports of Gujerat and Bengal were within the empire and the only portion of North India which did not accept the emperor's authority was the small State, of Mewar, whose Rana, the great Pratap, had refused to bend his knees to the "Turk" and had taken to his mountain fastnesses after the fall of Chitor.

Master of his dominions, with no opposition to his rule in any part of his state, Akbar was able to initiate his new policies. Already in 1562, when he was but twenty-two he had with due solemnity married a Rajput princess, the daughter of Raja Behar Mal of Amber and thus laid the foundation of the lasting alliance with the Rajputs, who constituted the most powerful political organisation in North India. Man Singh, the adopted son of the emperor's brother-in-law, was taken into service and received with high honour by the emperor. The results of this policy were far-reaching. In the first place it attached to the new empire a powerful section of the Hindu population and thus mitigated the foreign character of the rule. Akbar's aim was a national monarchy which his Hindu subjects did not consider as a burden on them. The "kings by profession," which the descendants of Genghiz were, had learnt this lesson in many countries. He followed up his marriage with a Hindu princess by the abolition throughout his dominions of the pilgrim tax, which the Hindus had to pay and which they considered to be a persecution of their religion. When it is remembered that not only Mathura from where this order was issued, but Banaras, Hardwar, Gaya and Ajmer and numerous other minor places of holiness lay within Akbar's territories, the great wisdom of this step will be easily recognised. This was followed in 1563 by the abolition of the poll tax on Hindus. The national monarchy had come into existence and though political power was with the immediate entourage of the court with its predominantly foreign nobility, no longer could the Hindus in the empire feel that they were merely the tax-payers, foreigners in their own land. It is well also to remember that these two reforms, the abolition of both the pilgrim tax and the poll tax, must have cost the treasury many crores of rupees annually as they were the two main sources of revenue, and consequently it was only because Akbar felt that the policy which he had in view, the creation of a national State, could only be achieved by such a sacrifice that effect was given to so far-reaching a decision.

The second result of the Amber alliance was to isolate the Rana of Mewar. The descendant of Mokal, Kumbha and Sanga who had for centuries fought against Muslim domination, was unlikely to accept the Moghul and in Rana Pratap this unbending resistance to the foreigner found a champion and a leader whose memory is still green in the minds of all Hindus. The alliance with Amber broke Rajput unity. The rulers of Marwar, Bikaner and Bundi hastened to the Moghul court and were received with honour and given appointments. The Rana was isolated and in successive campaigns made to feel the power of the empire. Akbar himself took the field against him and conquered Chitor, but though deserted by the great body of the Rajputs and reduced to extremities, Pratap held out to the last and the honour of Mewar was upheld.

The policy of employing Hindus in higher ranks which began with the appointment of Man Singh was also continued on a more liberal scale. Todar Mal had accompanied the emperor to Gujerat in 1573 and had done the settlement of that province. In fact on the historic ride to Ahmedabad, which he did in seven days, Akbar's personal party included fifteen Hindus (out of a total of twenty-seven). It is interesting to note that three of them were painters. Again, when Bengal was conquered and annexed the settlement of the country was entrusted to Todar Mal. A few years later Raja Man Singh who had become one of the premier grandees of the empire was appointed to this palatinate viceroyalty. Indeed a transformation in the character of the empire was visible to all, especially after the appointment of Man Singh to the important charge of Kabul which was a purely Islamic country.

The lower bureaucracy had at all times been predominantly Hindu. That was so even in Allauddin's time but the opening of the ranks of higher office to the Hindus was Akbar's own policy. By this stroke, he opened the doors of ambition to the Hindus of the best families, who instead of looking upon the new State as an enemy organisation began unconsciously to look upon it as providing opportunities for glory and distinction. The Hindu officials in Akbar's court were not all of them scions of royal families like Man Singh. Todar Mal, the great revenue minister, was of middle-class origin, and so was Birbal, the friend and courtier of the emperor. The policy of *carriere ouverte aux talents* converted the Moghul empire in one generation from a foreign government into a national State.

The emperor's religious policy strengthened this tendency. The house of worship which he built and where he carried on religious discussions admitted in the beginning only the Muslim divines: but in 1578 the exponents of other religions were also admitted, and soon the discussions became more intimate, being held in the hall of private audience. The five classes of the learned with whom Akbar had these discussions contained men from all religions: and among the few who, according to Abul Fazal, understood the mysteries of both worlds, he included not only his own father Mubarak, but Hindu and Jain saints. The reception accorded to Hiravijaya Suri, who was granted the title of Jagad Guru, may be compared with profit to the honour shown to the Taoist sage Chang-Chun by Akbar's great ancestor Genghiz in 1220.

Akbar's attempt to establish a new religion is only a matter of historical curiosity, but the departure from Islamic tradition is a matter of considerable importance. The empire became cosmopolitan in fact and Jesuit fathers, Parsi priests, Jain sadhus and Hindu sanyasis were received with equal favour, much to the disgust of orthodox Muslims. Akbar of course never openly broke with Islam. His so-called infallibility decree which offended the Muslims was no more than an attempt to set aside the pretensions of the Khalifs and to the end of his day, whatever Akbar's private beliefs might have been, he conformed to the creed of Islam.

The policy of conciliation stood Akbar in good stead when his throne was threatened from across the frontier. The ruler of

Kabul, Akbar's half-brother Mohammed Hakim, desired to repeat the achievement of Babar. Bengal and Bihar rose in revolt opportunely but Akbar's new allies stood firm. The Rajput forces were incorruptible and Akbar triumphed over his enemies without difficulty.

The new State developed without danger after the Kabul rebellion and when Akbar died in 1603 he left to his son a settled empire, a people attached to the dynasty by a special sense of loyalty, a treasury filled with money and an army which had not met with defeat. Afghanistan was a part of the empire which covered the entire area of India to the north of the Vindhyas. Gujerat and Bengal had been firmly secured and Sind which for seven hundred years had not come into Indian history had also been annexed. Kashmir became a province of the empire. Thus the entire area of North India formed the territory of the new State.

The singular fact, to which two thousand years of history had borne witness that when Hindustan is organised, the process of unification will steadily move to the South became clear in Akbar's policy also. It was not out of any desire to crush the independence of other States but because of the irresistible pressure of historical circumstances that Akbar embarked on his Deccan policy. The Deccan Sultanates after the battle of Talikotta had begun to fight among themselves. Akbar would have been satisfied if they had accepted his supremacy and even sent a mission to them with this offer. The Sultans chose war. Ahmednagar in spite of the resistance offered by Chand Bibi fell finally in 1600. The Deccan campaign had opened.

Akbar left to his successors three essential lines of policy: the maintenance of the national State; the conciliation of the Hindus, and the unification of India. The history of his three immediate successors can only be understood in terms of these policies. The first two principles were maintained perhaps not whole-heartedly by Jehangir and Shah Jehan but deliberately violated by Aurangzeb with results we shall see later. The last, the unification of India was the one great idea from which they never retreated but in which they never wholly succeeded. The interminable wars of the Deccan which drained the strength of the empire and which killed the great Aurangzeb were the direct results of the doctrine of Indian unity.

Salim, who succeeded Akbar with the regal title of Jehangir, was a candidate of the orthodox whom he had placated by ordering the murder of Abul Fazal, Akbar's friend, historian and adviser on theological matters. But as a monarch he followed the policies laid down by his father, brushing aside only the extravagances of the Din Ilahi. Though an orthodox Muslim he often visited Hindu religious men and showed them great respect as he himself testifies in his memoirs. The alliance with the Rajputs was even further cemented and the Deccan policy was carried on though not with any great vigour. The Persianisation of the court was even more pronounced in his time especially after the great influence that Nur Jehan and her family came to have on the emperor.

Shah Jehan who succeeded Jehangir followed the Deccan policy more vigorously. Under Jehangir the Deccan Sultanates, inspired by the courage and wisdom of Malik Amber, had united to resist the Moghuls. In 1633, Shah Jehan started a campaign in the South, captured Daulatabad along with Hussein Shah, the last king of the dynasty. The Sultans of Bijapur and Golkonda remained. The emperor himself arrived in the Deccan and the two Sultanates were simultaneously attacked. The Sultan of Golkonda accepted Moghul paramountcy, but the Adil Shahi kings of Bijapur resisted but were forced to yield finally and Shah Jehan had to be satisfied for the time being with the establishment of Moghul suzerainty. But the emperor was not so successful with his external possessions. He unsuccessfully intervened in Balkh on the pretext that it was a part of his hereditary dominions, and after a wasteful campaign had to retire to Kabul. Kandahar, the key to India, was lost to the Persians. But for these two unfortunate incidents the emperor's authority over the territories he had inherited was unquestioned.

The Moghuls were builders but Shah Jehan was the greatest of them all in this respect. A hundred years of settled government and prosperity had made the Moghul empire the richest State of the time and Shah Jehan was able to indulge in his taste for building. The Taj Mahal at Agra, the Red Fort at Delhi, the Jumma Masjid, the Moti Masjid—these are but the most magnificent of his numerous buildings. The love of display which was so strong a characteristic of the emperor found expression not merely in architectural conceptions of unexampled beauty but in the peacock throne whose magnificence has been sung by many foreign visitors.

Though Shah Jehan was a zealous Muslim and has to his discredit the demolition of a few temples, especially the one built by Bir Singh Bundela, he never alienated his Hindu subjects and moreover firmly adhered to the political alliance with the Rajputs. The number of Hindu officers in the imperial service was much larger than in the time of Akbar and Raja Raghunath who was his deputy revenue minister was a Khattri officer who had risen from the ranks. We have also a letter of the emperor himself to his son Aurangzeb when he was viceroy of the Deccan remonstrating with the prince against his policy of hostility towards Hindus. Shah Jehan fully maintained the national character of the State, and the clearest evidence of it is that when Aurangzeb rose in revolt, the imperial army which was sent to oppose him was placed under Jaswant Singh Rathore of Jodhpur.

Aurangzeb who deposed his father and succeeded to the throne after a disastrous fratricidal war was an emperor of a different kind. Perhaps the ablest of the Moghul sovereigns, a capable general, a good administrator and one who revelled in the details of organisation, Aurangzeb from the beginning was determined to restore the Islamic character of the State. To him Akbar's policy of a national State seemed to be the very negation of Islamic ideas. Even as a prince he had shown his hostility towards the Hindus, for example, by the desecration of the Chintamani temple at Ahmedabad in 1694. He was too cautious by nature to enforce his policy all at once. He started by enacting innocent looking reforms like the establishment of a censor of morals to put down un-Islamic practices among the faithful and the punishment of heretical ipinions, which concerned only Mussalmans. Islamic orthodoxy was thus restored. In the eleventh year of his reign all music was banished from the court. The Hindu customs which had found place in the court ceremonies like the weighing of the emperor in gold, the performance of the tilak on Rajas at their investiture were discontinued. Though these tendencies caused alarm among the Hindus, no positive action was taken against them beyond the destruction of a few temples here and there. It was in 1669 that he issued his first general instructions "to demolish all temples and schools of the infidels." From the time an active policy of temple demolition was followed and the great temples of Vishwanath at Banaras, Keshava Rai at Mathura and the much-pillaged temples of Somnath, to mention only the three most famous shrines, fell to his destructive enthusiasm.

A more important change was introduced by the re-imposition of the poll tax on the Hindus in 1679 more than a century after Akbar had abolished it. This was a complete reversal of Akbar's policy of the national State. Other differential taxation was also introduced such as customs duties solely on non-Muslims. A grave difficulty faced the emperor in the enforcement of these policies. The junior officialdom was practically exclusively Hindu, and the routine administration of the empire was dependent on the Hindu Quanungos, Peshkars and other lower officials. Logical even to the last, Aurangzeb ordered the replacement of these officials by Muslims but since such an official class did not exist among the Muslims the emperor modified the order so as to permit half the Peshkars to be Hindus and Hindu Quanungos were encouraged to become Muslims.

By 1680, with the introduction of *Jazia* or the poll tax, the national State ceased and the impression created by this revolutionary change is best expressed in the letter of protest that Sivaji addressed to the Emperor:

> "It has come to my ears that on the ground of the war with me having exhausted your wealth and emptied the imperial treasury Your Majesty has ordered that money under the name of *Jazia* should be collected from the Hindus and the imperial needs supplied with it. May it please Your Majesty. The architect of the fabric of the Empire, Akbar Padshah reigned with full power for fifty-two lunar years. He adopted the admirable policy of perfect harmony in relation to all the various sects. . . . The aim of his liberal heart was to cherish all the people. So he became famous under the title of world's spiritual guide. Next the Emperor Nuruddin Jehangir for twenty-two years spread his gracious shade on the head of the world and its dwellers, gave his heart to his friends and his hand to his work and gained his desires. The Emperor Shah Jehan for thirty-two years cast his blessed shade.
>
> "Through the auspicious effect of this sublime disposition, wherever he (Akbar) bent the glance of his august wish victory and success advanced to welcome him on his way. . . . The state and power of these emperors can be easily understood from the fact that Alamgir Padshah has failed and become bewildered in the attempt merely to follow their political system. They too had the power of levying *Jazia*; but they did not give place to bigotry in their hearts as they considered all men high and low created by God. . . .
>
> "How can the royal spirit permit you to add the hardship of the *Jazia* to this grievous state of things? The infamy will quickly spread from west to east and become recorded in the books of history that the Emperor of Hindustan coveting the beggar's bowls takes *Jazia* from Brahmins and Jain monks, yogis, sanyasis, bhairagis . . . etc. that he dashes down (to the ground) the name and honour of the Timurids."

This remarkable letter ends as follows:

> "If you imagine piety to consist in oppressing the people and terrorising the Hindus you ought first to levy *Jazia* from Rana Raj Singh, who is the head of the Hindus. Then it will not be very difficult to collect it from me, as I am at your service. But to oppress ants and flies is far from displaying valour and spirit.
>
> "I wonder at the strange fidelity of your officers that they neglect to tell you the true state of things but cover a blazing fire with straw."

The letter is important not only as a spirited protest against the *Jazia,* but as a classic statement of the doctrine of Akbar's national State. It provides the clearest evidence of the depth to which it had permeated the Indian mind during a period of hundred years and Hindus and Muslims alike understood the imposition of the *Jazia* as a definite reversal of Akbar's policy.

Naturally such a policy met with the widest opposition from the Hindus. Combined with the emperor's decision not to recognise a successor to Maharaja Jaswant Singh of Marwar, the greatest grandee of his time and the head of the powerful Rahtore clan, this act of re-imposition of poll tax broke the Moghul-Rajput alliance on which the empire had been built up. The Rana of Mewar and other Rajput leaders saw the fate that awaited them and their united forces challenged the empire. The war in Rajputana coinciding with the Maratha pressure in the South led to the ruin of the empire. The epic war of Marwar independence, of which the hero is Durgadas, demonstrated to the world the military weakness of an empire which had lost the support of its people and was engaged on many fronts.

To Aurangzeb the campaign in Rajputana was only a punitive expedition to bring his rebel vassals back to obedience. His main concern was with Deccan where a new power had arisen. Long ago when he was viceroy of the Deccan a young Maratha noble named Sivaji, the son of a military officer in the service of Bijapur, had risen to some prominence. He had occupied the strategic fortresses on the borders of Bijapur and a punitive expedition which had been sent against him under one of the premier chiefs of the Bijapur Sultanate had met with a disastrous end. In the quarrel that followed between the court of Bijapur and its recalcitrant feudatory, Sivaji had entered into negotiations with the Moghul governor and had thus come to the notice of Murad Baksh (1648).

In 1650, Aurangzeb had succeeded his brother as viceroy of the Deccan. The two great adversaries, the champion of an austere and unbending Islam and the disciple of Ramdas who had begun to consider it to be his mission to liberate the Hindus, stood face to face. Till 1649 Sivaji seems to have been only a spirited youth with local ambitions, an orthodox Hindu no doubt, but without a sense of national mission. In that year he came into contact with two remarkable men—Tukaram, the saintly poet of Maharashtra, a grocer by caste, who had given up his all and had become a wandering, minstrel singing the glory of God, and the religious leader Ramdas, who symbolised the revival of Dharma in Maharashtra.

The Maharashtra country had inherited great traditions. From the time of Satavahanas to the fall of the Yadavas of Deogir (1311) the area of Maharashtra had been one of the centres of Hindu culture. Though with three centuries of Muslim rule (Bahmani and Bijapur Sultanates) the glory that had created the temples of Ellora and Ajanta and the great Chalukyan architecture had vanished and the people had become depressed economically, they remained a hardy, honest and hardworking lot as Yuan-Chwang had described them in the seventh century. With the gradual weakening of Bijapur, the Marathas had come to have considerable influence in that State and in any case the small landed nobility had continued at all times to be Hindu.

The revival of Hindu religious feeling in the sixteenth century, which we shall deal with later, had also its political repercussions. In fact as we have noticed before the three hundred years of fight had not crushed the spirit of Hindu independence. With the battle of Talikotta the Muslim rulers of the Deccan had gained a notable victory but the successors of the defeated Ramaraja ruled from Penukonda and were till the middle of the sixteenth century masters of a powerful empire. Under Venkata II (1584-1614) the empire regained much of its ancient power and splendour and was able to resist the Muslim expansion to the south. In the North the policy of Akbar had deprived Hindu nationalism of its hereditary leaders, but the association of the Rajputs with the empire had in its turn helped the growth of their power as Aurangzeb discovered when he turned his arms to the conquest of Rajasthan.

By the middle of the century (1650) the central authority of the Vijayanagar kings had completely broken down and Hindu political independence had no visible national head. It is to this vacant position that Sivaji under the inspiration of Ramdas now aspired. Aurangzeb was however, for the time, more concerned with Bijapur. That kingdom which had absorbed Berar had under its Ottoman Sultans extended its authority from the Arabian Sea to the Bay of Bengal and was undoubtedly one of the richest in India, as much of the trade from the West came to its ports. Bijapur was even a more beautiful city than Agra and during the two hundred years of their rule the Sultans had ornamented and decorated it in a manner which astonished every visitor to the capital. It was an Indian Byzantium and at the time of Aurangzeb's viceroyalty it had reached a state of decay for which the luxury of the court was to a large extent responsible. Apart from the political pressure of unification which impelled the Moghuls to cross the Narbada and the Vindhyas and pushed them forward with demoniac determination, Aurangzeb personally had the further motive of destroying heresy in carrying on vigorously the campaign against Bijapur, the rulers of which, in spite of their Ottoman descent, professed the Shia doctrines. Aurangzeb's most vigorous efforts were not however able to reduce Bijapur when the news of Shah Jehan's illness reached him and he had to hurry back to North India. A singular incident however had given him a premonition of his trobules. During his attack on Bijapur, Sivaji to whom the future emperor had given no special attention, raided his viceregal capital (Ahmadnagar) and from Aurangzeb's own stable carried away a thousand horses. When Aurangzeb marched North the instructions he left to his officers were "to watch that son of a dog (Sivaji) who is only waiting for his chance."

The emperor's preoccupations in the north gave Sivaji the chance he was waiting for and he utilised the time to settle matters with Bijapur and to consolidate his hold on Maharashtra. In 1662, Sivaji's independence was recognised by Bijapur. Thus when the emperor was able to turn his attention again to the South (1663) it was with an independent prince of great prestige and rising power that his officers had to deal. Aurangzeb recognised this and the officer he chose to lead his forces against Sivaji was Shaista Khan, his own uncle, and the most important Muslim grandee of the empire. But Shaista was no match for Sivaji and the imperial army met with disaster. The next commander-in-chief was no less a person than the emperor's own son Muazzam but he met with no greater success. In 1664, much against his inclination, Aurangzeb nominated the most capable general in his service Raja Jai Singh to the southern command. Sivaji temporised and was invited to Agra on a safe conduct, but was kept under custody in the capital. Aurangzeb congratulated himself that he had solved the Maratha problem. But the mountain rat escaped and was soon back in his own territory. The emperor changed commands, sent reinforcements but nothing was of any avail. Aurangzeb himself was tied for the time to the north and Sivaji who had now, by the unanimous acclamation of the Maharashtra people, been crowned as king realised that once Aurangzeb was free from his entanglements the whole strength of the vast empire would be brought to bear on his State. Consequently he organised a great line of defence in the south conquering the Karnatak area and establishing a second capital in Ginji in the former Vijayanagar empire. When in 1680 he died he was the unquestioned monarch of the South, with both Bijapur and Golconda looking to him for help against attacks from the Moghuls.

The extraordinary impression that Sivaji created on his contemporaries, especially by his war with the empire, in truth a struggle between David and Goliath, may be best judged from the letter that the Shah of Persia wrote to Aurangzeb. "I learn," wrote Shah Abbas, "that most of the Zamindars of India are in rebellion. . . . The chief of them is the most impious Kafir Shiva who had long lived in such obscurity that none knew his name; but now taking advantage of your lack of means and the retreat of your troops he has made himself visible like the peak of a mountain, seized many forts, slain or captured many of your soldiers, occupied much of that country and plundered and wasted many of your ports, cities and villages and finally wants to come to grips with you."

The disputes with regard to the succession and the intrigues at the Maratha court convinced the emperor that with the death of Sivaji the Maratha problem had been reduced to its normal proportions, that of a frontier unsettled by an unruly tribe. It was essential to teach them a lesson but the empire need not stop its irresistible march towards the South across the Krishna. The campaign against Bijapur was pursued vigorously while the pressure against Shambu, the successor to the Maratha throne, was also kept up relentlessly. The attack on Bijapur united the southern forces, and even Shambu following his father's policy sent a contingent. The Sultan of Golconda also sent an army in support. The siege of Bijapur in the circumstances was no easy matter but the emperor himself arrived to take charge of the great move towards the South. Bijapur surrendered in 1686. Soon after fell Golconda, the capital of the Qutub Shahis which under Madanna, the Hindu minister, had successfully resisted the blandishments of the Moghul for over 15 years. Aurangzeb was able to congratulate himself that except for the Maratha State nothing stood between him and the unquestioned sovereignty of the whole of India. The unification of India under a single monarch which had so long been attempted but which never was actually achieved seemed to be within his grasp. Only the Marathas had to be crushed and to that supreme task he now bent his energy.

Shambu, the successor of Sivaji, was not cast in the heroic mould of his father: he was also weakened by court intrigues and internal dissensions. But he fought the Moghuls and maintained the national resistance with a degree of success which surprised Aurangzeb. Shambu however fell into the emperor's hands and was executed. Now at least, Aurangzeb must have thought, he would have peace. But what Sivaji had created was not a dynasty but a nation and a State. The Marathas mourned their king but organised resistance on the southern line established by Sivaji.

For the next twenty years the emperor chased his own shadow: marched up and down, attacked and conquered fortresses but the Maratha resistance only became stronger as years went by. It was a nation at war against an enemy. The Maratha campaign became what the Spanish campaign was to become for Napoleon, a running sore where his superiority in almost every calculable factor counted for nothing against a country in arms. After a strenuous campaign led by the emperor in person against Maratha strongholds, lasting for over six years, Aurangzeb returned to his provincial capital (1706) a broken and defeated man. Next year he died. The Marathas had not only not been put down but were in effective possession of a great territory and had attained enormous national prestige by their successful resistance.

It was not only in the South that Aurangzeb had been faced with a national rebellion. A year before his death the emperor received from a man in great straits, but who claimed the dignity of being a Sachi Padshah or true emperor, a letter entitled Zafar Nama or the epistle of victory. The writer was Govind Singh, the tenth Guru of the Sikhs who had felt the full weight of the empire, had seen two of his sons 'bricked in' alive by the emperor of Sirhind and was at the time of writing leading a hunted life with only a handful of followers. Govind was the tenth in the pontifical succession of the Panth founded by Guru Nanak (1469-1530). Nanak, a mystic singer and a follower of Ramananda and Kabir, had founded a pietist sect which preached monotheism and recognised no distinction of caste. Slowly this small community, recruited mainly from Jat cultivators of the Punjab, assumed a martial character. Amritsar, their headquarters, became a local capital and Guru Har Govind called himself Sachi Padshah, donned full armour and went about with a large armed retinue. The Sikh religion in spite of its original pietist character had from the beginning a nationalist tinge. Nanak himself had bewailed the fate of the Hindus by singing:

You perform Hindu worship in private,
Yet oh my brothers you read the books of
Mohammedans
And adopt their manners.

Guru Govind Singh succeeded his father when he was but a child; but from the first he was a determined enemy of the Moghuls as his own father Tej Bahadur had suffered martyrdom for pleading the cause of a few Kashmir Brahmins. In 1699, when the emperor was enmeshed in the labyrinth of the Maratha country, Govind took a step the significance of which but a few at the time would have understood. He established the Khalsa, transformed the community into a military organisation in which every member undertook if necessary to suffer the loss of life, family and honour in the service of the Panth. His power grew and it came into conflict with the Moghul governments of Sirhind and Lahore. Aurangzeb ordered stern measures to be taken and it was when the armies of Delhi had reduced the Guru to the position of a helpless exile that he wrote the Zafar Nama in which he proudly asked: "What is the use of putting down a few sparks when the flame is burning more fiercely than ever?" The flame that Govind Singh lit soon consumed the home province of the Moghuls—the Punjab.

Thus Aurangzeb died after raising against him the Marathas in the south, the Sikhs in the north and after alienating the strongest support of the Moghul State—the Rajputs. The loyalty of the Hindu population, so sedulously built up by his three immediate predecessors, existed no longer. He died a defeated man, but he died for an ideal—the unification of India. He was in fact the martyr for India's unity but the unity he desired to establish and for which he ruined his great inheritance was not the unity of a national State as Akbar had foreseen, but of an Islamic State—the rule of a conquering minority over India. It is that ideal which lies buried in the mausoleum at Aurangabad.

CHAPTER XVII

INDIA UNDER THE GREAT MOGHULS

THE social, economic and political development of India in the century and a half that lies between the accession of Akbar (1556) and the death of Aurangzeb (1707) shows some remarkable characteristics. The Moghul court with its Persianised rulers was a centre of cultural activity such as no North Indian court had been since the time of Bhoja, the Parmara emperor of Dhar. Not only the emperors, but the ladies of the royal household from Humayun's mother to Zebunissa, the famous daughter of Aurangzeb, were patrons of art and letters, cultivated people interested in beautiful things, gardens, paintings, carpets, fine buildings and in the encouragement of poets, scholars and thinkers. Akbar's generosity to scholars and his deep interest in religious and philosophical matters brought scholars from all parts of Asia to his court. The interest of the Moghuls in matters of the spirit was reflected in the higher officialdom and aristocracy. Abdur Rahman Khan-i-Khanan, the premier noble and the son of the regent Bairam Khan, was a scholar and poet not only in Persian but in Hindi and is counted even now among the masters of Hindi literature. The two brothers Abul Fazal and Faizi were noted writers and while both were interested in religious thought, as became the sons of Mubarak, Abul Fazal's contributions were more of a descriptive and political character while Faizi, his more learned brother, was a poet of distinction and earned fame as the translator of Hindu classics into Persian. Of the Hindu grandees at the court, Todar Mal, the revenue minister was himself the author or at least the active patron of *Todarananda*, a comprehensive work on Hindu Dharma Sastras. Prithvi Singh Rathore, the author of *Veli Krishna Rugminire,* was also one of the Rajput princes attached to Akbar's court. In fact Persian, Sanskrit and Hindi seem to have received equal patronage at the hands of the emperor and his nobles.

The greatest literary figure of the age and undoubtedly one of the great poets of India of all time, Tulsidas, lived outside the pomp and circumstance of the court, though he was a friend of Todar Mal, Man Singh and Abdur Rahman; but the revival of

Brija Bhasha and the great literary masters the language produced, Keshava Das, Surdas and Tulsidas, shed refulgent light on the greatness of the period. With the works of these three whose importance in the shaping of the Hindu mind of India cannot be overestimated, the Hindi language comes into its own as the fountain of spiritual sustenance to the people.

If literature found ready patronage at a court of which the shining lights were Abdur Rahman, Faizi, Abul Fazal and Man Singh, painting and architecture were encouraged and protected by the special interest of Akbar himself. Painting had always been a speciality of courts in India. From the evidence in Sanskrit literature we know that while mural paintings were considered the supreme examples of the painter's art, portraiture and pictures were cultivated as courtly hobbies of rulers and nobles. In *Sakuntala* and *Kaumudi Mahotsava,* the paintings of the beloved are part of the story. In the *Swapna Vasavadatta* of Bhasa, the portraits of the royal couple are sent as a present to Udayana by his father-in-law and in Gunadhya's stories many romances arise from seeing the pictures of heroines. Miniature painting was therefore an ancient art in India, though the earliest specimens have not come down to us. Akbar was so interested in art that he got painters to come from Persia and work for him. Persia after Beyzad was famous for its masters but the Indo-Persian school which Akbar founded had but a short life. It became Indian and the Moghul miniatures show how soon and how distinctively Indian genius asserted itself. Akbar's patronage of painters was so remarkable that in his lightning-like descent on Gujerat among the people whom he selected to go with him were three painters.

Nor were his son and grandson less enthusiastic. Jehangir in fact claimed to be the perfect connoisseur of painting and his memoirs contain allusion to the interest he displayed in encouraging the work of the masters in his employ. Even Aurangzeb in the earlier period of his reign seems to have encouraged painting as we know that he sent artists every six months to paint the portrait of a prince incarcerated in the Gwalior fort. Jehangir appreciated both Indian and Persian paintings and his *ateliers* produced some paintings of exquisite beauty. The work of the Moghul school now enriches the collections of most museums all over the world and is so well known that but little need be said here. From the list of the masters that have come down to us we know that it was pre-eminently an Indian school and Hindus and Muslims alike contributed to the artistic achievement of the period.

Abul Fazal mentions seventeen artists as being pre-eminent and of them thirteen are Hindus. The pictures executed by Hindu artists, Abul Fazal declares, "surpass our conception of things; few indeed in the whole world are found to equal them." Of the masters in Akbar's court Abdus Samad the Persian was the doyen: the great Basawan and Daswanth soon established the technique of the new school which ousted the popularity of Persian paintings. Akbar himself sat for the artists and the nobles of his court were commanded to have their portraits painted for the imperial collection.

The ancient Hindu school of painting did not get merged in the new developments. It had in fact an interesting revival as a result of the contacts with the Persian and Moghul styles and the so-called Rajput school which flourished in the Hindu courts of Central India, Rajputana and the Sub-Himalayan regions was the efflorescence of the earlier Indian tradition. The Moghul emperors and following them the Hindu and Muslim grandees had their libraries filled with albums and with illuminated books, the magnificence of which can well be imagined from the Jaipur collection. Each petty court imitated the Grand Moghul and the artistic harvest of the period was therefore rich enough.

The Delhi Sultanates and the provincial monarchies were, as we have seen before, great builders. The Indo-Islamic architecture is not therefore the special gift of the Moghuls, but the greater luxury and the unexampled wealth of the emperors enabled them to erect buildings of supreme beauty, lay out gardens which still give pleasure to millions, and even erect whole new cities. The city of Fatehpur Sikri, which Akbar laid out and built as his capital, has endured as an example of the mingling of Hindu and Muslim conceptions. Of the Taj Mahal, the Moti Masjid and the Red Fort and of the tombs of Itimad-ud-dowla little need be said. The Moghul gardens in Kashmir and even the gardens of the Amirs like Pinjaur near Kalka show a remarkable sense of beauty.

Equally important from the general point of view was the building activity of the great princes in this period. The domestic architecture of the Hindus underwent a very notable change. The great palaces that the Hindu grandees built in their capitals imitated the Diwan-i Khas, Diwan-i Am, Shish Mahal and the Baradari of the imperial palaces and the resultant architecture differed both from the earlier Hindu mansions and from the Moghul palaces. The great palace of Bir Singh Bundela, the old fort at Bikaner, the palaces at Udaipur, Jodhpur and Amber are among surviving examples of this great period of architecture.

The period also witnessed, as was but natural, a revival of temple architecture in the traditional style. With the growth of toleration under Akbar the restoration of old temples and the building of new ones became the recognised duty of Hindu grandees and merchants. Mathura again attracted the greatest attention but elsewhere also the restoration of temples was considered a pious act. The most notable of them, Bir Singh's temple, attached to his palace, was destroyed by Shah Jehan, but it is to be remembered that the majority of great temples that exist in North India today belong to this period.

The Deccan Sultanates have a special claim for remembrance for their architectural achievements. The Osmani rulers of Bijapur were great builders. The Gol Gombaz, whose dome is larger than that of the Pantheon in Rome; Ibrahim Rauja, the tomb of Taj Sultana; and the great palace of the Relic, gave to the city of the Adilshahis a glory which was greater than that of Agra or Delhi. The dome of Gol Gombaz was honey-coloured. Ibrahim Rauja in its dream-like beauty is the equal of the Taj and the delicacy and beauty of its work is in no way inferior to those of the great Moghul buildings. Of the tomb of Taj Sultana, the architect himself had it inscribed with blasphemous pride that heaven itself stood astounded at this building. The palace of the Relic, which housed two hairs of the Holy Prophet, adorned with fresco paintings by Italian artists, bore witness to the cosmopolitan taste of the monarchs of Bijapur. Beautiful gardens, magnificent public baths, and lovely palaces added to the beauty of the city.

The city of Golconda was no less famous for its architectural beauties. The green domes of the great tombs, the fine mosques and the palace whose galleries were adorned by fountains gave to the capital a magnificence which rivalled that of Bijapur. The wealth of Golconda was proverbial and the buildings reflected the riches of the kingdom, the refined taste of its Persianised kings, and the sense of luxury that pervaded India in the sixteenth and seventeenth centuries.

In fact the most noticeable factor in the life of the Indian courts and of the nobility of the period is the unexampled sense of luxury which even the court of Byzantium must have envied. Babar, though a man of refined tastes and one who appreciated the good things of life, had spent most of his time in the field to be an advocate of luxury. It was Akbar who started the Moghul court on that career of magnificence which even the Puritanism of Aurangzeb was unable to restrain or diminish. Even when the emperors travelled the magnificence was in no sense relaxed. The red tents which marked the imperial enclosures reflected the luxury of Agra and Delhi. It was the capital in all its magnificence that moved. Even when directing campaigns in distant parts the court bore no Spartan appearance. Nor was this confined to the emperors. Shaista Khan arrived in the Deccan for his southern campaign accompanied by four hundred dancing girls and all other paraphernalia of high life. Even minor officials, as testified by European witnesses, lived a life of luxury in the capital as well as in the camp.

In dress, in food, in methods of living, the higher classes showed the spirit of luxury. Brocades, printed silk and muslin were the ordinary dress of the great nobles. The austere food of the Hindus was replaced among higher classes by rich and special preparations, the pilaws, birianis and the varied and rich foods of Persia. In the houses of the Hindu nobility the great feasts were in imitation of the manner of the Persian and Central Asian Amirs. Rare fruits, mysterious decoctions, refinements of the culinary art to suit jaded palates, which the cosmopolitan society of Persia, long in contact with Rome, China and Egypt, had evolved, found their way into India and soon gained popularity with the richer classes among Hindus and Muslims alike. Even today the food that the great Rajput and other Hindu princes serve at their tables is predominantly Moghul in its preparations and famous dishes are known after the emperors as Shah Jehani Pilaw, Jehangiri Kabab, etc.

The manner of clothing also changed greatly. Early in the sixteenth century Nanak had bewailed the fact that the Hindus had adopted the dress and manners of the Muslims. The Album of Jehangir preserved in the Berlin Museum shows that even the rulers of distant Kutch and Nawanagar had in that emperor's time begun to put on the Moghul dress and the portraits of Rajput nobles from the time of Man Singh show that apart from the caste mark which distinguished the Hindu, the dress of both Hindu and Muslim nobles was practically identical. Of course the ordinary Hindu still wore his dhoti, as he does now, but the higher classes accepted the pyjamas and the chapkan as the ceremonial costume befitting their position. Every one of the Rajput princes whose painting has come down to us, except Maharana Pratap, is portrayed in his court dress and that is in itself sufficient evidence of the general acceptance of Moghul habits and manners by the higher nobility.

The acceptance of Muslim manners must have been fairly wide-spread, for we find the hookah specially denounced by Govind Singh. The drinking of wine had become general among the upper classes. The ceremonies of even Sivaji's court reflected the manners of Delhi. In short, the dress, social amenities, etc. which the Moghuls introduced ceased to be foreign and were accepted by the higher classes everywhere.

In the realm of thought, the Moghul period witnessed both a harmonisation and a revival. It is a strange fact that during all these years Indian Islam made but little contribution to the thought or culture of Islam in general. It was a one-way traffic all the time, the Muslim in India drawing upon the cultural sources of Islam from outside and giving but little to them. The only exception was literature. Indo-Persian literature has undoubtedly a few great names beginning with Amir Khusru, but it can hardly be said that the very considerable literature produced in India was accepted in the main stream of Persian or Islamic culture. They are a part of the heritage of India, an outstanding contribution by Indian Islam to the general treasury of Indian culture. In philosophy, religious thought and general scholarship Indian Islam's contribution to Islamic thought was negligible. There is no Averroes that India can claim. But Islam's influence on Hindu religion was very notable. Kabir and Nanak, two vital figures in medieval Hindu religion, were both influenced by the rigid monotheism of Islam and in both of them there is a mingling of Sufism and Bhakti. In no one was this more remarkable than in Dara Shukoh, the unfortunate son of Shah Jehan. Deeply versed in the mysteries of Sufism, Dara was an adept in yogic practices, and in the doctrines of the Hindu saints. His *Samudra Samagama* or mingling of oceans, his Persian Upanishad, and his recently published letter in Sanskrit to Kavindracharya testify to his deep knowledge of Hindu religion. In fact the influence of Hinduism on Indian Muslims seems to have been quite considerable. The translation of Hindu classics into Persian proceeded apace. Not a few of the leading Muslim scholars of the period seem to have known Sanskrit well, for we have Badauni's own statement that he was commissioned by Akbar to make a fresh translation of *Rajatarangini*.

In many ways the sixteenth and the seventeenth centuries marked a notable revival of Hindu intellect in North India. Of this movement Banaras was the centre. A new school of Dharma Sastra of which the leading lights were Nanda Pandita, Mitra Misra and Nilkanta Bhatta taught in the first half of the seventeenth century in the sacred city and their influence spread far and wide. Scholars from all parts of India collected at Banaras. In fact Banaras had never ceased to be the centre of Indian learning or the throbbing heart of Hindu religion: but in the sixteenth century it became the radiating centre of Hindu culture and once again a great university. In the volume of tributes presented to Nrisimha, a pre-eminent teacher of Advaita, we have the names of the great scholars who were then studying at Banaras under. him. The list is truly remarkable; it includes the names of scholars from all parts of India. Not only in Vedanta and Dharma Sastras was there a revival in Banaras: in secular studies also the sacred city took the lead. In the seventeenth century among the scholars who adorned the great centre of teaching were Khandadeva, the author of *Bhatta Dipika* and other *Mimamsa* works, Raghunath Siromani the logician, the author of *Didhiti*, and Kamalakara the astronomer. We have a description of one of such schools, of which there were many in Banaras, from the pen of Bernier who became the friend of one of the great Acharyas of the time, Kavindra Saraswati. "The town of Benares," says Bernier, "situated on the Ganges, in a beautiful situation and in the midst of an extremely rich and fertile country, may be considered the general school of gentiles. It is the Athens of India whither resort Brahmins and other devotees. . . . The town contains no colleges or regular classes as in our universities. but resembles rather the schools of the ancients, the masters being dispersed over different parts of the town in private houses, principally in the gardens of the suburbs, which the rich merchants permit them to occupy. Some of these masters have four disciples, others six or seven and the most eminent may have twelve; but this is the largest number."

Kavindracharya whose friendship Bernier cultivated was a poet and scholar of the greatest distinction and a yogi held in the highest esteem. He was a friend of Shah Jehan who had received and honoured him at his court and he was also one of the gurus of Dara who compares him in a Sanskrit letter addressed to him to Sankaracharya and the ancient teachers. Kavindra was the most famous teacher of the time in Banaras and seems to have been in charge of the education of the sons of Maharaja Jai Singh. Bernier visited him and this is what the traveller says: "When I visited him at Benaras he was most kind and attentive giving me a collation in the university library to which he invited six of the most learned Pandits of the town." Bernier saw a large hall entirely filled with books on all topics in Sanskrit. The libraries of Benaras were famous, but Kavindra's library was perhaps unique.

The Moghul emperors were great collectors of books. The imperial library was a treasure house of every kind of literature. In Akbar's time it consisted of 24,000 manuscript volumes many of which were specially copied out and illustrated for the emperor. The magnificent specimens that have come down to us like the *Shah Namah* of Shah Jehan, now in the Royal Asiatic Society's library, show what care the emperors had taken in regard to calligraphy, illustrations, etc. Akbar, Jehangir and Shah Jehan were great collectors of books and the nobles both Hindu and Muslim followed the fashion of the court. It is interesting to note that the great private manuscript libraries of North India all have their origin at this time, the Anup Sanskrit Library of Bikaner, the Pothi Khana of Jaipur and the great collections of Jaisalmer. Kavindra's own unique collection seems to have been dispersed after his death but many of them are still available bearing the master's ex-libris in the collections of Bikaner and Jaisalmer.

The period also witnessed the last efflorescence of Sanskrit literature in the north. In Akbar's court there were numerous poets whose works were appreciated by the court nobles. But the greatest Sanskrit writer of the period undoubtedly was Jagannatha Pandita honoured by Shah Jehan with the title of Kavirai. Jagannatha was the last of the great Sanskrit poets whose works attain a classic beauty in diction and sentiment. With him the language of Kalidasa was still a living and vibrant instrument and his *Ganga Lahiri* and other works have achieved a deserved fame and are rightly considered classics. Kavindra's library compositions, laboured and ornate, in no way on a par with Jagannatha's, deserve mention. Rupa Goswami, the author of the drama, *Vidaghda Madhava,* and other works, the playwright Giridharanatha and numerous others can be mentioned among the notable poets of Sanskrit during this period. Nor was scholarship confined to men. Vaijayanti collaborated with her husband Krishnanatha in the composition of *Anandalatika Champu* and Vallabhadevi is the reputed author of *Subhashitavali.*

It is however not in the mellifluous phrases of *Ganga Lahiri* nor in the laboured compositions of Jagadvijaya Chandas that we see the genuine poetic fervour of the period. It is to the inspired epic of Tulsidas, the moving poems of Sudras and other writers in the Brija Bhasha, to the Kirtans of Ramdas, to the Dhingal epic of Prithviraj that we should turn to appreciate the literary genius of India at the time. Indeed, after the great days of Kalidasa no century was so productive of the highest literature in India as the period of the great Moghuls. Tulsidas, the greatest of all Indian poets who wrote in the language of the people (1532-1623), may well claim to be the poet of India. Though a great Sanskrit scholar, he preferred to write in the vernacular, and defending his choice, he declared his language to be an earthen vessel which contained amrit (ambrosia) while Sanskrit was a jewelled and rare cup of extreme beauty which held poison. His *Ramacharita Manasa* is not only a magnificent epic singing the great deeds of Rama, but a scripture of the people to which the entire Hindi-knowing people from the Himalayas to the Vindhyas and from Lahore to Bengal turn for spiritual sustenance, a code of ethics constantly on the lips of all, from princes to peasants, and a truly fine expression of poetic genius. He gave to Valmiki's great story a popular appeal which made it one of the capital factors of Northern Indian life. It may be noted here that the same extra-ordinary fate overtook the Ramayana elsewhere, it being converted into a popular bible by Kambar in the Tamil country, Krittivasas in Bengal and Ezhuthachan in Kerala. As a recent scholar, Kissan Keane, has stated, "It is impossible to exaggerate the influence that the great words of Tulsidas have had on the lives and learning of his own countrymen. Above all Ramayana as a creation in literature and as an expression of religion stands supreme."

Tulsidas's *Ramayana* was the culmination of the great religious movement of which the great lights that preceded him were Ramananda, Kabir and Nanak. With him the spiritual ferment found a permanent and popular shape and the inchoate mass of Hinduism was saved from schisms and cults for the religion of *Ramacharita Manasa,* though it exalted Rama as the Supreme Being, was catholic enough to hold all sects.

The period also witnessed another remarkable expression of the Bhakti doctrines in the emotional Vaishnavism of Chaitanya, whose influence on Bengal and on Vaishnavite doctrines generally was profound. Chaitanya's doctrine was one of pure love and devotion to Krishna and Radha and he elevated Brindavan, the scene of Krishna's early manifestations, to the position of an earthly paradise. The movement produced a considerable literature in Sanskrit and still has much influence over a wide body of Indian thought.

Indian music shed glory on the reign of Akbar and his two successors. The great patron of music was Raja Man Singh Tanwar of Gwalior whose school of music was famous at the time. Tansen, who is acclaimed the supreme exponent of Indian music, was a favourite of Akbar and the art had the patronage of the emperors till the time of Aurangzeb whose puritan soul prohibited its performance at court and in Delhi. In all Hindu courts music was of course an essential part of life, and the Sultanates of the Deccan maintained an army of musicians—Golconda as many as

20,000. The classical Hindu tradition of music, as described in the *Sangitaraja* of Maharana Kumba in the fifteen century, underwent considerable simplification at the hands of the court musicians of the Moghuls.

The hilly tract of Bundelkhand deserves and honourable mention in the history of arts during this period. Owing to its inaccessibility, it had under its Chandela and Kalachuri rulers preserved an unbroken tradition of indigenous art in all its aspects, architecture, music and letters. Under the Baghela and Bundela kings of the medieval period music and literature flourished in this area. It was originally under the patronage of Ramachandra Baghela that the great Tansen came into prominence.

One curious change in the status of musicians may be noted. With the Hindus music was pre-eminently a religious art and devotion to it either professionally or otherwise involved no social degradation. In fact in South India even today many of the great masters are Brahmins of the highest social position. Maharana Kumba did not hesitate to call himself Abhinava Bharatacharya—the modern Bharata—and proclaimed his proficiency in all forms of music. In Muslim courts however music, though greatly patronised, became for the musician a degraded profession as the main body of the performers were dancing girls of ill repute. The position was analogous to that of actors and actresses in Europe till the middle of the nineteenth century. The degradation of the status of the musicians had the result of reducing the popularity of music with the educated middle classes who looked upon it as one of the luxuries of nobles. Education in music was discouraged among the ordinary people and as a result a distinction between the music of the schools and ustads and the folk music of the people arose which is still noticeable in North India. In the south, on the other hand, music continued to be the common heritage of prince and peasant alike.

The period produced some notable women in India, though the condition of women as a whole showed a marked deterioration, as a result of both invasions and of the rigidity of the system of purdah in Rajputana and the Gangetic valley. The great women we hear of during this period are princesses and noblewomen—Moghul princess Jehanara, the partisan of Dara; Roshanara, the partisan of Aurangzeb; Zebunissa, the daughter of Aurangzeb, whose verses under the name of Makhi have come down to us; Chand Bibi of Ahmadnagar and Tarabai, the regent of the Maharashtra kingdom. Nurjehan was of course a Persian but her strange career is of interest to Indian history. But these examples, remarkable as they are, give us no indication of the position of women in society. Jijabai, the mother of Sivaji, however is more typical. She is the type of the devoted Hindu mother, strong-willed and autocratic in the home, but wholly subordinating herself to the interests of her children. On the whole Hindu womanhood maintained its tradition, receiving its strength from religion and usage, but in proportion to the general advancement which the period shows, there is no evidence of progress.

Of the economic and industrial conditions of India during the Moghul times, we have ample evidence from a variety of sources. They have also been the subjects of detailed study by competent scholars so that the picture of the time can be filled up with a fair measure of accuracy. The main centres of the empire were connected by a reasonable road system. Sher Shah had completed the Grand Trunk Road which follows practically the same alignment as today from Peshawar to Bengal. This main road system was an inheritance from the Mauryan times, though the importance of Kanauj at the time took the line from Sirhind across the Gangetic valley in a more northerly direction. Bengal was one of the main provinces of the empire and communication with it had at all times to be in an efficient state. Another important road connected Agra with Ahmedabad and from there to Surat, the gateway to Mecca and to the commerce of the world. This road passed through Bayana and Gwalior and was the main commercial route of the empire.

Caravanserais, dharamshalas at convenient distances, long avenues of trees over large stretches, piaus or places for providing water and other conveniences existed on these roads. A constant stream of wheeled traffic proceeded from the main centres to the capital. Normally, the journeys were safe enough and effective action was taken by local authorities to keep the roads clear of thieves, dacoits, etc., though we have occasional records of certain areas acquiring a bad name in this connection. Along the Ganges the waterways were very popular and fleets of river-boats sailed down this great highway at frequent intervals from Allahabad to Bengal. The boats were of considerable size and bottoms of two hundred tons carrying goods were not unfamiliar sights on the river.

The Deccan campaigns which were, as we have seen, a regular feature of imperial policy kept the road to the south in a state of reasonable repair Reinforcements had constantly to be sent, changes in command were frequent and the generals being men of the highest position had to keep up a regular communication with the court. A relay service was also maintained for official purposes and when, as in the last years of Aurangzeb's reign, the emperor was in camp in the Deccan the maintenance of easy and rapid communication became a matter of supreme importance.

Lahore, Delhi, Agra, Ajmer, Allahabad and Banaras were the main cities of the empire. Lahore was a great city. Agra was the main capital but after Shah Jehan, Delhi assumed that role.

We have the evidence of the European visitors about the conditions of Indian cities. All witnesses are agreed that Lahore and Agra were among the greatest towns of the world at the time. Delaet, the Dutch writer who made an interesting summary of all the information available about the empire of the Moghuls, quotes authorities and declares that Lahore in the Moghul period was a greater city than London or Paris. Of Agra with its fine river front where all the nobles had their mansions, with its citadel which was undeniably the most magnificent and luxurious royal residence of the time, with the architectural beauty of the Taj Mahal and the other great buildings, it is perhaps enough to say that its claim to pre-eminence was undisputed. Delhi comes again into prominence with the construction by Shah Jehan of his new city and the compulsory residence of Aurangzeb there during the imprisonment of Shah Jehan in the Agra Fort. Allahabad, where Akbar erected the great citadel, soon assumed importance, because of its strategic position and the value of its river-borne trade to the new European trading centres on the Bengal coast.

The main ports of the empire were Surat, Cambay and Satgaon. Surat was the emporium of Western trade and the gate to Mecca, for the pilgrim ships sailed from there. Like all great ports it was a cosmopolitan city, where the merchants of all countries met and traded. In the seventeenth century, Portuguese, Dutch, French and English merchants had their factories there. In fact it was the main English factory at the time, the rather insignificant seed of the great empire which was to grow from it two centuries later. In the port it was not an uncommon sight to see over a hundred ships of all nationalities at anchor. The city had its own separate administration under a governor, who kept magnificent state and was accompanied by war elephants, guards and State banners and other insignia of high office when he went out into the city.

Surat was well provided with fine dharmashalas and rest houses and the merchants and bankers of the place maintained gardens and pleasure parks outside the city walls. Money changers were much in evidence and the banias of Kathiawad performed their duties of banking there as they do now with inherited skill and caution. The prestige of Indian banking stood high and the hundis of the banias were honoured at all trading centres. The prosperity of the port was such that its customs revenue was one of the main sources of the imperial treasury.

In the sixteenth and seventeenth centuries India was one of the main industrial countries. The manufacture of cotton cloth was undoubtedly the staple industry of the country and it was not confined to any particular area. The whole country participated in this industry, though specialised work was naturally limited to certain areas. Thus Chanderi in Central India was famous for its fine cloth, Masulipatam for its prints, Surat for its borders, Banaras for its rich brocades for which there was great demand and Dacca for its fine muslins. Cloth of every quality was woven as India was the sole supplier of cotton cloth to the areas east of the Cape of Good Hope, the Middle East, Burma, Malaya, Java, etc. Woollen goods formed only a small part of Indian manufacture. Kashmir shawls were then as now a luxury product. The manufacture of carpets was introduced by Akbar and though it attained great perfection, no export trade in it seems to have developed. Silk-weaving was a localised industry but seems to have flourished greatly from very early times.

Among other industries ship-building may be specially mentioned. The Moghuls maintained a naval station in the Bengal waters and constructed their own ships. The great traffic on the Ganges and on the main rivers led to the growth of this industry while in Cutch, Cambay and other port towns ships of considerable size were also built. Indian ship-building had a high reputation at the time and even the Portuguese had some of their best ships built in India.

The prestige of India stood high in the outside world. Even before Vasco da Gama's voyage to India, Hindustan was fairly well known in Europe. Many Europeans had previously visited India. But their knowledge was hazy. With the arrival of the Portuguese more about India came to be known in Europe. Before the time of Akbar the connection of the Portuguese was mainly with the powers on the west coast, Bijapur and Calicut and with the empire of Vijayanagar: but when Akbar invited the Jesuit priests to his court and encouraged merchants to visit Agra information about the great monarch began to spread in Europe. During the hundred and fifty years of the rule of the great Moghuls India's name stood high in the world and she took rank then with the most civilised countries and with most powerful nations.

CHAPTER XVIII

SEA POWER ENTERS INDIA

THE only Indian State which had a proper appreciation of sea power was the Chola empire. The oceanic policy of the Chola emperors, as we noticed before, led to the establishment of bases in Nicobar and territorial authority over the coastal areas of Malaya. The hundred years' war that followed with the naval power of the Sailendra kings resulted in the breakdown of the Chola State, and in the thirteenth century the Bay of Bengal was again under the exclusive authority of the Sailendras who even invaded Ceylon. Sailendra power, however, collapsed with the rise of the empire of Java, and by the fifteenth century the navigation of Indian waters was in the hands of the Arabs. Local Indian rulers, the most important of whom were the Zamorins of Calicut and the Sultans of Gujerat, maintained naval forces which controlled the trade with the Red Sea ports and with the Persian Gulf, but their authority was local and an oceanic sense was altogether absent from their policy.

In 1498 a naval power with its base in Europe entered the Indian waters. The arrival of Vasco da Gama at Calicut heralds the dawn of a new epoch when India is drawn into world politics and the rivalries of distant kingdoms. Vasco da Gama claimed for his master the sovereignty of the Indian seas and he immediately came into conflict with the powerful ruler of Calicut. Withdrawing from that port, the Portuguese established themselves at Cochin whose ruler, owing to the rivalry that existed between him and the Zamorin, gave them help and support. The naval engagement (1503) that followed was indecisive in point of fighting but was decisive from the political point of view. The Calicut fleet which had to meet the Portuguese intruders was not a high seas navy. It was effective for fighting in coastal waters where its lightness and superior mobility gave it an advantage. But it was helpless in dealing with an enemy who was equipped to roam the oceans. This weakness of Zamorin's naval power was demonstrated by the action off Cochin. When in the next year the Portuguese returned in greater strength the Zamorin had to fall back on the defensive. An attempt to drive the intruders away from the Indian seas with the help of the Sultans of Egypt and Gujerat proved fruitless as the Egyptian admiral Mir Hussein after a first victory failed to drive home his advantage and returned to his home waters. The Portuguese had come to stay.

With Alfonso Albuquerque (1510-1516) the position underwent a material change. He established a system by which the entire Indian Ocean was controlled from three points, Malacca, Goa and Socotra. After an unsuccessful attempt to reduce the Zamorin, Albuquerque attacked and conquered Goa and its immediate vicinities which he converted into an impregnable base. He captured Malacca and thus ensured entry into the Pacific and controlled at the same time the eastern entrance to the Indian Ocean.

With the conquest of Malacca and the establishment of friendly relations with the ruler of Arakan, Albuquerque's oceanic strategy reached its completion. He had set out to build up a commercial empire based on an unchallengeable position in the Indian Ocean. The coast-line of Africa was already under Portuguese domination and what Albuquerque had to secure was a system of strong points which would cover the main areas. By the annexation of Socotra, by political suzerainty in Ormuz and by holding Malacca he established a system of control which remained unshaken as long as the Portuguese naval power remained strong enough in Europe. To enable this policy to be carried out successfully it was essential that there should be a territorial base in India which could act as the central point of Portuguese power. The conquest and partial settlement of Goa and its development as a metropolitan city with the complete paraphernalia of government was therefore the foundation of all his schemes. In short, Albuquerque's strategy may be summarised as (*a*) direct rule over Goa and its colonisation by mixed marriage, (*b*) fortresses and bases at strategic points, and (*c*) subordinate alliance with rulers of coastal areas of strategic importance. By these simple methods Albuquerque built up an absolute mastery of the Indian seas which endured for a hundred years. Further, in its essentials it marked out the grand strategy for all the naval powers who entered the Indian Ocean from the West.

The Portuguese never had an empire in India. Their territorial possessions which they vaingloriously called the "State of India" were at no time much larger in extent than they are today. What they did have was the empire of Indian commerce. At the time of their arrival, Calicut, now only an unimportant district town, was a great emporium of trade. Most of the trade of South India including cotton goods, notably calico which takes its name from the port, all the pepper trade which was a monopoly of Malabar, a great portion of the trade with the Red Sea ports including the valuable coral trade, pearls from the Gulf of Manaar passed through Calicut. When Ma-Huan saw it in 1425, it was a great and flourishing city. So were Surat and Cambay. But with the arrival of the Portuguese the entire position changed. The King of Portugal claimed to be "the lord of navigation" and his representatives in India denied to others the right of navigation on the high seas. As Barroes, the Portuguese historian, says: "It is true that there does exist a common-right to all to navigate the seas and in Europe we recognise the rights which others hold against us; but this right does not extend beyond Europe and therefore the Portuguese as Lords of the Sea are justified in confiscating the goods of all those who navigate the sea without their permission."

After the Egyptian admiral Mir Hussein's departure from Indian waters in 1509, the Portuguese proceeded to enforce this claim which they were in a position to do, especially after Albuquerque's establishment of the sea empire. Any ship sailing without their *cartas* was treated as a pirate and was liable to capture and confiscation. Thus by one stroke the Portuguese became the masters of Indian commerce. Those who suffered most by this crude system of monopoly were the Arabs who had the lion's share of the carrying trade in the century immediately preceding da Gama's arrival. The Arab sea trade with India was totally ruined and India's maritime commerce passed into the hands of the Portuguese.

There is very little to recommend the Portuguese from any point of view. Devoid of scruples or sense of honour, overweening in their pride, indolent and with no sense of morality, they produced no statesman or administrator of outstanding ability except Albuquerque during the period of hundred and fifty years when they held the mastery of the Indian seas. But they made some contribution to the life of India. Garcia da Orta's treatise on the medicinal plants of India is the first systematic study of an important subject. The introduction of printing and the establishment of seminaries for the training of Indian priests at Verapoly and at Goa are notable contributions to enlightenment. The ornate Manuelesque architecture which they popularised on the West coast and the bungalow type of building they introduced are also worthy of mention.

Ardent Catholics, who believed fervently in their mission as the messengers of Christ, the Portuguese can also claim some recognition in the field of religious work. The Catholic church sent out to India during this period two very notable personalities. Francis Xavier and Alexis de Menzes. Xavier was one of the original members of the Society of Jesus, a disciple of St. Ignatius Loyola. He came out to India with the object of reclaiming for Christ the heathen population of the areas under Portuguese influence. He achieved some success and his body lies in the Church of Bom Jesus in Goa in a tomb supplied by the Grand Duke of Tuscany, where it is said to work miracles. De Menzes, who became the Archbishop of Goa, was not interested so much in the conversion of heathens as in removing Hindu influence on the ancient Christians of Malabar and of bringing them into the mother church. His synod of Daimper (Udayamperur, 1599) is an important event in the history of Indian Christianity, more important than is now recognised for it brought the majority of Syrian Christians into the Catholic Church and made India the most Catholic country in the East outside the Philippines, a position which it maintains even today. In spite of State assistance and a hundred years of missionary work in the interests of Protestantism, the Catholic Church maintains its primacy in India and has more members than all the other Christian sects put together. The ecclesiastical architecture of India, especially in the south, is Portuguese. The cathedral at Mylapore and the numerous churches on the West coast bear witness to the enthusiasm of the Portuguese in matters of religion.

The Portuguese trade monopoly was primarily of advantage to the mother country, but it was also of importance to India. In the first place it provided a world market for Indian goods, especially spices and muslin, on a scale unknown before, and secondly it introduced into India the products of Europe and China. The trade in chinaware became an important part of Portuguese commerce. Another important aspect of Portuguese trade was the supply of Persian horses to Vijayanagar. The external trade of the great Hindu kingdom was practically in the hands of the Portuguese and friendly relations were maintained over a long period with the court of "Narsinga" as the country was called.

The degradation of Portuguese life in India after the first twenty years of pioneer effort is affirmed by all authorities. Luiz Camoen's Sonnet on Goa is the earliest record we have of the pitfalls into which sudden wealth had led the Portuguese. As time went on, the successors of Vasco da Gama, Duarte Pacheco and Albuquerque, living on the tribute of the seas, sank into a state of indolence unusual even in India, moral depravity for which it will be difficult to find a parallel, and a luxury which eclipsed even the neighbouring courts of Golconda and Bijapur. The sense of security which the mastery of the seas gave to the Portuguese was their undoing. There was no one to challenge their authority on the high seas. Whatever the admirals of the Zamorin might do in the coastal waters of Malabar, India's trade was theirs and no one was there to question it, especially as Philip II of Spain, the only great naval power in the Atlantic, had also become the king of Portugal.

From this slumber they were rudely awakened when in the beginning of the seventeenth century, the Dutch and the English arrived on the Indian seas in quick succession and the French followed a little later. It was a naval truism of the time that whoever controlled the Atlantic controlled the Indian Ocean also; that the mastery of the Indian Ocean was determined by the strength of the navies off the coast of Europe. After the defeat of the Spanish Armada, European nations, especially the Dutch and the English, awoke to the fact that the power of the Portuguese in Indian waters could be challenged. Linschoten, who had been private secretary to the Archbishop of Goa, was the inspirer of the Dutch East India Company. The first Dutch fleet, consisting of four ships, sailed for the East in 1595. This voyage opened the way for regular commerce and, in spite of Portuguese opposition, the Dutch were able to establish themselves in Indonesia. Malacca was captured in 1641, thus opening the Eastern door to the Indian Ocean. Albuquerque's system had not failed, but his successors had not been able to defend it. Once Malacca was in Dutch hands the attack on Ceylon was easy enough. In 1654 Colombo fell and the smaller settlements on the Malabar coast came into Dutch hands by 1663. The Portuguese monopoly had ended by the beginning of the century; their political power vanished by the Dutch occupation of Ceylon.

The English East India Company was established in 1603 and after a considerable interval the French also entered the field. The British interests were originally centred in the Indonesian islands but after the massacre of Amboyna (1623) the company turned its attention to Indian trade based mainly on Surat and Masulipatam. The Indian Ocean thus became a cockpit of naval rivalry, faithfully reflecting the position in Europe. The Portuguese fell into the background and the first round of the fight was between the Dutch and the British which ended only after the naval power of the Dutch was eclipsed in Europe following the accession of Louis XIV.

With Colbert, France also entered the fray. The original idea of the great French minister was to establish French power in Ceylon and with this object a considerable fleet was sent out to India under Jacob de la Haye in 1570. Though Trincomalee was obtained from the king of Kandy, by the time the French arrived there, the Dutch had already taken possession of this famous harbour. De la Haye returned to France, but he left behind him Francois Martin, who established the settlement of Pondicherry.

The actual fight for dominance of the Indian waters between England and France came later with the appearance of La Bourdonnais at the head of an effective fleet. But in spite of his, and later Suffren's, victories, the sporadic nature of French naval power in the Atlantic left the unquestioned mastery of the Indian seas to Britain, which after the treaty of Utrecht had become the dominant naval power of Europe and the mistress of the seas.

An interesting period of Indian naval activity under the Angreys of Suvarnadurg may also be mentioned here. Sivaji realised the importance of a navy and actually organised one. Under the Peshwas the Maratha navy passed into the hands of a leader of remarkable ability, courage and enterprise, Kanoji Angrey, who established his headquarters at Suvarnadurg and entered the lists against the naval powers then active in the Arabian Sea. Soon he established a mastery of the coastal waters and the weight of his power was felt by all the European powers in succession. From Kanheri, his island base, only sixteen miles ouside Bombay, Kanoji began to levy chauth (the Maratha tribute of one-fourth of revenues on the territories conquered by them). This conflicted with the permits issued by the British and the *cartas* of the Portuguese and in the struggle that ensued the British naval might proved ineffective and had to suffer losses and failure a number of times. Enraged at their continuous failure the British allied themselves with the Portuguese and the fleet, this time led by a squadron of the Royal Navy, attacked Angrey in his stronghold (1722). The viceroy of Goa sent a force of 5,000 men to support the attack. But victory lay with Kanoji and the allied forces had to withdraw to the safety of their bases. The Dutch fared no better in their conflicts with him, and as an English historian says: "Victorious alike over the English, the Dutch and the Portuguese," the Maratha admiral sailed the Arabian Sea in triumph.

His successors carried on the policy of Kanoji and till Clive and Watson led an expedition to Suvarnadurg and captured that fortress in 1756, Maratha naval power was a factor of importance on the Konkan coast. Again, it is necessary to emphasise that the activities of Angrey had no oceanic importance. The authority of the Maratha admirals was confined to the territorial waters, and they never ventured out into the open sea in order to meet their enemies. The British naval power was, therefore, supreme on the high seas, though their exclusive authority on Indian waters dates only from the departure of Suffren in 1784.

The Moghul empire even at the height of its power was helpless on the sea. Akbar with his Central Asian tradition had no appreciation of sea power and actually saw the ocean only after the conquest of Gujerat. The empire was essentially continental except for its outlet at Surat and the smaller sea-ports in Bengal; and the idea of a navy seems never to have struck him and his successors. In the conflicts which the empire had with the European factories at different times, the imperial authorities were powerless to enforce their decrees. The English company's factories at Surat, for example, defied the ban on coral trade from the Red Sea which under the laws of the empire was closed to all foreigners; but Jehangir could do nothing about it. Shah Jehan did build a small coastal navy in Bengal and used it effectively against the Portuguese but by that time the successors of Vasco da Gama had ceased to be a major naval power in the Indian waters. In general the recurring fights between the Moghuls and the naval powers were fights between the elephant and the whale, the one helpless against the other, outside its own element. The imperial authorities had to watch with impotent rage their pilgrim traffic being interfered with, the ships of their merchants pillaged and confiscated on the seas. The European powers, on the other hand, had to put up with the insolence of local officials, interference with their trade and occasional attacks on their factories.

It is also to be remembered that sea power on an oceanic scale became a problem only in the sixteenth century. It is Vasco da Gama's arrival in India that created the problem, for, the earlier exercise of authority on the seas was purely coastal, unless as in the case of Sri Vijaya or the Cholas there were territories on both sides of the sea. The arrival of Europeans in India and in the Pacific raised the problems of bases, fuelling stations and repair facilities. As the movement was from Europe via the Cape to India, the organisation of the route was the first step towards naval power. When the foreigner appeared all of a sudden, India could not realise the significance of what had happened, and was able to put up only a local defence. Further, the historic pressure from the north had turned all attention to security of land frontiers. Never previously had India faced the problem of a control of all the waters washing her shores.

The importance of sea power in relation to Indian development became apparent from the beginning. The monopoly of trade drained the wealth of India to the countries of the West. But more than that, politically it became clear that the sea powers, safe under the protection of the guns from their navy, could not be ejected and would in time, when circumstances permitted, be able to enlarge their hold and increase their influence. It is an established historical fact that as against a well-organised land power, a naval power cannot maintain a land empire; but it is an equally obvious fact that where no such land power exists, the naval bases tend to become the nuclei of empires. For a hundred years the Portuguese with all their might on the sea could not break the power of the Zamorin; nor could the Dutch in the hundred years that followed. When the Moghul empire was still powerful, neither the English nor the Hollanders nor the French could do more than carry on their trade; but when the central authority weakened and some of the provinces became the scene of civil wars, the factories which had concealed their political ambitions were in a position to stand forth and influence events in an effective manner.

CHAPTER XIX

THE BREAK-UP OF THE NATIONAL STATE

In 1794 Poona witnessed a strange and impressive ceremony. The Peshwa, the actual head of the Great Maratha empire, was invested, in circumstances of solemn ceremony, with the insignia of certain dignities conferred on him by the emperor of Delhi. The insignia were received with the tokens of the highest respect, and with suitable formalities indicating the gratitude of the recipient of such imperial favours. The "emperor" whose Khillat was thus received was a prisoner of a servant of the Peshwa, was the sovereign not even of his palace whose sanctity an Afghan adventurer had violated, when he even laid his hand on the descendant of Akbar and had his eyes put out. A prisoner of Scindia, living on the charity of the Marathas, the emperor had been solicited by his captor to honour his master with certain dignities and titles, which the Peshwa thus received in a solemn Durbar.

An even stranger event happened a few years later in 1799 when Srirangapatam was occupied by the forces of the British and of their ally the Nizam, and the usurping Sultan of that State lay dying of honourable wounds in his own fort. The first thing that Mir Alam, the representative of the Nizam with the allied forces, did, was to drive to the Jama Musjid and have the *kutba* read in the name of the shadow emperor of Delhi—a formal protest against Tippu having dared to substitute his own name for that of the Padishah.

The poor emperor of Delhi counted for nothing; but the tradition of Akbar, the idea of the national State had survived, so that the head of the Maratha confederacy which ruled without question most of Hindustan as an independent sovereign power and who held the person of the emperor as prisoner, was honoured to accept a title from him, and the people of Mysore who had never been the subjects of the Moghul empire felt that a wrong had been righted when the *kutba* was read in the emperor's name. The empire by ceasing to be a fact had become an accepted idea.

When Aurongzeb died the Moghul empire extended only up to the Tungabhadra. A martyr to the idea of Indian unity, though not of the national State, he had died fighting for it. But the empire which only his personality held together fell to pieces with surprising rapidity. The usual wars of succession, and the rapid change of emperors gave the State no chance to recover or to exert its authority over the provinces. The one statesman of ability which the Delhi court produced at the time, Asaf Jah Nizam-ul-mulk, after vainly attempting to stem the tide retired to the viceroyalty of the Deccan, which he governed in a state of semi-independence. The Marathas under the guiding genius of Rajaram and Tara Bai had resisted successfully Aurangzeb's last and vain effort to put down Maratha nationalism, and under the Peshwas, the first of whom, Balaji Viswanath, assumed authority on delegation from King Sahu at Satara in 1713, were ready to move forward and bring under their control areas which had till then been under the occupation of the Moghuls. The appointment of Balaji as Peshwa is an important date in Indian history. The capital of the Maratha State was transferred to Poona, the original jagir which saw the growth of Sivaji's power. The new State, freed from the fear of a war of annihilation by the Moghuls, was organised both for settled government at home, and for aggressive adventures in the fertile areas to the north of the Vindhyas. The cabinet of Asta Pradhans became the government of the State and by 1724 Gujerat was already conquered and a military colony settled there under a Maratha general Damaji Rao Gaekwad.

The picture of India in 1725, eighteen years after the death of Aurangzeb, is a strange one. The sway of the empire extended theoretically up to Tanjore, and a Governor of the Carnatic was established at Arcot. In 1724, Nizam-ul-mulk had moved to Hyderabad and assumed the Subaship of the South claiming authority also over the Carnatic. The Marathas, safe in their own homelands, had extended northwards, conquering and annexing Gujerat and planting a colony there. Already in 1714 by agreement with the emperor they were in legitimate occupation of Khandesh, Gondwana and Berar. The Rajput rulers, so long the ornaments of the Delhi court, had withdrawn to their own States, consolidated their principalities and settled down to active government. The ablest among them, Jai Singh of Amber, devoted his talents to the construction of a magnificent city, all in pink, with avenues wider than those which Haussmann conceived for Paris a hundred and thirty years later. He extended his authority over minor princes and jagirdars and even celebrated a sacrifice in the manner of ancient Hindu kings. The Punjab was in a state of disruption, with the Sikh confederacy actively assisting in the process. Imperial authority had totally broken down in that vital province. Sadat Khan had taken over the rich province of Oudh which his nephew Safdar Jung, made Wazir of the empire in 1748, was to turn into an independent State. Murshid Quli, appointed by Aurangzeb Nawab Nazim of the great province of Bengal in 1705, was at the zenith of his power which he transmitted to his son-in-law, Shuja-ud-din Khan. The emperor at Delhi, still the heir of a great and effective tradition and the source of all valid title to authority in India, became less and less the wielder of effective power.

There were also in existence in 1725 a number of fortified places on the coastline of India occupied by foreign merchants. The most important of these, apart from the Portuguese possessions, were Surat, Madras, Masulipatam and Fort William, all centres of great trading activity belonging to the English East India Company which also owned the island of Bombay which had come to Charles II in his dowry; Pondicherry and Chandernagore, where the French were settled; Cochin, Tranquebar and Negapatam and certain stations on the Hugli where the Dutch had settlements. In Surat the company's factory was strongly and solidly built and had withstood the threat of Sivaji. Fort St. George in Madras, no less than Fort William, was a stronghold capable of effective defence especially with the support of a navy. Pondicherry was also well guarded. Behind these fortifications, the foreign merchants, with their accountants, writers and packers lived a life unconnected with the main currents of Indian life, and dealing only with the crowds of banias that collected to do business with them, and not interfering with what was happening around.

The pattern of political life as we see in 1725 is hardly changed with time except for the growing weakness of central authority when in 1739 the shepherd boy who had assumed the title of Nadir Shah and ascended the throne of Persia, invited by the weakness of the central government, and tempted by the fabulous wealth of India, descended on the plains at the head of a great army. There was hardly any resistance as the Punjab had already become a scene of anarchy. The imperial government in great panic and confusion appealed to its great viceroy to come and help: but no help came. Nadir Shah entered Delhi, put a large portion of the population to the sword to satisfy his whim, with ironic courtesy exchanged in token of eternal brotherliness his astrakhan for the Moghul crown with enormous hanging emeralds, and quietly appropriated to himself the treasures of Delhi, including the Kohinoor and the Peacock Throne. Nadir Shah seems to have been a born humorist for on his departure he issued letters the

Hindu rulers advising them "to walk in the path of submission and obedience to our dear brother" (the despoiled Mohammed Shah) and threatening "to blot them out of the pages of the book of creation" if they persisted in rebellion.

After this becoming gesture of Islamic solidarity the Shah marched back to Persia. Delhi lay prostrate. The imperial treasury had no money; the army did not exist, and the wretched emperor, on whom the torn and decayed mantle of Akbar had descended, wrote letters couched in terms of command to his overgrown viceroy vainly supplicating them for help. The regulator of the empire, Nizam-ul-mulk, while not renouncing his allegiance, proclaimed his intention of considering the Suba of the Deccan a hereditary possession of his family. The nominal prime minister, Vazir Sadat Khan, followed suit and founded his dynasty which was to write new chapters in the history of human degradation in Lucknow. The greatest threat, however, came from the Marathas. Peshwa Baji Rao, who had succeeded his father and had been invested with full powers of a Regent by Sahu, watched with growing interest the state of affairs in the north. In 1740, the Marathas took the final decision to fight for the succession to the Moghul empire.

In 1723, Baji Rao had decided that the future of the Marathas lay in attacking Delhi and assuming the government of Hindustan. "Let us strike at the trunk of the withering tree and the branches will fall themselves." "Thus, should the Maratha flag fly from the Krishna to the Indus," he is reported to have declared in council. What lured them to the north was not merely the chimera of imperial power but the feeling, never absent from the mind of the orthodox, of recovering the sacred places of Hinduism, especially Banaras, from the control of the Mussalmans. To reach the Ganges and to re-establish Hindu authority over the sacred cities of Kashi, Prayag and Gaya seemed to the Chitpavan Brahmins in Poona not merely good religion but good politics. With Baji Rao, Hindu Dharma was an important factor and his idealism found support in the great Hindu leader of the north of the time, Jai Singh II of Amber, the astronomer king, and among the champions of Hinduism in Bundelkhand. Baji Rao crossed the Narbada and reached the vicinity of the imperial city, but turned back to meet Nizam-ul-mulk, who was marching north to the support of the emperor. In the battle of Bhopal the Nizam was defeated and he returned quietly to his capital.

In the results that followed, this decision of Baji Rao was most momentous. If the Maratha power had consolidated itself in the south and organised a national State south of the Vindhyas in the period between 1730 and 1740 they might have conserved their strength and developed along other lines. As it was, they marched north without safeguarding either their flanks or their rear, allowed Nizam-ul-mulk to consolidate his territory, and Hyder Ali to organise the Mysore State. If Sivaji's plan had been followed, South India would have been organised as a new Vijayanagar before the Maratha cavalry expanded northwards. That decision was not made. Baji Rao marched north. From their homelands, the Marathas fanned out in all directions. Holkar established himself at Indore and Scindia planted the Maratha standard at Gwalior. Lesser generals received jagirs at other important centres. The Bhonsles spread out from Nagpur and from there conquered the province of Orissa and the Maratha cavalry reached even the frontiers of Bengal. Hindustan became a happy hunting ground for the Deccani horsemen.

The government at Poona did not have at its disposal an effective machinery for administering so vast an area. The personnel required for the effective government of the territories over which the Maratha cavalry spread so quickly could not be commanded by the authorities in Poona, and, therefore, the system of great jagirs had to be evolved. Small military colonies were planted at important centres, and Gwalior, Indore, Nagpur, Dewas and Dhar became cantonment areas under the great generals who also were put in charge of territorial administrations. In short, they became military viceroyalties and a crude system of government was thus established in the areas that passed under the control of the Marathas.

Soon, Delhi itself came within the sphere of their influence. In 1757 they attacked Delhi and dictated a peace to the puppet emperor. Raghunath Rao, their general, attacked Lahore and captured it in 1758 and annexed Punjab to their dominions, and carried their flag to the fortress of Attock. But their hold on the Punjab was weak, and their forces were dissipated in vain attacks on garrisons in the Gangetic plain. These aggressive activities in the Punjab brought down Ahmed Shah Durrani, the Afghan king, and a trial of strength became inevitable. The Afghan and Indian forces met in 1761 at Panipat. The battle went against the Marathas. The carnage was immense. The report to the Peshwa stated. "Two pearls were dissolved, twenty-seven gold mohurs have been lost and of the silver and copper the total cannot be cast up." As a defeat it was complete, though the Marathas recovered soon enough from its effects. After his victory Ahmad Shah went back to Kabul and the Marathas fell back on Gwalior to reappear again in Delhi soon afterwards.

The importance of the battle of Panipat has been greatly overrated. Its true significance lay in the fact that it stopped Maratha expansion into the Punjab, and perhaps gave the British in Bengal a much-needed respite, and Hyder Ali in Mysore an opportunity to consolidate his conquests. But by confining Maratha activities to the area south of Delhi, it enabled them to strengthen their hold on Central India and convert it into a proper dominion which under the descendants of the Scindias, Holkars and the Pawars it continued to be for nearly two hundred years.

It had another political effect which passed unnoticed at the time. Till 1761, the wars in Hindustan were commanded by chiefs sent out from Poona. Sadashiv Rao Bhao commanded at Panipat. When the recovery came it was the local viceroys that carried out Maratha policy—a system which weakened the central government and led to the disintegration of the empire, when it had to fight the power of the British.

After 1761 the Maratha power in the north became stabilised under the great feudatories, still obeying the mandates of Poona and following a unified policy dictated from the headquarters. The generals emerged by slow degrees as dynasts and Madhoji Scindia who escaped from Panipat when he was a stripling, succeeded to the command of the Maratha forces in the territories immediately to the south of Delhi. The case of Holkar was similar and around Indore in the most fertile regions of Malwa he built up a State. The sprawling territories of Nagpur extended across the peninsula to Orissa and included the forest regions of Bundelkhand.

In the south also events were shaping towards a great transformation. Nizam-ul-mulk, the regulator of the State, who had refused to regulate its affairs and had left the capital for the security of his southern viceroyalty where he saw the opportunity of carying out a kingdom for himself, died peacefully in Hyderabad in 1748. Anwardin, the Nawab of Carnatic, followed him shortly afterwards. A so-called war of succession followed in which for the first time the French, who had a settlement at Pondicherry, and the English, from their settlement at Madras, gave support to the rival candidates. The French settlement was under Dupleix, who had been appointed governor of Pondicherry in 1742. A man gifted with boundless imagination and a taste for grandiose schemes, but with no capacity for execution beyond an undoubted ability for tortuous intrigues in degenerate courts, Dupleix showed soon after his accession to power a desire to interfere in the affairs of others. As war was going on between England and France in Europe, La Bourdonnais, the French governor of Mauritius, had arrived in Indian waters with the object of attacking English shipping. He succeeded in driving the English squadron back into the Hugli and then in capturing Madras itself. The French leaders fell out after this. La Bourdonnais agreed to return the town to the British on the payment of a ransom, but the governor, Dupleix, repudiated the treaty, and took measures which clearly indicated his hostility to the English company. When, therefore, Dupleix interfered in the succession to the Carnatic governorship, for which there were two claimants—Mohammed Ali, destined to become famous as one of the shadiest characters in history, and Chanda Saheb—the English at Madras realised that if political influence passed on to the French their own position in South India would become untenable. Dupleix installed Chanda Saheb on the seat of Carnatic governorship receiving in return a Moghul title, a profitable jagir and magnificent presents, an example which was not lost on an enterprising but unscrupulous clerk at Fort St. George by the name of Robert Clive. The English company, therefore, interfered to support the rival claims of Mohammed Ali, captured by a bold stroke the fort of Arcot, which surrendered without a fight to the motley force that accompanied Clive. The capture of Arcot meant nothing, but a more significant victory was achieved when Clive withstood a siege of fifty-three days in conditions of great severity. Dupleix saw the work for which he had intrigued break down before his eyes. He retaliated with an attack on Madras, which, however, proved abortive, as the French and their allies broke up camp before Clive had even arrived. A British puppet was installed safely as the Moghul Governor.

The French schemes vanished into thin air and except for the enormous financial gains of Dupleix and a grossly exaggerated fame in history for him as a statesman, the French had indeed but little to show for their troubles. With their failure in the Carnatic they had also lost the game in Hyderabad. Muzzafar Jung, the French candidate to the Nizamship, had obliged Dupleix with a grant of the hinterland of Fort David. Nazir Jung his opponent whom the English supported was murdered. The grateful Muzzafar made his ally Dupleix the governor of the South over the lands extending from the Kistna to Cape Comorin, in fact the legal successor to the Vijayanagar empire, over large areas of which, e.g., the Mysore territories, the Moghuls had exercised neither legal nor factual authority. Chanda Saheb was to have been his feudatory. But Clive's intervention upset all this. After this the French in India only continued to intrigue and never played an effective part. When later, as in the case of Hyder Ali, the French forces tried to co-operate with the enemies of the British, it was only in a subordinate capacity and not as political and military principals. The English on the other hand had become, by the victories they had achieved in the Carnatic, a political force. They had realised their strength in warfare against the undisciplined forces of the country powers. They had also discovered a method by which political power could be exercised through puppet monarchs. In fact Indirect Rule, which the British empire was to develop in later years, had come into being by the accidental circumstances of intervention in Arcot.

Elsewhere also the pattern of things was changing. In the table-land of Mysore where a viceroyalty of the Vijayanagar empire had been stabilised into a State under the dynasty of Wodeyars, a new military power had taken birth. Taking advantage of the internal dissensions in the capital, Hyder Ali, the Naik of Dindigul, had assumed the duties of commander-in-chief and had in a short time become the source of all power in the State, though under the cover of being an officer of the Hindu ruler. The military genius of Hyder became evident enough when out of the chaos, which preceded his usurpation of authority, he evolved not merely an ordered State but a disciplined and powerful army.

In 1757 the picture that India presented to an observer was that of different forces taking shape, not one of which had the appearance of finality or stability. The Marathas had covered the whole of North India up to the Ganges, lured by the sacred places of Hinduism and the prestige and authority of Delhi, but except in their home provinces in the Deccan, they were not a stabilising force but only added to disorder and confusion. In the great provinces of the Moghul empire, administration had broken down to a degree which was altogether unparalleled. The reasons for the great breakdown, which resulted in so much chaos and anarchy were not far to seek. Akbar had centralised the administration of the Moghul empire. The provinces were governed directly by officers sent down from Delhi. Under the ancient Hindu empires, local administrations continued in the main in the hands of Rajas who had accepted the suzerainty of the empire and obeyed the orders from the Centre, but carried on without any serious diminution of their prestige or authority. When the strong hand of the Centre was removed, the local rulers regained their independence, and consequently there was no breakdown or anarchy. The centralisation of Akbar added to the strength, resources and prosperity of the empire. But once the Central authority ceased to function, there was no local authority which received the unquestioned loyalty of the people. The bureaucratic administration of the provincial governors, never indeed efficient or strong, counted for little. With no dynastic loyalties, succession inevitably became a matter of dispute and the viceroys, while trying to convert their offices to hereditary princedoms, could count neither on the inherited loyalty of the people nor on the support of strong armies. Thus in the great provinces of the empire, Deccan, Carnatic and Bengal, the administration was nominal and of the weakest character when the great personalities who had originally come down from Delhi, Nizam-ul-mulk, Anwardin and Alivardi Khan, disappeared from the stage.

CHAPTER XX

THE FIGHT FOR EMPIRE

ALIVARDI KHAN, viceroy of the great province of Bengal, died in 1756. His successor Siraj-ud-Dowla was a young man, who under normal times might have died after a life of useful service to the empire. But the times were different. He had neither a valid hereditary claim nor an effective official right to the post he occupied. He was merely the candidate of a faction. Also new forces of which he had no knowledge had come into existence which required able and more experienced hands to handle them. The growth of European trade in the main port towns of India had brought into prominence a class of bania merchants who were fabulously wealthy and were in close contact with the European factories, for the companies' enormous business passed through their hands. They were mainly Gujeratis in Surat, Chettis in Madras and Marwaris in Bengal. The last named, residents of distant Rajputana, were bania merchants who had been attracted to Calcutta by the new possibilities opened to them for trade by the growth of English, French and Dutch interests on the banks of the Hugli.

The Bengal factories so far had had a chequered career. Under Job Charnock, who was a coarse and wilful but strong man, "deeply tinged with native habits of thought and action" (having married a Hindu widow whose Sati he had prevented), the trade flourished and the factory attained some prominence. But they were foolish enough to quarrel with Aurangzeb and suffered for the time the loss of the Bengal trade. In 1690, Charnock founded the city of Calcutta where, in the words of Hamilton, he "now reigned more absolutely than a Raja and only wanted much of their humanity." In 1696, leave was obtained to fortify Calcutta and the company also obtained a Zamindari, thus becoming both a landlord and a merchant under the Moghul governor.

During the first half of the eighteenth century the position of Calcutta improved and the banias crowded into it, as the trade of the province was truly enormous. The company's position vis-a-vis the Nawab Nazim of Bengal was that of the humblest servant, for, in 1715, we see John Russell, the president, in addressing the

Moghul governor describing himself as "the smallest particle of dust," "whose forehead rubbed on the ground," "on receiving the word of command." The company's prosperity increased further when an imperial firman permitted them to buy land and they were confirmed in their Zamindari. Under Alivardi Khan the province enjoyed peace and settled government and the business of the company and of the great Indian merchant princes who traded with them flourished greatly. When Siraj-ud-Dowla became Nawab Nazim, he had succeeded to a situation which it would have taken a far acuter mind to grasp and deal with. That situation was that while the Moghul viceroyalty conferred only the title to power the actual authority had passed to the great Hindu merchant princes and their allies in the fort that dominated the Hugli. A quarrel arose between the company and the Nawab about the fortification they were erecting. In the fighting that ensued Calcutta was captured and the English who had remained back imprisoned. This is the story of the Black Hole, evidence in regard to which is conflicting and scanty. Howell, an early expert in war propaganda through horror stories, was a known liar and clearly the incident was exaggerated out of all proportion, though no doubt the Nawab was not particularly kind in his treatment of the prisoners. A British force under Watson and Clive, whom the defence of Arcot had made famous, arrived soon after in Bengal as war had broken out with the French. There was as yet no quarrel with the Nawab whose neutrality the English were anxious to secure. But the Hindu merchants in Calcutta and Murshidabad had made up their minds to engineer a change. Jagat Seth, the first of the great succession of Marwari millionaires, whose wealth is still legendary, had been insulted by Siraj-ud-Dowla and he offered through Ami Chand, another Marwari in close relation with the company, to have the Nawab replaced. An alliance was struck between the head of European baniadom, the English company, and the Marwari merchants who commanded the wealth of Bengal. The Nawab's fate was sealed.

Events moved forward rapidly to the strange climax of Plassey which is popularly said to mark the establishment of the British empire in India. The Nawab was betrayed, his side losing only five hundred men as Mir Jafar made no attempt to fight. It is to the Seth's house that the victorious commanders adjourned to celebrate the victory and there it was that Ami Chand was told that he had been cheated. Plassey, unimportant as a battle, was politically important as the company became the Zamindar of 24 Parganas, nearly nine hundred square miles of territory to the south of Calcutta, and became also the king-maker in Bengal. The legal position had not been changed, as the territory was held only under the normal tenure and the Nawab Nazim continued to exercise nominal sway. The puppet Nawab ruled, however, only in name and from 1757 to 1772 for a period of fifteen years we have the unparalleled instance of a country subjected to organised loot and plunder by a mercantile company and its servants, assisted and encouraged by the Hindu commercial classes who shared the loot with them. There is no instance known in history where a great province was swept so clean of its wealth. The Nawab's treasury was there to be requisitioned at the whim of the Council. Every servant of the company and everyone who claimed the protection of the company roamed about at will and traded free of customs duties which others had to pay. In a remarkable document some of the leading Bengali Zamindars petitioned the Council and stated:

> "The factories of the English gentlemen are many and many of their Gumasthas are in all places and in every village almost throughout the province of Bengal. . . . They trade . . . in all kinds of grain, linen and whatever other commodities are provided in the country. In order to purchase these articles they force their money on the ryots and having by these oppressive methods bought the goods at a low rate, they oblige the inhabitants and shopkeepers to take them at a high price, exceeding what is paid in the markets. They do not pay the customs due to the Circar. . . . There is now scarce anything of worth left in the country."

In 1765, the company's forces met and defeated at Buxar the troops of the Moghul, and Clive, who had come out as governor of Bengal, obtained from the emperor the diwani or the right to administer the revenues of Bengal, Bihar and Orissa. By this act, the East India Company became in effect a sovereign power on the mainland of India.

Clive was a gangster who had achieved glory, a confessed forger, liar and cheat, whose military achievements compared to those of the generals of the time were wholly ridiculous. The State he founded and administered for seven years was nothing more than a robber State, the one object of which was to extract as much as possible from the territories it was supposed to administer. English historians prefer to draw a veil over the period between 1757 and 1774 but it has to be emphasised that at no period in the long history of India including the reigns of Toramana and Mohammed Tughlaq did the people of any province suffer so great a misery as the people of Bengal did in the era of Clive.

Elsewhere also conditions were changing. The Marathas recovered soon from their defeat at Panipat, and their authority was now well established in Hindustan. Madhoji Scindia, who had succeeded to the command of Gwalior, was slowly building up a State which in a short time was destined to dominate Delhi and control the Gangetic valley up to Allahabad and Kora. Raghoji Bhonsle was no less unmindful of his interests in the Nagpur area, and the events in Bengal had helped both these chiefs to realise that great changes were taking place which required constant vigilance.

The experiment of putting a saint to govern an infant predatory State which had hardly established itself was risky enough; but when the saint was also a young widow, and the State itself was set in surroundings of unparalleled anarchy, it might have been thought that the experiment was foredoomed to disaster. And yet this is what the Marathas did at Indore. Ahalyabai who was selected for the regency of the Holkar State, was an undisputed saint, who was canonised by universal acclamation in her own lifetime. The State which she was called on to rule had hardly been established for twenty years, and the people over whom she was to rule pretended to no loyalty to the military authority which she represented. Her State was surrounded by those who were bitterly opposed to the power of Holkar. Yet, the experiment succeeded. And we have the authority of Sir John Malcolm, diplomatist, administrator, historian and one of the leading actors in the drama of the era immediately following, that the success of Ahalyabai in the internal administration of her dominions was truly wonderful. The fame of the piety of Ahalyabai Holkar was enough to keep even plunderers and free-booters away. People in distant parts, far away from her own dominions, revered her name, and the hold she established over her people, alien though she was to Central India, was such that even the sins of the Holkars have been redeemed in a measure by her saintliness.

In the south, Hyder Ali had consolidated his power in Mysore and had even dictated peace to the company at the gates of Madras. The Nizam, shorn of much of his territory, was still an important power, with considerable French forces at his command. In the Maratha homelands life flowed normally.

The appointment of Warren Hastings as the governor-general of Bengal may be taken as the beginning of England's fight for supremacy in India. Hastings was not one of those, like Clive, who had graduated in chicanery and experimented in fraud. Personally honest, though unscrupulous, without any ethical or moral considerations when the requirement of the State and the safety of his tenure were concerned, he was a wise and far-seeing statesman, liberal in his administration and sympathetic to the people. His regime as governor-general saved the Company. The country powers, the Marathas and Hyder Ali, had awakened to the threat which the new State in Bengal meant to them and Hastings had `to meet numerous combinations, all potentially dangerous, to the Company as a State. The Bombay government had roused the watchful Marathas whose policy was then being guided by the great Nana Fadnavis, the last great statesman of independent India. The company's forces surrendered disgracefully, repudiated their engagements, tried again their strength against the Marathas, but failed to obtain any results and were content to sign a treaty which left the two powers at peace for twenty years. When Hastings retired from office the danger to the Company's political power had passed; more, he had by cautious diplomacy generated in the mind of the two of the most powerful Maratha chieftains ambitions of founding independent States. Madhoji Scindia's vaulting ambition was encouraged and in the treaty of Salbai, his semi-independence was recognised by the governor-general. With the Bhonsle Raja of Nagpur, Hastings kept up a friendly correspondence, weakening the allegiance of that officer to the central power. But while Nana Fadnavis held the reins at Poona these intrigues did not bear fruit but the seed of dissension had been sown which was to bear a rich harvest in years to come.

Madhoji Scindia was the leading Maratha chief in the north and it was through his good offices that the treaty of Salbai had been negotiated. After this diplomatic achievement which strengthened his own position, Scindia began to organise battalions on the company's model with the help of a remarkable Savoyard, Comte de Boigne. With these new forces he held the whole of Hindustan in fee, broke the power of the Rajput rulers, and occupied Delhi itself, taking under custody the blinded emperor Shah Alam, a pitiable figure living in penury in surroundings of shadowy magnificence. It was at this time that he obtained from the emperor the title of viceregent of the empire for the Peshwa, and went to Poona as the Moghul's representative to invest his master with the insignia and khillat, which was done after obtaining the consent of the puppet Raja of Satara. Madhoji died in 1794 and was succeeded by his nephew Daulat Rao. The next year witnessed the last act of Maratha greatness, when at Kharda the united forces of the confederacy under its great chiefs overwhelmed the Nizam's army, trained by Raymond and led by the Nizam's Wazir.

A curious incident during the administration of Hastings deserves notice and that is the Sanyasi rebellion. The order of Sanyasis was organised by Sankara in the ninth century and till Akbar's time seems to have taken no interest in politics. During the early years of Akbar's reign, armed Muslim Faqirs attacked and killed a number of Hindu Sanyasis and though the matter was represented to the emperor by Madhu Sudan Saraswati, the authorities afforded him no redress. Madhu Sudan Saraswati then initiated a large number of Kshatriyas in seven out of the ten orders (the three excluded ones being Tirtha, Asrama and Saraswati) and placed on them the duty of defending religion and dharma. In Moghul times we have numerous instances of conflicts in which these Hindu Templars fought the Muslim Faqirs. When the anarchy, misgovernment and plunder of Bengal reached its height in the years following the establishment of the robber State by Clive, the Sanyasis rose in rebellion and were put down only with great difficulty. This strange incident showed the awakening life of Hinduism in the anarchy that fell over Bengal with the breakdown of Moghul government and the assumption of British power.

Cornwallis who succeeded Hastings consolidated the administration, evolved order out of the chaos in which his predecessors had left the government of Bengal and introduced into the affairs of the company a non-mercantile attitude which gave it a prestige and authority which the bania traditions of a trading corporation did not possess. His permanent settlement brought peace to distracted Bengal. The conquest of an empire was not his object, nor that of his successor, Lord Teignmouth. But with Wellesley a new era begins. Cornwallis had reformed the administration. Fifteen years of peace had restored the prosperity of the company and their service began to attract men of a superior calibre. The Kirkpatricks, the Metcalfes, the Malcolms, and the Elphinstones of the generation, sent out to India by the Scottish clannishness of Dundas, were men of a different stamp from the miserable crowd of corrupt adventurers who had adorned the service of the company in the time of Clive. With such suitable instruments in his hand Wellesley was in a position to play at high politics. In a short campaign the governor-general reduced the power of Mysore and exiled its usurping dynasty. After two years of low intrigue meant to heighten the discord in the Maratha camp, already at loggerheads after the death of Nana Fadnavis, the power of Sivaji's empire was destroyed in the battles of Assaye and Laswari and the Peshwa reduced to the position of a subordinate ally. By 1803, Britain had become the paramount power in India, with such Indian rulers as were left to rule their own territories looking up to the company's authorities in Calcutta for favour.

The Moghul empire had vanished. The descendant of Akbar exercised his sovereign powers within the city and surroundings of Delhi under advice from a British Resident. In this capacity he developed a great trade in titles, for, with the loss of his power, the doctrine of the national State had found its consummation. There was no ruler in India in 1803 who did not accept the sovereignty of Delhi. The descendant of Rana Pratap was a tributary to *Ali Jah,* Dowlat Rao Scindia. The ruler of far-off Travancore, where no Mussalman conquerer had ever trodden, the claimant to Chera succession, sported with respect the very minor honour of Shamsher Jung awarded to him by the Nawab of the Carnatic. The East India Company, the real sovereign of practically the whole of India outside the Punjab, claimed its authority legally under Moghul firmans and called itself the East India Company *Bahadur.* In fact, the doctrine of the unity of India was taken over by the British from the disembodied idea of a national State which the Moghuls represented at the beginning of the nineteenth century.

The glittering noblemen, who succeeded one to the other at regular intervals to the gadi at Fort William, deposed rulers, annexed principalities and retired to the obscurity of the House of Lords, are, from the point of view of Indian history, but fleeting shadows on her stage. From the point of view of the history of the English in India, they are no doubt important; but in the context of Indian history, these governors-general signify nothing. The bare political facts may be summarily stated. In 1812, the company's trading activities in India were terminated by Parliament and the East India Company became merely a machinery by which the British Parliament administered India. In the period between 1813-1818, the Marquis of Hastings reduced the power of Scindia and Holkar by bringing the States of Rajputana under British political control and also annexed the territories of the Peshwa in the Deccan. The whole territory of India to the east of the Sutlej passed under the sway of the company, though over much of it the government at Calcutta exercised only a suzerainty through the Indian rulers who had been brought into the system of subsidiary alliance which Wellesley had perfected. By the Charter of 1833, the last vestiges of the company as a trading corporation were eliminated and the responsibility for civilised government in India was accepted by the British which led to the appointment of Macaulay as law member of the Council of the Governor-General. A scheme for the education of Indians was also considered and given effect to. In 1845-48, the Punjab where the Sikhs under a notable ruler, Ranjit Singh, had established a great military power, was annexed in the anarchy that followed that ruler's death. The territories of Oudh, towards which the authorities at Calcutta had cast covetous eyes for many decades, were also annexed and brought under direct rule. From the Indus to the Brahmaputra, from the Himalayas to Cape Comorin, in the whole of the traditional territory of Bharata Varsha, the Union Jack flew in unquestioned supremacy. The unity of India which the sacred writings of the Hindus had postulated centuries before Christ, but which neither Asoka nor Akbar was able to achieve, and which the Marathas had not even conceived, had in fact come into being. The doctrine of the national State which the mind of India accepted in the eighteenth century was realised through the force of British arms.

Two out of the governors-general during the half century between Wellesley and the great rebellion deserve mention: Lord William Bentinck and the Marquis of Dalhousie. Bentinck was the governor-general who abolished Sati, the first act of a social reform by legislation in Hinduism. Dalhousie was a masterful personality remembered now only for his numerous annexations, especially of Oudh. But his achievements in the sphere of administration are more notable than those of any other governor-general or viceroy. The Central Legislative Council of India owed its existence to him. The first railway line was laid by him. The first telegraph line was due to his direct initiative and the half-anna postage was his reform. The great Ganges Canal, the first of the mighty irrigation schemes, was his handiwork. The Grand Trunk Road in its modern shape was begun by him. In fact politically and administratively, Dalhousie is the greatest of India's proconsuls. His humane interests were no less notable. At his own personal cost he maintained the Women's College which his colleague Bethune had founded. The great Roorkee Engineering College owes its existence to him. India owes a heavy debt of gratitude to this great Scotsman.

Underneath the placid surface of Anglo-Indian administration other forces were taking shape. The dispossessed classes still had great prestige with the masses. The Muslims of upper India felt legitimately that from a ruling class they had in one generation become a dispossessed and uninfluential population. Of the great empire of the Moghuls, only the king in Delhi remained as a pitiable pensioner, even his innocent trade in titles having been prohibited (1830), and his dignity humiliated by the authority exercised in the capital itself by the Resident.

The Suba of Oudh, raised to the status of a kingdom early in the century, had been the sole survival of and the continuing testimony to the greatness of Islam in India. In spite of the opression, misrule and obvious degeneration, Oudh represented to the Mussalmans of North India the greatness of Islamic rule. With its annexation the last vestiges of Muslim authority had vanished and from Delhi to Murshidabad the Muslims felt that their sun had indeed set.

The Marathas in North India had also not contemplated this transfer of power with equanimity. Their position was no doubt different. The great Houses of Scindia and Holkar still held vast tracts of North India in sovereignty. It was the annexation of Satara, Nagpur and Jhansi that they felt as irretrievable blows to their prestige. The two great people who had lost the empire of India were in a sullen mood and the disaffection soon manifested itself in an open rebellion which began as a mutiny of three Indian regiments in Meerut (10th May, 1857). Within forty-eight hours Delhi had been occupied and Bahadur Shah the Moghul, proclaimed Emperor of India—the last act of the national State. The whole of North India excepting the Punjab, especially Oudh and the Gangetic valley, threw off the British yoke. It was a general disorder that followed, not an organised rebellion under a government whose authority was accepted by all. At different places different leaders held authority each on his own and only nominally subordinate to the emperor. In Delhi, itself there was no unity of leadership, Mirza Moghul and Bakht Khan quarrelling about their right to command. But the disorders engulfed practically the whole of Hindustan. During the first four months the British authorities, taken by surprise, were paralysed and unable to act. If during that period a reasonable Central government could have been established and the activities of the rebels co-ordinated, the British would have found it difficult to maintain their position in the interior and they could have been compelled to withdraw to their coastal fortifications. In the absence of any such co-ordination the great rebellion became merely a matter of local uprisings which the centrally directed campaign of the British authorities had but little difficulty in overcoming in time.

It is true that all the leaders of the rebellion came from among the great dispossessed: but all were united in the object they had in view: the expulsion of the British and the recovery of national independence. In that sense the "mutiny" was no mutiny at all, but a great national uprising. That large areas and powerful princes kept aside from the movement does not in any way detract from its national character, for clearly they were waiting on events and after the first enthusiasm, it was plain enough that the rebellion had little chance of success. Quislings there were in plenty, notably Salar Jung of Hyderabad, but neither he nor anyone else would have found it possible to restrain the enthusiasm of the people if the leaders of the mutiny had organised a Central government and instead of besieging small garrisons as at Lucknow had won victories against British forces. This they were unable to do and the rebellion actually fizzled out.

The movement produced some remarkable leaders: Tantia Topi, Azimulla Khan, Lakshmi Bai of Jhansi, and Khan Bahadur Khan. The only serious campaign of the war was against Tantia Topi, in whom the Marathas had produced a leader of ability, who in conjunction with the heroic Rani of Jhansi, a truly noble figure in the history of the nineteenth century, fought well-ordered battles. For the rest it was a question of hunting down rebel groups. With the defeat of the combined forces of Tantia and Lakshmi Bai, the military aspect of the rebellion ended. The White Terror that followed was mainly political meant to strike fear in the heart of Indians so that another such rising might not take place.

The mutiny finds an unusually large place in British histories of India, mainly because of the Great Fear it generated in the minds of the British at the time, and the permanent danger to their position which the uprising disclosed. The authorities recognised that the maintenance of power in India by a small racial minority, unconnected with the people and strangers to them at all times, required overwhelming superiority of force, constant vigilance, and the acceptance by the subject people of a moral superiority which for a long time went under the name of prestige. Racial solidarity had to be created and maintained. A racial religion was the result with all its paraphernalia, pilgrimage centres like the Cawnpore Well and the Lucknow Residency, and its temples, the ugly mutiny memorials which occupy a prominent place in every city, and its saints and martyrs. On the Indian side also, the mutiny loomed large. The rebels had been put down with a heavy hand. The atrocities of the White Terror rankled long in Indian minds and poisoned the relationship of the two races for decades to come.

Seen in true historic perspective, the mutiny is important only from two points of view. In the first place it was the last effort of the old order to regain national independence and honour, and though stained by cruelty, it was a heroic effort of a dispossessed people to reassert their national dignity. In the second place, it is the Great Divide in modern Indian history, as the policy, practice and ideals of the government that followed differed fundamentally from the government of the company which it displaced. The Crown took over the government of India in 1858, and the East India Company vanished from the stage of history.

If one were asked to name three Englishmen from the pre-mutiny period, who are likely to be remembered in Indian history, as different from the history of the English in India, the choice is not likely to fall on the governors-general, commanders, or administrators whose names now loom large in Anglo-Indian text-books but on Edmund Burke, William Jones and Macaulay. Of these Burke had never even visited India; but the moral indignation which one of the greatest minds of the time felt and expressed in undying words against the oppression, tyranny and corruption by his countrymen in India can well be claimed, as Morely does claim, to have put an end to a period when moral considerations did not enter into the government of India. Burke's voice which resounds through history was raised not solely against the high crimes of the company's most distinguished governor-general but it was raised in the interest of justice to the people of India. The epic quality both of his sympathy towards the people of India and of his hatred of oppression, and the moral indignation that he voiced changed the course of history, for since then a moral tone comes into Indian administration and the robber State of Clive dies an unmourned death. The tribe of Benfields and Macphersons, who lived on the ruin of Indian peasants, and the officers who lived by the plunder of the country and returned home as Nabobs to corrupt English public life were no longer the power they were before the impeachment of Warren Hastings. Burke is the father of the liberal tradition in India.

Sir William Jones held high office but his claim to an honoured place in Indian history is based on more permanent factors. Arriving in India in 1783 he along with Colebrooke establish in the very next year the Bengal Asiatic Society. It was through him and Charles Wilkins, the translator of the *Bhagavad Gita*, that the treasures of Indian literature came first to be known to the world. Jones' translation of *Sakuntala* may be said to mark the beginning of European interest in oriental culture; a movement the full effects of which were to become evident as time went on. Today it can fairly be claimed that the literature, art and philosophy of India and the East have become the common inheritance of civilised man, though its permeation into the texture of European thought has been slow and not very widespread. But the number of learned societies that exist in every European country, to study, edit and interpret Indian texts is in itself proof that the work of "Asiatic Jones" in translating *Sakuntala* and in founding the Asiatic Society of Bengal were acts of momentous significance.

Apart from opening the door to Western appreciation of Indian culture, Sir William Jones' work had very remarkable effects, on India itself. To a people who had sunk so low as the people of Bengal had in the eighteenth century, the work of Jones and his Orientalists came as a balm. The national self-esteem of India which had touched its depths at the end of the eighteenth century received its first aid to recovery in the appreciation which Indian literature received at the hands of the most renowned men in Europe. Jones can well be acclaimed in this sense as one of the fathers of the Great Recovery which followed in the nineteenth century.

Thomas Babington Macaulay is not a popular name with educated India and yet on a true appreciation of values, it will be seen that it is the genius of this man, narrow in his Europeanism, self-satisfied in his sense of English greatness, that gives life to modern India as we know it. He was India's new Manu, the spirit of modern law incarnate. The legal system under which India has lived for over a hundred years and within whose steel frame her social, political and economic development has taken place is the work of Macaulay. An examination of his *Minutes* which have recently been edited will show how even those elementary principles of law which we now take as axiomatic, e.g., that the accused is to be considered innocent unless proved guilty, had to be fought for and established by him against the opinion of his colleagues. The establishment of the great principle of equality of all before law—in a country where under the Hindu doctrines a Brahmin could not be punished on the evidence of Sudras and even punishment varied according to caste and where, according to Muslim law, an unbeliever's testimony could not be accepted against a Muslim—was itself a legal revolution of the first importance. Few indeed who compare Macaulay's code with its great predecessors, whether Manu, Justinian or Napoleon, will be ready to cavil at the claim that the Penal Code as drafted by the Law Commission under his guidance was a great improvement on previous systems. The imposing and truly magnificent legal structure of India under whose protection four hundred million people live is indeed a worthy monument to Macaulay's genius.

A no less important contribution to the development of Indian life which Macaulay made was his famous minute on education. Divested of the narrow prejudices against Hindu civilisation and of the shelf of books for which he was prepared to exchange the entire treasures of oriental literature and the cheap rhetoric about "seas of treacle and seas of butter" which marred that famous document, its main thesis of an education based on the New Learning and through the medium of English was, in the circumstances of the time, the most beneficently revolutionary decision taken by the British government of India. The exaggerations in Macaulay's minute need not concern us now, but some idea of the importance of the decision which was forced on the British government may be gained by considering what the results of the alternative policy would have been. The particularisms based on vernaculars would have grown so greatly as to break up even the idea of an Indian unity. Much of the New Learning on which India's Great Recovery has been based would not have been available to us. No doubt the scientific development of the West would have reached us secondhand, but participation in the scientific work of the world would have been but a distant ideal. By going in for education in English, India joined a world community. Besides, what was the alternative? Even the most advanced Indian languages of the time, excepting Sanskrit and Persian, had not reached the level of literary standard for secondary education. Education up to university standards would have been impossible without decades of preparation, which would have required an army of men trained in English and familiar with the new learning of the West. This, after all, is what Macaulay's system has done. It has developed the Indian languages to standards in which a university education is now becoming possible. But without the universities teaching in English and producing the army of workers, such a development would hardly have been possible. The great colleges, universities and schools of India, which have attained a position of some eminence in the world of learning, are the direct result of Macaulay's system.

Another significant contribution of the period was the awakened interest in Indian history and the rediscovery of Buddhism. For seven hundred years Indian history had been considered as starting only from the invasions of Mahmud and the records of history were only what the Muslim historians had left behind. The great work on Indian history, the deciphering of inscriptions, the collection of material from foreign sources, the reconstruction of the lost pages of India's annals through numismatics, etc., belong to a later period. But Duff's *History of the Marathas,* Wilk's *History of Mysore,* and Tod's *Annals of Rajasthan,* all written by officers of the company directly connected with contemporary events created an interest in historical studies among Indians and a pride in their past which were in time to produce remarkable results.

CHAPTER XXI

THE GREAT RECOVERY

By 1848, India had been unified. Ten years later the Crown and the British Parliament assumed responsibility for the direct government of India. The period that followed, extending to very nearly a century, can well be described as the period of the Great Recovery. Before we survey the outlines of the movement, which has given to India her present place in the world, the features of Anglo-Indian administration during the time may be briefly alluded to.

During the time of the Company a great administrative machinery had been gradually built up, the foundations of which were laid by Cornwallis. The period that followed the mutiny witnessed the growth and development of this administrative machine which has no parallel in the history of the world. Neither the Byzantine nor the Chinese empires, both typically bureaucratic, produced anything comparable to the great administrative services built up in India, both at the centre and in the provinces. The great all-India services, the I.C.S., the Indian Police, the Indian Audit and Accounts Service, the provincial services (especially Revenue and Judicial Services) created an administrative machinery which shouldered the burden of governing three hundred million people, which no government had actually faced before. The organisation of such a vast machinery which felt itself competent to deal not only with the work of government, but with famine, plague, floods, etc., was possible only because of the historic tradition of bureaucratic government in India, inherited from the time at least of the Mauryas. Only a small fractional percentage of the services was European. The rest was at all times recruited from the same class on which the previous empires of India had also depended: the Brahmins, the Kayasthas and the Khatris in the north, and the Brahmins and certain other literate castes in the south. Without the loyal assistance of this class, which under its changing rulers had governed India for two thousand years, the organisation of the great bureaucracy would not have been possible.

With an administrative machinery so organised the Government was able to take up the work of administration on a scale which

14

no Government, outside Russia, in recent times, had undertaken. Railways and telegraph lines knit the country together. Great irrigation schemes were undertaken, notably in the Punjab and in the United Provinces. Peace reigned over the land, and law was administered as between man and man under a system of jurisprudence which was enlightened and comprehensive. The land revenue system was overhauled and though an uneconomic system of landlordism prevailed in many parts, the settlement and assessment of lands and the Government demands from the ryots were clearly defined. In fact for a hundred years India had a peaceful administration.

The educational policy of the Government was not progressive, but the great universities in the provincial capitals and the system of Government colleges helped to create a large and fairly well educated literary class. The weaknesses of the system were many but all the same it provided for middle-class education and was thus responsible for the creation of a large body of like-minded people all over India, who talked the same language, had the same point of view and were able to think in terms of India. The progress was even slower in respect of medical welfare and public health measures. Generally speaking these activities were confined to urban areas.

In short, from the point of view of actual administrative work, the British Government was one of the best in the world: but from that of organisation for national welfare its work fell far short of what could have been legitimately expected. Industrial development was neglected, if not, as often alleged, sacrified in British interests. Even agriculture was not the subject of much governmental interest till Lord Halifax's regime. The arts and crafts of India fell into decay, and the standard of life showed no signs of improvement. It was the theme of the first generation of Indian economists that India had actually been impoverished by a system of veiled commercial and economic exploitation and that the wealth drained from India was the cause of the misery of the masses. Whatever the truth of this charge, it is undeniable that the government of India from 1858 to 1921 confined their activities mainly to the collection of revenue, the maintenance of peace and the defence of India's frontiers, the three minimum essential functions of government, and undertook schemes neither for the reorganisation of society, nor for raising the moral and material standards of the people, nor for increasing the national wealth of the country. They provided the appurtenances of civilisation but did not undertake the work of civilisation themselves.

The growth of popular political institutions, though tardy, may also be credited to the British Government. The Legislative Council was enlarged in 1861 to include some nominated Indian members. Lord Ripon's reform of local self-government laid the basis of local and municipal self-government, which soon took firm root in India and became the groundwork of democratic institutions in higher spheres. Representatives elected from provincial legislatures sat in the Imperial Legislative Council at the end of the century. It was, however, only with the Minto-Morley reforms that the councils began to reflect popular opinion. Though these beginnings were moderate and did not in any effective measure introduce democratic methods of government in India, they undoubtedly provided a most valuable training ground in parliamentary work and produced some men of remarkable ability, who made their mark in municipal administration and parliamentary life. The Montagu-Chelmsford reforms took it a step further, introducing the principle of direct election in the provinces and the Centre, and partial responsibility in provincial government. By the 1935 Act the provinces became practically self-governing.

The most notable achievement of British rule was the unification of India. British rule may be said to have given substance to the idea of a national State which India had inherited from the Moghuls. True, one-third of India was ruled by its own princes. Over large tracts, British authority was no more than nominal in the period immediately following the mutiny. But a conscious process of unification was set afoot, the object of which was not merely to secure the effective exercise of British authority in Indian States, but weld the whole of India into one country. Railways, posts and telegraphs, currency, salt administration—these were the main external forms through which this unity was achieved. The doctrine of paramountcy by which the Central Government claimed over-riding powers over the States as also authority for the Crown over the rulers was the method and machinery by which this far-reaching change was effected. The deposition, in 1875, of the Gaekwad of Baroda, the greatest Hindu prince and the oldest ally of the British, the punishment of the Jubraj of Manipur in 1895, and the declaration of policy contained in Lord Reading's letter to the Nizam: these are the landmarks in a forward movement, which claiming the imperial pretensions of the Moghuls, successfully reduced the independence of the States to an absolute and open dependence on the British power. The assumption of the imperial title by the Queen and the three imperial

Durbars at Delhi demonstrated to the world the achievement of this unity.

It is only after the first Great War that the British authorities began to doubt the political wisdom of strengthening the movement for unity. But the conspiracy of princely and imperialist interests (Butler Report, 1929) which sought to separate British India from the States by accepting the Leslie Scott thesis that the relationship of the States was with the Crown of England came too late to disrupt the unity that had already been achieved. A legal separation of the Crown Representative from the Governor-General was possible, but the economic, fiscal and administrative tentacles of the Central Government bound the States too closely to allow any separation. The unity of India which was the result of a hundred years of effective administration defied the legalism of British lawyers and the narrow dynastic interests of the princes.

In other fields their achievements were notable. In 1837 James Princep discovered the clue to the inscriptions of Asoka. This was an event which revolutionised Indian history for it provided the key to a systematic study of ancient India. In 1860, Alexander Cunningham was appointed the first Director of Archaeology and Fergusson's monumental work describing the magnificent architectural monuments of India laid the foundations of a revival of Indian interest in Arts. The appointment of Dr. Hultz as epigraphist to the Government of India was the beginning of the great work of reclamation of Indian history. The deciphering of the ancient Indian scripts, and the official search for inscriptions all over the country and their publication gave India the first corpus of material from which her history could be reconstructed. It is almost an epic story and its significance in creating among Indians a historical sense, a pride in their achievements and in their nationality cannot be overrated. Today when we talk of the Mauryas, the Guptas, the Chalukyas and the Pallavas, let it be remembered that the story of these great ages of Indian history was recovered to us by the devoted labours of European scholars in the service of the British Government in India.

If Indian history was thus recovered, so was, in a sense, two other main streams of Indian thought, Buddhism and Pali literature. For a thousand years Buddha had been forgotten and the great literature of Buddhism in Sanskrit itself neglected and ignored. To the Hindu, Buddha was but one of the minor avatars of Vishnu. It was the work of European scholars that repatriated the Sakyamuni. Asoka whose name seems to have been expunged from Indian history was restored to his honours, and today holds a position in the minds of Indians higher than that of any monarch—the result not of Indian researches, but the work of European scholars.

Even the revival of Sanskrit studies on modern lines in India is due largely to the activities of the British Government and the scholars patronised by them. The Queen's College at Banaras was the first serious attempt to teach Sanskrit in a systematic way to young India and it is a fact worthy of note that even the great religious classics of India, the Vedas, the Upanishads and the Dharma Sastras like Manu and Baudhayana have been made available to a much wider circle in India than ever before, through the critical translations of European scholars.

"Hindu Stuart," who stole the statues from temples, was perhaps the first European to appreciate the beauty of Indian sculpture, but in due time the taste spread first among the European critics before India awoke to her own artistic treasures. The truth which we should not forget is that except in the field of music and literature the Indian people, over large areas, had ceased to be the heirs to their own culture. In the beginning of the nineteenth century, Ellora, Ajanta and Mahabalipuram meant nothing to Indians; nor did the magnificent sculptures of Elephanta and the temples of Orissa or the Chola bronzes speak to us. Our craftsmen no doubt preserved the traditions but in the miseries of the latter half of the eighteenth century and the denationalising tendencies of the nineteenth century, Indians at least in the north had become strangers to their own inheritance. It is to men like Havell and Coomaraswamy, an Anglo-Tamil born and bred in England, that we owe the revival of our artistic sense. These are undoubtedly achievements to the credit of Britain whose value will greatly increase as time goes on. When the viceroys and governors whose statues adorn public places, and whose wives are commemorated by having their names inscribed on public buildings are forgotten, India will remember Fergusson and Havell, Hindu Stuart and Marshall.

The great industry of the British period after the mutiny was the manufacture of quislings. A table of salutes was made, and what Gibbon calls the "artful gradation of hopes and honours" became a major factor in British policy. "The vain dictionary of titles" was sedulously searched for such magnificent titles as "Farzand i Khas i daulat e Englishia," the beloved son of the British Empire, "Indir Mahender," the supreme lord of lords, "Siphar e Sultant," the shield of the Empire, etc. As Lytton exultingly reported, by these methods the conservative aristocracy was rallied to the empire. The princes and the great landowners vied with each other to be considered the most loyal among the Queen's subjects. Great rulers became petitioners for decorations from the emperor and felt themselves honoured when empty military ranks were conferred on them. The middle classes looked upon the empire as an opportunity more than a burden and Rai Sahibs, no less than Knight Grand Commanders, felt themselves to be pillars of an empire. But this systematic attempt at demoralisation succeeded only for a short time. By the end of the nineteenth century the spirit of India had recovered, and the nation had found its soul. It is to this aspect that we should turn now.

The second half of the eighteenth century had witnessed over large areas in India a breakdown of civilisation which has but few parallels in the history of the world. In Bengal and in the Gangetic valley there was anarchy of a kind comparable only to the conditions of Germany during the Thirty Years' War. Punjab was in a state of military upheaval, when that fair land was well-nigh turned into a desert. Only in Maratha homelands, in Mysore and in the extreme south did normal Indian life continue. In out of the way places like Rajputana, Mysore, Tanjore and Travancore, art and scholarship continued to be cultivated. In fact India at the end of the eighteenth century in its most widely populated areas and traditional centres of culture lay prostrate and gasping. Religion was degraded and demoralising. India's soul was sunk in deep pessimism.

The new century witnessed a rebirth. The conquest of Bengal by the Europeans brought about a sudden change in the position of Hinduism. Under the Muslims Hindu religion was at best tolerated. The change of authority brought freedom to the Hindu religion. To the Englishmen of the day, Hinduism and Islam were both heathen religions, and as the Company had no religious interests, Hinduism, for the first time in five hundred years, stood in a position of equality in its own territory. Also new wine began to be poured into old bottles. The opening years of the nineteenth century produced a man who may legitimately be called the father of Indian Recovery. Ram Mohan Roy (1772-1833) was born of a Brahmin family which had received some distinction in the service of the Nawab Nazims of Bengal. After a very liberal education which included the study of Sanskrit, Persian, Arabic and English, he entered the service of the Company and rose to high office.

But essentially Ram Mohan was a humanist and a religious reformer and left the service of the Company to devote his time to the service of his people. Profoundly influenced by European liberalism, Ram Mohan came to the conclusion that radical reform was necessary in the religion of Hinduism and in the social practices of the Hindus if the country was to emerge from the slough of despondency. The founding of the Brahmo Samaj was the result.

The religious work of Ram Mohan Roy was too intellectual, too unrelated to the tradition of Hinduism, too deeply imbued with modern ideas to have any great effect on the people as a whole. But it provided the middle classes of Bengal with spiritual sustenance at a time when they were most inclined to despair and thereby it arrested a dangerous threat to Hinduism. The universal religion which he was anxious to found did not survive him, for in the next generation, under the inspiration of Maharshi Debendranath Tagore and of Keshab Chander Sen the spirit of Hinduism reasserted itself and the Brahmo Samaj became mainly a social influence rather than a separate religious sect.

Great though Ram Mohan's services were to the cause of religious reform, his claim to be remembered in Indian history is as the originator of all of the more important secular movements in India. He was in fact the first modern man in India. His services to the cause of the abolition of Sati are well known. He was the first feminist in India and his book, *Brief Remarks Regarding Modern Encroachments on the Ancient Rights of Females* (1822), is a reasoned argument in favour of equality of women. He argued for the reform of Hindu law, led the protest against restrictions on the press, memorialised Government against the oppressive land laws and in written memoranda submitted to the Joint Select Committee, argued the case for the association of Indians in Government. A great and fervent educationalist, it is noteworthy that he was strongly on the side of those who argued in favour of an English system of education in India.

The revival of Hinduism in its own natural form was not long delayed. The British Government till 1875 was mildly pro-Hindu, looking upon the Muslim as their implacable enemy. One governor-general even boasted that he had avenged the sack of Somanath by his destruction of Ghazni and by recovering the gate of the historic temple. Hinduism showed new signs of revival and the new education which Macaulay hoped would dissolve the Hindu faith helped in its revival. But these tendencies were not visible to the eye till after the effects of the mutiny had passed. In 1853

Karl Marx with uncanny acumen had written: "All the civil wars, invasions, revolutions, conquests . . . in Hindustan did not go deeper than its surface. England had broken down the entire frame-work of Indian society, without any symptoms of reconstitution yet appearing. The loss of his old world with no gain of a new one imparts a particular kind of melancholy to the present misery of the Hindu and separates Hindustan ruled by Britain from its ancient traditions and from the whole of its past history."

But the revival was not slow in coming. Dayanand Saraswati, a Sanyasi from Gujerat, was the first to preach an aggressive, reformed and militant Hinduism. His Arya Samaj was frankly an attempt to re-establish Hinduism on a Vedic basis. It was an appeal to the alleged pristine purity of Vedic Hinduism. Dayanand's polemics and his notable book *Satyartha Prakash*, a commentary on the Vedas, gave an effective strength to Hinduism, where it had long ceased to be a living force—the Punjab. As a phase of nationalism and as an expression of resistance to Christian and Islamic doctrines, Arya Samaj is very important. As a proselytising sect, with a great urge for social service (its educational effort in the Punjab is remarkable), Arya Samaj is still an important factor in the Hindu resurgence of the north. But its repudiation of Puranic mythology, its open objection to the worship of idols, and its insistence on rejecting all the other sacred books of Hinduism except the Vedas, restricted its influence to those areas where Hindu culture in its widest sense had generally disappeared. The revival of Hinduism had to come from the general body of Hindu tradition and of this movement Vivekananda was the prophet.

Vivekananda (1861-1902) was a young Bengali graduate, one initiated in the New Learning, who had become a disciple of a mystic saint, Ramakrishna Paramahansa, who is now accepted by his followers as an avatar. Initiated Sanyasi, Vivekananda on the death of his master in 1886 took to the life of a wandering preacher spreading the gospel of Vedanta all over India. The most notable thing about him was his flaming patriotism, his zeal for reviving the greatness of Hinduism and the motherland. A tour in America and Europe gave him a greater sense of social values and his fervent declaration, "I do not believe in a religion that cannot wipe out the widow's tears or bring a piece of bread to the orphan's mouth," is the reaction of what he saw in the West. Again, on his return he does not hesitate to declare: "I consider the great national sin is the neglect of the masses and that is one of the causes of our downfall." Vivekananda's success in America, and his militant presentation of Hindu thought and his courageous proclamation that Vedanta was the religion for all, gave to the Hindus generally a sense of pride in their religion. For the first time people in India felt that there was no reason to be apologetic about Hinduism. This feeling was also helped by the growth of the Theosophical Society which under Col. Olcott and Madame Blavatsky began to preach a Hindu revivalism in a European garb. By the end of the century Hinduism stood erect before the world, fully conscious of its own greatness and powers and ready if necessary to challenge the teachings of rival religions.

The sense of Hindu greatness was also awakened and fortified by the recovery of Indian history. By slow and patient labour European scholars had begun to reconstruct the lost story of India's greatness. The synchronism of Chandra Gupta and Alexander, once established, made a beginning. The deciphering of Asoka's inscriptions was an equally important step forward. Gradually the Hindu awoke to the fact that his was not a race whose destiny it was to be conquered by foreign people, but one which through many centuries had to its credit great achievements in every sphere. The names of great monarchs whose memory had died out long ago came to light. The story of the founding of empires, of the extension of Indian civilisation across the seas, of the unique monuments of architecture, gave to Indians a sense of national pride which they had lost for many centuries.

The great work of Sir William Jones also began to bear unexpected fruit in India. The cultivation of Sanskrit in Europe opened the eyes of Indians to the great riches that their ancestors had left to them. It may sound strange but it is none the less true that it was the enthusiasm of Max Muller, Monier Williams and others for the culture of India that gave the first impetus to the modern study of classics in India. Also it was through the translations published by European scholars in English that the new middle classes began to know of the higher things in their own thought. The *Sacred Books of the East* published under the inspiration of Max Muller and the study of Indian philosophy in the West gave added impetus to the sense of nationalism that was daily growing in India.

The transfer of political authority to the English people brought about inevitably certain social changes which were not immediately visible. The Indian bureaucratic classes, the Kayasthas, the Brahmins, the Khatris and others in the north had always been dominated by a feudal nobility or the warrior classes. With the growth of the British power the feudal nobility lost in importance.

The Rajas and Maharajas in the conquered areas had *no power* left to them. The military classes also fell into discount since in the Indian army they had to be content with lower ranks. The substance of power and influence therefore passed to the castes from whom the vast army of officials was recruited, who also provided the recruits to the learned profession. Ram Mohan Roy himself came from one of such families. When English education became more widely prevalent, the differentiation of this class from the rest became obvious. In the period after the eighties of the nineteenth century, it is the voice of the lawyers (W. C. Bonnerji, Pherozeshah Mehta and others), teachers (Surendranath, Gokhale, Tilak), administrators (Raja Madhav Rao, R. C. Dutt, etc.) and journalists (G. Subramanya Iyer, Motilal Ghosh) that came to be heard. The liberal profession and the officials were recruited from the same classes. Apart from service in Government, the only openings then available to them were those of law, journalism, teaching and medicine. These new middle classes, better educated, with wider appreciation of the immediate requirements of the country, and a greater sense of solidarity stood for modern India. The old nobility living on their past in dilapidated mansions but pretending to a social eminence which had but little to back it lost ground every day. True that after the nationalist turn which the middle classes began to take, the British Government consciously embarked on a policy of bolstering up the aristocracy and of an alliance with them as the loyal and conservative elements in the country but those classes had fallen so far backward and lost credit with their own people that ultimately the alliance did only harm to the British.

The building up of a new India in all except the industrial sphere was the work of this class. It is they who organised and led the nationalist movement. They were the advocates of new learning and the torch-bearers of new India that was shaping. Of the names included in G. Parameswaran Pillai's *Representative Indians*, there is only one who belonged to the old ruling classes. The rest—and among them some of the most remarkable—are those who rose from the ranks of the middle classes. They include names of eminent administrators, scholars, lawyers, professors, industrial magnates. The New Society was of the people, and did not derive its tradition or inspiration from the governing classes of the past.

The organisation of political life which was their main achievement began even in the days of the Company but was interrupted by the mutiny. The earlier institutions such as the British India Society (Calcutta, 1843) and the British Indian Association (1851) were meant to voice the grievances of the people and to work for their political uplift. But this work was interrupted by the violent suppression of the mutiny which awed India into silence and utterly demoralised her people for a generation. But by 1875, the revival of Hinduism, already alluded to, began to be reflected in political trends. The Indian Association of Calcutta was formed in that year, and at about the same time, the Sarvajanik Sabha of Poona and other similar organisations came into existence in the major cities. The voice of India also began to be heard through Indian newspapers. In the beginning of the eighties there were no less than four hundred and seventy-eight papers mostly in Indian languages. Among them may be mentioned the *Amrita Bazar Patrika, The Hindu* and *The Tribune* and such noted champions of earlier days as the *Bengali* and the *Indian Mirror.*

The existence of numerous institutions in different parts of India working for the same cause—the political advancement of India—led naturally to the formation of a single all-Indian body. The Indian National Congress was founded in Bombay on December 28, 1885. Seventy-two representatives had gathered from different parts of India. It met under the presidency of W. C. Bonnerji, a distinguished lawyer of Calcutta. It is noteworthy that most of the people, who gathered at Bombay, and the next year at Calcutta, were the representatives of the new learning and of the new classes that had developed. They represented a Western and liberal point of view and were great admirers of the British. At the third Congress a young graduate from Allahabad made his debut, whose golden voice held the audience spell-bound. He was Pandit Madan Mohan Malaviya, the very embodiment of the Hindu spirit. All the same it may be said that the earlier Congressmen were liberals in spirit and were not consciously representatives of the Hindu idea. With the next generation, however, the movement changed in spirit. Hindu nationalism, especially in Maharashtra and in Bengal, was coming definitely to the fore, and with their new-found consciousness of religious greatness, their nationalism was not only more extreme, but was in spirit revivalist and not liberal. Maharashtra had always been the centre of a strong Hindu tradition. The Maratha spirit which was unbroken was revived under the inspiring guidance of a wise and learned man and thinker Mahadev Govind Ranade. Soon, however, it found a more militant leader in Bal Gangadhar Tilak, a staunch and orthodox Hindu, learned in Sanskrit, and a philosopher capable of a new interpretation of the *Gita,* and also a supremely able political tactician and organiser who knew what he wanted in the realm of politics.

He wanted nothing less than the freedom of India. Like Sivaji three hundred years ago, he desired to base the national revival on Hindu Dharma. He resuscitated the benevolent elephant-faced deity Ganesh, the Remover of Obstacles, and organised a cult for him which was but a thinly veiled political movement. The Sivaji movement had also the same object. But Tilak went even a step further: he provided a philosophic basis for Hindu nationalism by the traditional method of an interpretation of the *Gita*. His *Gita Rahasya*—or the secret of the *Gita*—written in jail is a book of supreme importance from the point of view of Hindu nationalism. It taught the doctrine that action is the fulfilment of life, and purposive human effort should be the object of the Karma Yogi. In the context of Indian politics—as indeed in the context of the *Mahabharata* battle—the injunction, "Therefore, son of Kunti, arise and fight" could have only one meaning, and Tilak drove the philosophy home by his agitational methods. Thus the second phase of the Congress, the nationalist movement, was frankly Hindu and revivalist. Tilak, Lajpat Rai, and Motilal Ghosh took pride in their orthodoxy while the younger and more radical group led by Aurobindo Ghosh imported even a fervent religious mysticism to their politics. In fact at the beginning of the twentieth century, the more extreme expressions of nationalism had taken an even more pronounced Hindu character. The terrorist group took vows before the great goddess and the ceremony of Virashtami showed the close connection between the cult of Bhawani and the organisation of the new nationalism based on the use of force. It is a remarkable fact that all through the history of India, it is Bhawani that is the object of worship in times of aggressive action. Not only Sivaji but Guru Govind Singh also claimed to have received the blessings of the Mother and a mysterious sword and the tenth Guru's book in the *Granth Saheb* gives great prominence to the Devi's fight with all powers. The secret organisations which spread fast in Bengal had this background and the cult of the bomb also extended to Maharashtra and the Punjab. The middle class movement which the Congress represented and which was only unconsciously Hindu was out of its depth in dealing with a movement of this character and there was every danger in the period that followed Lord Curzon's viceroyalty, that the Congress would cease to be a vigorous force in Indian politics.

The death of the Congress had often been foretold. In 1900 Lord Curzon had reported to Whitehall, "The Congress is tottering to its fall and one of my great ambitions while in India is to assist it to a peaceful demise." There were other viceroys who felt no less certain of the imminent dissolution of the Congress, which in fact has not happened yet: but if in the beginning of the century the Congress did not break up, Lord Curzon himself was to a large extent responsible for it. His partition of Bengal, an administrative and political arrangement fully justified by the events that followed, gave Bengal a great opportunity for a spectacular agitation. The movement which the people of Bengal started united the different sections of nationalist opinion on an aggressive platform of boycott, Swadeshi and Swaraj. The new technique of the boycott of British goods as a first step in the movement for the achievement of Swaraj (or independence) gives to the movement of 1906 its revolutionary character. For the time it united all the forces of nationalism, which, with the defeat of the Russians at the battle of Tushima, had begun to see the vision of a new liberated Asia. The Japanese victory over Russian imperialism had a psychological effect which it is impossible to exaggerate. The spirit of nationalism and of Hindu revival stood triumphant and in great expectations in the first decade of the twentieth century.

The Great War of 1914-18, though it interrupted the growth of the national movement, gave added impetus to the national spirit. The Congress that emerged from that period was under the revolutionary leadership of Mahatma Gandhi. No longer a middle class movement, it set itself to organise the masses, and the revolutionary cry of no compromise with imperialism and the programme of nation-wide non-cooperation, gave to the Congress for the first time its claim to speak effectively for the people of India.

The period of cooperation with the Muslim League and the interlude of the Khilafat agitation should not blind us to the fact that the strength of the Congress lay primarily in the Hindu revival and in an integral nationalism based on the Hindu masses. The Mahatma himself embodied in his person certain aspects of Hindu spirit. His commentary on the *Gita* shows the original source of his inspiration. While in no way interested in the subtleties of metaphysics or in the forms and rituals of religion and its worship, Gandhiji was all the same a religious leader of the masses and his Mahatmaship, so universally accepted by the people, was but a reflection not only of his saintly character but of his life as a Karma Yogi. Under him, though in a different way, the Congress represented the resistance of Hinduism as a whole to alien domination, though the political purpose of the Congress and its general outlook in regard to the future of India was entirely non-sectarian.

With Gandhiji's final assumption of leadership after the Amristar tragedy, India enters a period of determined struggle with the British power in India. The events of that period of heroic sacrifices and the consequent upsurge of the masses cannot be dealt with here. After twenty-seven years of ceaseless fight, Britain finally accepted the principle of India's complete freedom, and in August 1947 the country regained its freedom and entered the international world as an independent state.

The economic recovery of India during the second half of the nineteenth century was also a fact of great significance. The period of the robber State (1757-1773) saw the British provinces depleted of their wealth. The extension of British territory in the first quarter of the nineteenth century witnessed the spread of ruin all over India. It was noted with surprise by British administrators like Monroe and Elphinstone that the areas which were under Tippu and the Marathas seemed under indigenous rule to have enjoyed a measure of prosperity which the territories directly administered by the company did not. Many European administrators noted with dismay the decay of the countryside which followed British annexation. The Governor-General, Lord William Bentinck, in a famous minute in 1829 noted "the gloomy picture of the effect of a commercial revolution, productive of so much present suffering to numerous classes in India and hardly to be paralleled in the history of commerce." The misery of the Indian peasant and artisan and the ordinary classes may be read in the graphic pages of Romesh Dutt's *Economic History of India under Early British Rule* and in his *India in the Victorian Age.*

India had been all through her history a great industrial country. Before the nineteenth century her textiles were famous all over the world. Her production of iron and steel was notable. Shipbuilding flourished in the ports of the west coast. In fact so late as 1840 Montgomery Martin had testified before a parliamentary enquiry that India was as much an industrial country as an agricultural one. But a great and ever-widening gulf had come between India and the rest of the industrial world. Indian technology fell back in the vital period between 1770 and 1860. While European and especially British technology made rapid strides, India lagged behind with her industries bound up with a decaying village system. Indian industry of the past was based on craftsmen; and the inelastic character of caste organisation which had overspread the craft guilds made any adjustment of industry to modern conditions impossible. In the result Indian economy became unbalanced and the country began to be rapidly impoverished. The commercial organisation of England was not slow to take advantage of the economic anarchy that followed. India became the safe market for the ever-expanding British trade of the nineteenth century.

The economic recovery of India was slow. In the external trade of the country some communities, notably the Parsis, had begun to share even before the government of the company had ended. The civil war in America gave an impetus to textile industry in India on European lines and slowly India built up her present position as a producer of cotton textiles. Other major industries followed—steel and iron, cement, sugar—and Indian capital, shy in the beginning, began to be invested in industrial enterprises. British possessions in Asia, especially Burma and Malaya, and the African territories afforded opportunities for Indian capital and once again Indian firms made their appearance in these areas which not many centuries before had witnessed the spirit of Indian mercantile adventure.

Another factor which helped the recovery of the Indian mind was the phenomenal growth of Indian vernacular languages—a result no doubt of the new education through the universities. Before the introduction of English education in India, some of these languages, notably Tamil and Hindi, had literatures which were truly classical. But they had not developed as vehicles of modern thought. The new educational system required suitable textbooks in the lower classes and the growth of all the great modern Indian languages starts generally with the production of textbooks for the new schools. With the continuous pouring of old wine into new bottles secular literature of a kind previously unknown in India began to appear and mould the opinion of the common man in an increasing degree. This literature was patriotic, the novels of Bankim Chandra and the plays of Dwijendralal drew their inspiration from Indian history. The songs of Bharati and Tagore were intensely nationalistic; and so were the earlier poems of Iqbal. Bengali soon took its place as a great modern literature with a comprehensive outlook on life, and rich in its varied aspects and it produced at least one writer of world significance. The part played by Urdu in the consolidation of Islam will be treated separately, but other languages like Hindi, Gujerati and Marathi and the great Dravidian languages in the South—Telugu, Tamil, Malayalam and Canarese—had equally significant developments. It is, however, necessary to emphasise that the growth of these languages led to an integration of linguistic nationalities in India, to the emphasis on the fissiparous tendencies of particularism, so that, moved by their pride in their language, the Gujaratis, the Marathas and the Canarese, for example, began to feel different from each other in a way they had never done before.

The growth of the scientific spirit is another aspect which requires notice in connection with the recovery of Indian spirit. In the nineteenth century India had made no contribution of significance to the world of knowledge. A new spirit was abroad, however, and with increasing opportunities India began to claim recognition in these fields also. The discoveries of Ramanujam in the field of pure mathematics were the first real contribution of new India in this field. Soon, however, research workers in physics, chemistry and other sciences began to make a name for India in the world, reflecting the intellectual stature of her people.

CHAPTER XXII

ISLAMIC INTEGRATION

BEFORE the nineteenth century Islam in India was not separately organised. Hindus and Muslims lived together, professing their different religions. The political power of Islam was a sufficient guarantee for the religious faith and the necessity for the Muslims to organise separately was never felt. Muslim officers freely entered the service of Hindu rulers, and even at Panipat where the Maratha forces met the Afghans, the Hindu side had numerous Muslim soldiers and captains, and it was Ibrahim Gardee's artillery that played the greatest havoc on the Afghan forces. The Maratha governor of Lahore in 1758 was Adnam Beg. In the same way, when Babar invaded India, the Afghans allied themselves with the Hindus to resist the invader. But in the nineteenth century the position took a sudden and disastrous turn for the Mussalmans. They found themselves deprived of all power and authority in the country. Their downfall was so sudden and so marked that it was impossible for anyone to overlook it. The Muslim divines of the period were openly bewailing the loss of the glories of Islam, and this spirit of depression produced a theological leader of importance in Mohammed Shah Waliullah of Delhi. One of his disciples, Ahmad Shah of Rai Bareilly, may be said to be the founder of Indian Wahabism, a puritanical sect which desired to purge Islam of the weaknesses which had gathered around it. The Wahabi movement was a religious revival though it had a radical background. It was in no sense anti-Hindu and its political warfare was against the British authorities who put it down with severe measures.

The period of extreme Muslim depression was between 1833 and 1864. The new code of Macaulay displaced the Muslim criminal law which had been applied in Northern India for many centuries. Nor was Muslim civil law left untouched, for an Anglo-Mohammedan law was taking shape which amended the sacred *Shariat*. The abolition of Kazis proclaimed to the world the supremacy of British law. In the field of administration Islam suffered a severe blow by the abolition of the practice of using Persian as the court language. Politically the kingdom of Delhi had been reduced to vanishing point, and the only symbol of Muslim authority in North India was the kingdom of Oudh, itself in the last stages of disintegration. Its annexation meant the loss of everything in Upper India, and Islam after six hundred years of power, found itself reduced to a position which was altogether depressing.

During this period the Muslims found themselves looked upon as the enemies of British authorities in India. Lord Ellenborough declared in an official communication to London that "the race (of Muslims) was fundamentally hostile to us and our true policy is to reconciliate the Hindus." The discontent of the dispossessed noblemen, the Maulvis who had lost their political influence and the general resentment at the degradation of Islam under British rule led to constant outbreaks in North India. The blame for the mutiny was also laid at their door because the Maulvis had issued a *fatwa* supporting the rebellion and also because Bahadur Shah had been proclaimed emperor. In many places the Muslim hostility was marked. Till 1864 this attitude of looking upon the Muslims as irreconcilable to British authority was accepted as the true basis of British policy.

To a patriotic Muslim the situation would have seemed to be truly desperate. The classes to which Islam could have looked for leadership, the nobility and religious leaders, had been rendered wholly powerless. The economic position of the community was fast deteriorating. At no time was the community economically broad-based or strong. Its financial position had been based on Islam's political power and the loss of authority meant also general ruin. The authorities looked upon the Mussalmans with suspicion if not active hostility. The avenues of preferment were also practically closed to them as they had not taken to the new learning and especially to the study of English which had displaced Persian. More than all, they were a minority, and ran the risk of becoming totally depressed, if the situation was not seen in true perspective and the decay arrested. On the other hand, it was obvious that the Hindus were forging ahead. The alliance of Hindu merchants with the Company which gave Bengal to the British, still continued as the Hindus had not yet come to be identified with seditionists Placed on a footing of equality, Hinduism had already begun tc show signs of a great revival. Islam had to find a new policy or perish.

The man who saw this most clearly was Syed Ahmed, a noble of the Moghul court, whose father had held a titular office of high rank near the emperor. Syed Ahmad, though offered the same rank and position as his father, elected to join the service of the

Company as a judicial officer. During the mutiny he rendered notable services to the British. When the depression of Islam was at its height, he assumed the leadership of the more moderate elements who saw that the future of Islam could only be safeguarded by an integration of the Mussalmans of India into a single community, by a period of co-operation with the British to enable them to retrieve their lost position, and by an encouragement of English education. The view that Syed Ahmad was unpatriotic in his activity is entirely wrong. It is even a greater injustice to him to say that he was anti-Hindu in his attitude. In fact Sir Syed was intensely patriotic and his relations with Hindus were extremely cordial. But he realised that Indian Islam lay helpless and without a period of consolidation and organisation, it would undoubtedly fall into the background.

He, therefore, set himself to woo the British. Maulvi Karamat Ali of Jaunpur had already declared that the Muslims were not bound by their religion to rebel against the British, a doctrine which the *fatwas* of eminent Muslim divines had promulgated in the first period of hostility. The British Government were also ready for a change of policy. In 1872, Sir William Hunter published his book on the Indian Mussalmans which pleaded for a better understanding of the Islamic point of view. Syed Ahmad's activities, therefore, found strong support in official quarters. In 1875, the M.A.O. College was founded at Aligarh, as the central educational institution of the Indian Mussalmans, with the support of the leading Muslim gentry of North India and the active co-operation of Salar Jung, the prime minister of Hyderabad. The British Government thought that they had achieved a notable success in rallying the Muslims to their support. The Aligarh movement had strong British official and non-official support from the beginning. Sir Syed had wisely decided from the very beginning that he should have the co-operation of sympathetic Englishmen to organise the college and create a special *esprit de corps*. And he found a remarkable helper in Theodore Beck who was fully in sympathy with his ideals and threw himself whole-heartedly into the work. He gave to Aligarh a missionary spirit. Under him it fulfilled a dual purpose: it created in the generation that followed a spirit of Anglo-Muslim co-operation which no doubt paid immediate dividends to both sides and it also converted Aligarh into an intellectual general staff for the work of Islamic integration.

The Aligarh movement, which is the central factor of Islamic renaissance in India, had two very important results. It was the first step towards the integration of Indian Islam. The dispersed Muslim population in different parts of India had now a central institution which provided them with a common intellectual background, and fostered a common ideology. It was the "Aligarh man" who was the spearhead of the Muslim movement in every corner of India. In the second place Aligarh elevated Urdu to the position of a national language for Indian Islam. Urdu had been the common language of the official classes, Hindu and Muslim, for over three hundred years. Aligarh, by adopting it as its compulsory language for matriculation, made it the language not only of the U.P. but in theory at least the language of the Muslim educated classes everywhere as Persian had been fifty years before. Thus provided with a separate language and a special ideology the Muslims were able in due course to claim to be a separate nation.

By 1894, Syed Ahmad was able to convince the British, as Strachey officially declared, that the upper classes among the Muslims were a source of strength to the Government. By his opportune declarations against the Congress Syed Ahmad also cemented this alliance: but it is necessary to emphasise that there was no conscious anti-Hindu feeling in all this. The Aligarh movement soon found its reflection in every province and State. Hyderabad, Bhopal and other Muslim States recruited their services from the graduates of the M.A.O. College. Anjumans were started in every town where the doctrines of Aligarh were preached and the cultivation of Urdu encouraged. A Muslim press, mainly in Urdu, also developed at the same time. Indeed, it could well be claimed for Syed Ahmad that not only had he arrested the disintegration of Islam but in the course of a generation had restored it to a position of great importance and undoubted influence.

The new century saw other developments. Syed Ahmad's opposition to the national movement was mainly on the ground that Islam required time to organise. The growth of an integral nationalism in India, which was the main feature of the first decade of the twentieth century and which was mainly a reflection of revived Hindu feeling, frightened both the British Government and the body of Muslim landholders who was behind the Aligarh movement. The Muslim youth on the other hand was stirred by the call of Islam. All the Islamic countries were then in ferment. The teachings of Jamaluddin Afghani had revived a sense of Islamic solidarity in the Arab countries, while under the young Turks, Ottoman power was showing signs of invigoration. Young Islam in India led by Maulana Mohammed Ali, was turning towards the doctrines of Pan-Islamism. The Aligarh movement was split in two, the older leaders supporting the policy of Syed Ahmad, unconcerned generally with Islam outside India and rallying to the British side against the onslaughts of the Congress; the younger looking for inspiration to Constantinople and Cairo, and pursuing a frankly anti-British policy on the ground that Britain was ranged against Islam everywhere in the world. The older leaders represented the landholders, the nobility and generally the vested interests while the younger represented the new middle classes.

In 1907, when the question of political reforms became urgent in India, and the Minto-Morley scheme was on the anvil, the Government of India took the decision, at the request of a Muslim delegation led by the Aga Khan, to introduce separate electorates for the Muslims. The two-nation theory which Sir Syed Ahmad had tentatively advocated when he declared that Hindus and Muslims were the two eyes of India had found its consummation. Islamic integration was complete, for everywhere in India the citadel of nationalism was permanently breached and the separation of Islam from the body politic of India proclaimed in words which could not be misunderstood. From 1907, there could be a Hindu-Muslim alliance but no united national movement.

From separate electorates to Pakistan was but an easy and natural evolution. Forty years had, however, to pass before the policy of two separate States could be formally enunciated. The reason was obvious. The matter became a live issue only when it became clear that power was going to be transferred. Also by 1909, the younger group had become anti-British and their interest lay in an alliance with Hindu nationalism. Events in the Islamic world outside India made such an alliance inevitable. Britain's agreement with Russia over the Persian question dividing that ancient empire into two zones of influence, her open support to Italy in the latter's war of aggression in Tripoli against Turkey and finally, the humiliation of Turkey in the Balkan wars, caused the wave of anti-British feeling to rise high in the minds of the younger generation. Dr. Ansari led a medical mission from Indian Muslims to Turkey during the Balkan wars. The elder Muslim leaders though sympathetic to Pan-Islamic doctrines were so closely allied to Britain that a breach between the two sections was unavoidable. The Muslim League, which had been founded by the pro-British party led by the Aga Khan, was captured by Mohammed Ali, and in the special circumstances created by the war it moved towards an alliance with the Congress. The Lucknow Pact was not a step towards a Hindu-Muslim settlement; it was an alliance between two parties. After the war, the Khilafat movement brought the Hindus and Muslims again together. But the alliance was dissolved and after a period of uncertainty, when it was clear that power was going to be transferred to India, Islam declared for separation. Under Mohammed Ali Jinnah, the revived Muslim League representing an integrated Islam proclaimed its adhesion to the doctrine of two nations.

It is not to be understood that alongside with the great movement for Islamic unification, there was no spirit of national Indian awakening among the Muslims. From the beginning of the Congress movement there have been many Muslim leaders of standing associated with it. Mr. Jinnah himself was at one time a leading figure in the Congress, and the appeal of a united nationalism found its echo in many Muslim hearts. But broadly speaking Islamic opinion after the mutiny was dominated by a sense of political fear and was organised for protection.

CHAPTER XXIII

INDIA AND THE WORLD

With the arrival of Vasco da Gama the era of geographical isolation forced on India by the impenetrable barrier of the Himalayas may be said to have ended. But the monopoly of the sea route first in the hands of the Portuguese and then of the British limited India's direct contact with the European world. It was essentially a contact through a middleman. India's moral isolation continued up to the first decade of the twenieth century, though by the end of the nineteenth century Indians had begun to travel extensively in Europe, and Indian students to frequent English and European universities. With the progressive changes in the means of communications, especially the aeroplane and the radio, the influence of the world on India began to increase considerably. Education in English enabled India in an increasing measure to participate in the thought of the world.

The first Great War had a very great influence on the Indian mind. The weakening of the moral authority of Europe, the increased prestige of Japan, and the transfer of the world conflict to the Pacific brought new factors which profoundly affected the mind of India. But perhaps the greatest single event which influenced the political and moral development of India during the century was the Russian Revolution. The assumption of power by the proletariat not only in Moscow, but across the border of the Pamirs, had a profound effect on the youth of India. Before the end of the first Great War, there was hardly any labour or peasant organisation in India. The period between the two wars witnessed the phenomenal growth of the labour movement, of the peasant (Kisan) agitation and the establishment of a Communist Party. While middle class nationalism was indigenous in its inspiration, though strengthened by outside influences, the organisation of labour was primarily the reflection of a world movement. Its revolutionary ideology is derived from Marx and Engels, and the trade union organisations are modelled on their counterparts in England.

While the labour movement is anti-imperialist and anti-communal, its socialist ideology is revolutionary in regard to the social, political and economic organisation of India. The secular nature of socialist thought, and the principle of historic determinism which is basic in the teachings of Marx make the movement a determined opponent of the Hindu social system, and generally of the traditional structure of Indian life based on the joint family and the personal laws of Islam and Hinduism. This revolutionary character gives to the socialist-labour movement an importance which cuts through the religious division of Hinduism and Islam, for, to the socialist, the enemy in the first place is capitalism, whether of the Hindu or of the Muslim, and in the second place organised religion, which socialism considers to be merely a defensive organisation of capitalist society. In the result, the growth of socialist, communist and kisan organisations which is one of the central facts of the last twenty years, tends to break down the exclusive nationalism of both Hindus and Muslims and may in the long run bring about a different type of national feeling based on economic divisions.

During the first Great War, Indian nationalism became in a measure an international issue. The Imperial German Government recognised a provisional Government of India with Raja Mahendra Pratap as President. In the period before the wars revolutionary groups had been working in different centres in Europe and America. The Gadhr or the Revolutionary party which had its headquarters in San Francisco, was a powerful group which was supported mainly by the Sikh settlers on the West Coast. In England a group of intellectuals led by Vinayak Savarkar and Virendranath Chattopadhyay worked among Indian students, while Shanji Krishna Varma worked in Paris and built up contacts with European revolutionary movements. The London group was broken up and dispersed following the murder of Dr. Lalkaka and Curzon Wylie; but the French and German groups continued their activity. During the war, their activities were curbed in America and France, but Lajpatrai and Rashbehari Bose in Japan carried on systematic national work which was to bear fruit later.

However, till the rise of the Gandhian movement the impact of Indian nationalism on the world was small. Because of its revolutionary character and the uniqueness of the methods employed by Gandhiji, the non-cooperation movement attracted wide attention. It also began to enter into friendly relations with nationalist movements everywhere, with the Irish republicans, with the Wafd in Egypt, with the Istiqal party in Morocco. Indian participation in the League against Imperialism is also a fact worth mentioning.

With the countries of the Far East also India began to develop political relations during the period. The visit of Rabindranath

Tagore to China re-established the ancient cultural links with this country. Slowly the Congress built up political relations, which laid the foundations of a close friendship between India and China.

Official India also had begun to play a role in international affairs. As one of the participants in the war of 1914-18, India was a signatory to the Treaty of Versailles, and an original member of the League of Nations in whose activities she participated regularly through delegations which contained also non-official representatives. She participated also in other important international conferences like the Washington Conference and the World Economic Conference. In fact it may legitimately be claimed that in the inter-war period, India through popular and official activities achieved a position of some importance in international affairs.

In the world of culture also, India made notable progress during this period. The award of the Noble Prize for literature to Rabindranath Tagore in 1913, was the first international recognition of this cultural development of modern India. Recognition came to her also in the field of science. J. C. Bose's discoveries with regard to plant life may be said to be the first important contribution of India to modern science. Ramanujam's discoveries in Mathematics, the award of the Noble Prize in Physics to C. V. Raman are the other major facts which indicated India's changed position in the scientific world.

A significant reactions of world opinion has been in the women's movement. Ram Mohan Roy's plea for the rights of Hindu women in the eighteen-twenties was itself based on the first reaction of European ideals on India. But the Hindu and Muslim revivalism which provided the nationalism of the nineteenth century with its strength did not devote much attention to the liberation of women from the shackles of ancient customs. The Brahmo Samaj, influenced as it was by European thought, did much to break down the barriers of custom which prevented Hindu women from taking part in social life. The movement for social reform which had considerable vogue at one time was concerned more with the prevention of child marriage, permission to windows to remarry and other necessary changes in Hindu life. It had also a strongly puritanical bias which led its adherents to such extremes as opposition to traditional dances and music.

It should, however, be remembered that apart from social custom and usage there was no general opposition in India at any time to the participation of women in public life or in welfare activities. In fact the work of women pioneers like Ramabai Ranade received wide public support. But the organisation of a women's movement as such was the result of impact of world forces. Once the All-India Women's Conference came into existence its activities soon assumed a national range. Under such leaders as Sarojini Naidu, poetess, orator, politician and president of the Congress, the movement gathered momentum, and it may well claim to be one of the great factors welding India together into one nation.

CONCLUSION

What does this bird's-eye view of the panorama of Indian history show? The school of thought which looks upon history as a system of national apologetics has but little justification in its favour. Nor can the history of any country be considered as a grand procession of great men, or a majestic stream of progress, broadening with every age, and from precedent to precedent. But the history of a country has little value unless it deals with the conscious effort of a people to achieve a civilisation, to reach better standards, to live a happier and nobler life. Indian history from the earliest days is the record of such an endeavour. As in the history of every other people, it has its ups and downs. There are periods when the lamp of faith has burnt brightly and the consequent achievement have been notable; there are other periods, when the will of the people had slackened, their faith grown dim and their achievements had been of little value to themselves and to the world. With all such ups and downs, it is the continuous purpose of a people that makes a history. That such purpose has existed is clear enough by the maintenance of a continuous civilisation through at least thirty centuries, because a civilisation cannot continue unless there is a conscious effort in every succeeding generation to carry it forward, or at least to maintain it unimpaired. The organisation of Indian civilisation in its domestic and social structure, in the philosophic background, which held it together, was the work of the period prior to Buddhism, for we see it fairly well established during the ministry of Buddha. That the system in its essentials should have been inherited by the Indians of the twentieth century was rendered possible only by the conscious effort of the Indian people during all the succeeding centuries, withstanding alike the forces of internal disruption and of external pressure. The remarkable continuity of effort in the interpretation and adjustment of Dharmasastras which constitute the steel framework of this civilisation is the outstanding factor in Indian history.

Indian history is of necessity predominantly the history of the Hindu people, for though other and potent elements have become permanent factors in India, the Hindus still constitute over eighty per cent of her population. Besides, what is distinctly Indian has so far been Hindu. Islamic contribution is not specially related to India and is a part of a world culture to which Indian Muslims belong. To the extent it is Indian, as in the case of Moghul painting or Indo-Saracenic architecture, the differentiating characteristic is the interaction of Islamic and Hindu cultures. In essence, therefore, the history of Indian effort towards the building up and maintenance of a specially Indian civilisation has to be the history of the Hindu mind and its achievements.

The dynastic history of any country with a record of five thousand years can never be a source of much inspiration. Not that India has lacked great monarchs or inspiring leaders. A few figures like Asoka, Akbar, Krishnadevaraya and Sivaji stand out by the nobility of their character and the massiveness of their achievement. But the military conquerors, the political architects, and the other great men around whom national histories cast their halo are of no great significance unless they are moved by a faith or motivated by an ideal which carries humanity forward in its march. Indian history has her ample share of such great men, statesmen and conquerors from Chanakya to Nana Fadnavis, from Chandra Gupta Maurya to Aurangzeb. Their glory and their greatness are no doubt important; but in Indian history, as in the histories of other peoples, what counts in the end is the achievement of the people, the faith that moves them to great deeds, the endeavours that preserve society as a living organism, fit for the common man to live in.

The difference between one age and another lies clearly in this important fact. There is no such thing as a golden age, which is but the chimera of a defeated people. Compared to the life in India in the nineteenth century when the first efforts towards her recovery of the lost spirit were being tentatively organised, life under the Guptas, or under Akbar and in the Vijayanagar Empire was undoubtedly backward. What is it then that makes us proud of the Gupta Empire under Chandra Gupta or the Moghul Empire under Akbar or the Vijayanagar Empire under Krishnadevaraya? The answer is simple. It is *not* that oppression was less, economic life more secure, inequalities less glaring; but the people of those time were engaged in high endavours with a conscious feeling of their destiny. The people in the Gupta Empire felt, perhaps vaguely, a national pride, an impulse to move forward, a yearning towards achievement, which not only saved India from foreign invasions but left us immortal monuments in literature, art and architecture. The undoubted feeling of the people in Akbar's time was that they were living in a new age. This is reflected not only in the political enthusiasm of the time but in the art and architecture of the period, in the poetry of Tulsidas, and in the music of Tansen. In the same way, the people of Vijayanagar realised for three hundred years that they were the champions of an idea. It is when national idealism fails and faith grows dim that decay sets in. India had many such periods, when anarchy prevailed, the social system reached the verge of breakdown and the achievements in the realm of the mind became mean-spirited. It is her glory that there was sufficient faith and vision left even in the period of the greatest misery to enable her to recover.

Today India stands on the threshold of a new era, when her spirit, revived by a century of effort, and strengthened by the assimilation of new ideas and ideals faces the world. The great question for the future is: Can India by her conscious effort carry forward to greater summits of achievement the spirit she has inherited through the five thousand years of unbroken succession?

SUPPLEMENT

INDIA AFTER INDEPENDENCE

On the 15th of August, 1947, a new chapter opened in Indian history. After a century of political chaos and social anarchy that followed the breakdown of the Moghul empire and nearly 150 years of foreign rule, India again emerged as an independent nation. The British withdrew from India as a result of political agreement which, however, had two special characteristics. The first was the partition of the old Indian empire into Pakistan and India. The Muslim majority areas in the west of India consisting of Baluchistan, the North-West Frontier Province, Sindh and a part of the Punjab, and on the east, the larger portion of Bengal were constituted into the new state of Pakistan. Secondly, Britain released the princely states of India from the obligations of Paramountcy which had during the period of British authority created a facade of political unity. The creation of Pakistan as an Islamic state had large-scale repercussions in India as it led not only to the uprooting of millions of men on both sides of the frontier, but in generating in India a demand for a "Hindu" state. The demand for a Hindu *pada padshahi,* or a Hindu empire as a counterpoise to Pakistan which found a following among considerable sections of people was a grave menace to the ideal of a secular democratic state to which the national movement had been committed from the beginning. It required the martyrdom of Mahatma Gandhi (assassinated on the 30th January, 1948) to awaken India to the serious disruptive consequences of this movement, which the nation unequivocally disowned and the government put down with vigour.

The withdrawal of British authority also brought to the forefront the problem of the princely states. As we have seen, at all known times in the past the concept of Indian unity was that of a *samrajya* or empire with vassal princes exercising local authority in areas outside the direct administration of the imperial government. This system had been inherited by the British, and during their period of authority there were more than 600 princely states over which the British Crown did not claim sovereignty. They varied in size, population and resources from Hyderabad with over 80 thousand square miles, a population of 18 million and very considerable material resources to the demesne of the petty chief of a few square miles in Kathiawad and Simla Hill states. About twenty of these princely states were substantive sovereignties, having regular administrations and maintaining considerable military forces. They stretched across India and the facade of unity under the British had been maintained by the doctrine of Paramountcy which claimed overriding powers for the British Crown. It was the contention of some of the more powerful princes, which the British government accepted, that all the rights of paramountcy which the British Crown exercised over the princely states would lapse with the end of British power and that the princes would revert to their original position of independence. Such a development would have meant utter political chaos. The first notable achievement of independent India was the integration of these princely states with what had formerly been British India to create the union of India. The achievement was spectacular, for even before the actual date of independence, all the states within the territory of India (excluding Hyderabad) and having common frontiers with Pakistan and India (excluding Kashmir) had voluntarily entered into agreements creating thereby a single states from the Himalayas to Cape Comorin. Though it was the firm but sympathetic policy of the national leaders that brought about this result, credit is also due to the patriotism and vision of many of the leading Indian princes who recognised that the days of feudal power had passed and that their future lay with the Indian Union. It may also be emphasised that the willing acceptance by the vast majority of princes of the changes in India was the consummation of a long process started afted the mutiny which had through administrative developments, educational policies, customs arrangements and more than all by the growth of an Indian national sentiment which affected the people of the princely states in the same manner as the people of British India, had even while preserving the forms of partial independence and separateness, created a union of mind. In Hyderabad alone it required a police action to bring the Nizam in line with the rest of the princes. Kashmir, a state continguous to both India and Pakistan hesitated for a time but when Pakistan sought to force the issue by an unofficial invasion by tribesmen from the frontier, the Maharaja acceded to India (November 1947).

For the first time in history, India was united into a state obeying a single authority whose writ ran from the Himalayas to Cape Comorin. Neither the Mauryas nor the Guptas, nor the British at the height of their power, exercised sovereignty over the whole of this territory. Also, though the new state of Pakistan had been carved out of the old Indian empire, the Indian Union without question continued the historic identity of India and represented its civilisation and traditions. Two small areas under foreign occupation, the French and Portuguese settlements, alone remained to complete the territorial unity of India. France realising the changed situation negotiated (1954) a settlement by which her possessions were peacefully handed over to India. The liberation of Goa, Daman and Diu took place in 1961.

The Constituent Assembly to which the sovereignty of India was transferred endowed the new state with a constitution federal in structure and democratic in character. The former provinces of India and the territories of Indian rulers were constituted into states united together under a federation which was invested not only with residual powers but also the rights of intervention in cases of breakdown. An outstanding feature of the constitution was the provision of fundamental rights like freedom of speech, of worship, of association which could be enforced through courts of law. The structure of government was that of parliamentary responsible government with elections based on adult franchise. The central parliament was bicameral, a house of the people (Lok Sabha) and a house of the States (Rajya Sabha) with financial authority exclusively in the hands of the former. The head of the Union was the President elected by the members of central and state legislatures. Governors, nominated by the central government, nominally headed the governments of the states where also authority was vested in the cabinet enjoying the confidence of the legislature. A supreme court with authority to pronounce the validity of legislative enactments, to uphold the fundamental rights provided in the constitution, to maintain the balance between the federation and the states and to hear appeals from the state high courts is another important feature of the constitution.

As the constituent states of India were in the main successors to British provinces and princely states which had come into existence by the accidents of history, the new government after a comprehensive examination of all the relevant factors reconstituted them on the basis of language, culture, traditions and historic identity. Thus, for the first time the Andhras, the Tamils, the Marathas and other major linguistic groups in India were constituted into states, merging into them the neighbouring princely units connected with them by language and culture. The re-constituted structure of the Indian federation consisted of 16 states including the proposed new state of Nagaland. Apart from this, there are also certain union territories (Himachal Pradesh, the federal capital Delhi, Andamans and Nicobars, Manipur, etc.) for which the federation has a direct responsibility.

The government which took over from the British authorities

was a national coalition under Mr. Jawaharlal Nehru in which were represented all the major political parties. But after the first elections which returned the Congress party in an overwhelming majority, strictly party cabinets were established at the centre and in the states in order that there may be undivided responsibility in matters of policy and administration. As in the succeeding elections also, the Congress maintained its majority practically undiminished, Mr. Nehru continued to be Prime Minister shaping both the internal and external policies of government, that the post-independence period may legitimately be called the Nehru age.

The internal policies of the government reflected the liberal revolutionary urge of the national movement. It sought simultaneously to modernise Hindu society through the reform of its laws and institutions, to raise the living standards of the common people by a rapid industrialisation of the country, through planned reconstruction of economic life and to transform the rural life of India both by the abolition of large-scale land-holdings and through a comprehensive scheme of community development and national extension service. The demand for the modernisation of Hindu society, though not a part of the political movement, had an earlier history and had developed on parallel lines with the national struggle. The abolition of untouchability was an important plank in the Mahatma's platform; the claim of women for equal rights and opportunities had also the strong support of the Congress. Therefore, the constitution itself abolished the practice of untouchability in all its aspects and also provided for equality of rights and opportunities for women. The general problem of modernisation of the laws and institutions of the Hindus was taken up after the new parliament had been elected on the basis of adult franchise and the decade that followed (1952-62) was rendered remarkable by a series of legislative enactments which brought Hindu society on level with other modern societies. The Hindu marriage law was a notable reform in many respects: for the first time there was a uniform marriage law affecting Hindus all over India. Polygamy, which was permitted under Hinduism, was abolished.

Marriages between different castes were made legal contrary to the doctrines of Hinduism. Also the new law provided for divorce, which as official Hindu theory had considered marriage to be sacramental was a radical change so far at least as the Brahmins and the other higher castes were concerned. The Hindu succession code was equally far-reaching. It provided, among other things, for equal rights of succession for daughters, again something totally at variance with the theory of Hindu law. Briefly, it may be said that the post-independence period inaugurated a reorganisation of

Hindu society which provided it with modern laws and institutions.

In the economic sphere, India was, at the very beginning of her independence, faced with many major problems. The first was a menacing deficit in food production whose seriousness was increased by a steady growth of population at the then rate of 5 millions a year. The emphasis during the first stage of government's activity was on reforms of land tenure, the improvement and modernisation of agriculture, and the provision of irrigation facilities. Systems of uneconomic land-holdings by intermediaries like zamindars and jagirdars between the government and the cultivator were abolished all over India, giving a direct interest to the peasant in the cultivation of land. Large-scale irrigation schemes were undertaken in every state, bringing millions of acres under cultivation as in Rajasthan or ensuring them against the vagaries of an uncertain monsoon. The most important of these projects which are mainly of a multi-purpose character, are the Bhakra Nangal, Damodar Valley, Hirakud, Chambal, Koyna, Tungabhadra and others which together irrigate more than 40 million new acres of land. The production of foodgrains was during this period increased by nearly 80 per cent.

Though the emphasis during the first few years was on land reform and agriculture, the government realised from the beginning that a rapid programme of industrial development was essential if India's economy was to be modernised and a noticeable improvement in the living conditions of her people effected. The government, therefore, embarked on a programme of planning with the object of creating in India the conditions of highly industrialised self-sustained economy under a system in which the basic industries were organised and managed by the government itself. The emphasis in the first five year plan was on agriculture and related projects like fertilisers and irrigation. The second plan devoted much greater attention to basic industries like steel, heavy chemicals, production of machinery and machine tools. The third plan continues the programme on a more intensive scale. One notable feature of the industrial programmes which the government has been able to put through has been the financial assistance and technical cooperation received from other nations notably U.S.A., the Soviet Union and Britain.

This rapid programme of industrialisation which has been a notable feature of the post-independence period led naturally to a great increase in scientific and technical education. During the British period education was mainly in humanities and though after the Montagu-Chelmsford reforms when education came under the control of elected Indian ministers, there was some improvement in the situation, the number of technically trained personnel, especially at higher levels, and research facilities in pure and applied science were inadequate for a country of India's size and requirements. A significant feature of the Nehru government's activity since independence has been the establishment of institutes of technology and other facilities for training in the highest technical skills in different parts of India. Encouragement of advanced research in pure science has also been a major activity of government. In the field of atomic energy, India has been able during the last ten years to make substantial progress. The current (third plan includes the erection of an atomic power plant of 3,00,000 Kw. at Tarapore near Bombay which would signalise India's definite entry into the atomic world.

A third and equally far-reaching achievement of the government is the transformation of India's rural life through the community projects and national extension service. 82 per cent of India's population lives in the villages, which weighed down by old customs, social practices and a primitive handicraft-economy and backward agriculture constitute the most difficult problem in any scheme of modernisation. No plan of industrialisation could touch more than a fringe of this problem. Also it was obvious that in the conditions of modern life, a reconstitution of the self-sufficient village of past was neither practicable nor desirable. The Government of India, therefore, decided on a comprehensive plan, briefly described as community projects, the main features of which were the grouping of villages into sizeable communities, generally between 80 and 90 villages, the formulation of a plan for each such community providing for education, better sanitation and housing, rural communication, encouragement of cooperation, improved methods of cultivation, local irrigation, development of rural industries and, the establishment of rural industrial estates. While the government provided technical assistance and guidance the objective was to develop local leadership at the village level in order to secure popular cooperation in the realisation of the programme. This scheme which brings modernisation and improved techniques to the doorstep of every villager has already covered over 450,000 out of 550,000 villages of India. It will cover the whole of India in 1963 and will thereby effect a rural revolution parallel to the changes taking place in urban life.

Though this revolutionary programme at the time of its origin was meant to modernise the villages and to enable them to share in the new life that India was creating for itself, it has now in the course of its first ten years of existence developed also a new political pattern. This is what is known as *Panchayati raj,* under which the village units through their own elected *panchas* are to be entrusted with a large measure of self-government. The villages will thus again constitute the basis of government in India, the main difference being that unlike in the past these will be wholly democratic in structure. The village communities of the past were status and caste dominated. In most places the village officers were hereditary. The *Panchayati raj,* which was first introduced in Rajasthan in 1960 and has now spread to most states and will soon cover the whole of India, is on the other hand based on adult franchise, without reference to sex, caste, community or status. It is thus not only a great endeavour to take the democratic processes to the lowest level, but to provide a catalytic agent for the dissolution of caste and other allied institutions based on traditional status. The panchayats are provided with their own revenue sources and are in effect governments with responsibility for all aspects of village life. One major activity entrusted to the panchayats is cooperative farming on a voluntary basis, in order to enable the generally uneconomic and fragmentised holdings of the villages to be cultivated jointly on modern scientific lines.

Above the village panchayats are the *zilla parishads* and the block panchayat *samitis* which supervise the work of the villages and coordinate it for the whole block. While the general supervision and guidance will no doubt remain with the state governments, the responsibility for the carrying out of rural programme will now be entrusted with block *samitis.* This is something more than what is generally known as local self-government. It is a process of democratic decentralisation under which increasing responsibilities are placed on the people themselves, an attempt to create a democratic system in which the participation of the people is more direct than what mere representative government could ensure. This new system brings the villages into the very centre of the picture and is in keeping with the traditional policy of India.

The working of democratic institutions directly by the people, and the creation of an industrial society require an educated population. When India became independent, more than 80 per cent of her people were illiterate. Admission to the universities numbered only 300,000. The sustained effort of the government has sent over 80 per cent of India's children to schools and the current five-year plan visualises universal compulsory education for all children between six and eleven years of age. No less spectacular has been the rise in university education. The number of universities has more than doubled itself and enrolment in colleges has passed the million mark. A University Grants Commission created by a central statute ensures standards, equipment and development along proper lines.

The policy of the government in education, public health, employee-employer relations, betterment of the conditions of working classes, the uplift of the under-privileged like scheduled tribes and the erstwhile untouchables has been determined by broad recognition of its responsibilities as a welfare state. Though public health, like education, is within the sphere of state and not federal activity, the central government has, with the cooperation of the states embarked on a number of schemes for the general improvement of health in India including the control of malaria, the eradication of contagious diseases like small-pox and cholera which used to take a heavy toll of Indian life and similar measures. The policy in respect of labour seeks to ensure that the industrial revolution now taking place does not involve the exploitation of the working classes, and that the profits of industry are in a measure shared by the workers, that the conditions of work in factories and mines are humane, that housing facilities and medical care are available to them, and their right to collective bargaining for wages in fully respected. The uplift of the tribal population spread in hilly tracts all over India and of the former untouchables is a responsibility placed by the constitution itself on the central government. A large tribal population living away from the rest of the community and following its own ways and traditions has always been a feature of Indian life. They were not interfered with, but left in a large measure to themselves though there was always a steady pressure against them by the plains people, confining them more and more to less accessible areas. The new government of India from the beginning accepted a special responsibility to safeguard their interests, protect their culture and provide them with special facilities for education and employment. In respect of the former untouchables also a similar policy of special encouragement in respect of education, employment in public services, representation in elected bodies, etc., has been followed.

It is a policy orientated to socialism that the Nehru government has been following in internal matters. The utilisation of the powers of taxation for ensuring better distribution of wealth, the direction of industry through the dominance of the state-owned or state-controlled industries (the public sector), the control of banking, through the supervisory powers of the Reserve Bank and the special position of the State Bank of India, the state's participation in insurance, shipping, external trade, etc., have already created in India a socialist pattern of administration, though its effects in the form of a welfare state have only begun to penetrate to the lower levels.

FOREIGN POLICY

India's foreign relations have been, from the beginning, under the personal direction and control of Nehru who functioned also as foreign minister. The policy which he has followed could only be understood in the special circumstances of the period. The year of India's independence witnessed the emergence of the sharp division between the United States and the Soviet Union. From the time of its origin all the states aligned themselves with one or the other thus leading to the organisation of the international world into two hostile camps. India alone, to start with, stood out of this grouping and followed a policy of independent action. She was soon joined in this policy by a number of the newly independent states of Asia, like Burma, Indonesia, Ceylon, and this policy of non-involvement became in course of time a recognised alternative to alignment with the contending power blocs.

While maintaining an attitude of independence India sought to build up relations of friendship and goodwill with the states in both the blocs. As a member of the Commonwealth, her relations with Britain were in some senses more intimate, though in some major issues especially the Suez intervention, she took a line in opposition to the official policy of Britain. Also, India's attitude towards colonialism and the liberation struggles of subject peoples differed basically from that of Britain. With America also her differences have been significant, especially in regard to the Korean War and the Japanese treaty in both of which India's approach differed fundamentally from that of the United States. Between the Soviet Union and India also the relations have been cordial on the basis of mutual respect and understanding of each other's problems, though naturally their approach has been different on many important issues. Generally speaking, India has been able, within the frame-work of her policy of non-alignment, to build up for herself a position of friendly understanding in the international world.

The major exceptions have been the relations between India and her two neighbours—China and Pakistan.

With China the relations started well. The revolution in China found much sympathy in India and the attempt of the American government to isolate the People's Republic was resisted by the Indian government which was among the first non-Communist states to recognise new China. During the Korean war the Chinese point of view aroused considerable sympathy in India and the relations between the two states developed satisfactorily leading to the treaty in regard to Tibet which included in its preamble the famous *Pancha Sheela* or the five principles of co-existence. But soon afterwards the situation began to deteriorate. The territorial encroachment of China in the Aksai Chin area of Ladakh, the claim that the boundary between India and Tibet is undefined with consequent pretensions to parts of territory on the Assam border (known as the MacMahon line) led to the growth of a hostile feeling in India towards China. Equally the feeling in China towards India showed a marked change with the developement of pro-Tibetan opinion among Indian politicians at the time of the Khampa rebellion. Chou En-lai's visit to Delhi to discuss the troubles arising out of these border disputes, did not bring the situation any nearer settlement, and when in 1962 the Chinese asked for a renewal of the Tibetan treaty, the Indian government felt compelled to point out that in view of continuing Chinese occupation of Indian territory it did not feel that it could enter into negotiations for the renewal of a treaty which in any case had not functioned satisfactorily from the point of view of India, because of the numerous restrictive conditions that had been imposed on Indian traders in Tibet.

Other issues which aggravated the situation were the evasive attitude of China towards India's position in Bhutan and Sikkim, the obvious attempt to get Nepal, which is bound by special treaty with India, to move into the Chinese orbit (e.g., the construction of a Khatmandu-Lhasa road) and the offer to negotiate with Pakistan a settlement of the boundary dispute in respect of the occupied areas of Kashmir in the Karakorum. All these seemed to indicate a general attitude of unfriendliness towards India which naturally had its reaction on Indian policies.

The relations with Pakistan were governed by the tragic events that followed the partition. Throughout the period they continued to be hostile, both countries suspicious of each other's motives, policies and actions. There were four factors which in differing degrees helped to keep the two countries in an attitude of undiminishing hostility. First, there was the bitterness of the millions of refugees on both sides who were uprooted from their homes and had lost their all in the migration. This, of course, is a diminishing problem but for the first few years it created a great deal of bitterness. The second issue related to the utilisation of the water of the Indus river system, a major problem which affected the economic life of millions in East Punjab and Rajasthan in India and of West Pakistan as a whole. This question has now been settled to mutual satisfaction through the mediation of the World Bank. The third and fourth issues are much more complicated. Pakistan, it will be remembered, was created, according to the version of its leaders, as a homeland for Indian Muslims. But even after partition there were 35 million Muslims left in India. Pakistan's attitude towards them, which the Indian Muslims as a whole resent and repudiate, has been that of a kind of guardianship. Every minor local incident in which a Muslim is involved is played up as a communal issue, and the alleged plight light of the Indian Muslims, the disabilities they suffer from, the desecration of their mosques and religious places—these are the fables on which Pakistan opinion is fed. More than this, Pakistan seeks to influence the opinion of Muslims in other countries with propaganda about the persecution of Muslims in India. This assumption that the Government of Pakistan is in someway the trustee of the religious interests of Indian Muslims, vitiates the political relations between the two countries.

More than all these is the question of Kashmir. Following a short period of futile negotiations backed by political pressure, Pakistan organised an unofficial invasion of the state. The Maharaja's government then turned to India and acceded to the Indian Union, placing on it the responsibility of defending the state. After the invaders were pushed back from the valley by the Indian army, the government referred the matter to the Security Council which negotiated a cease-fire between the parties, leaving about a third of the territory in Pakistan's hands. No political settlement of the issue has so far been reached though many attempts have been made by the Security Council to get the parties to reach an agreement. India has stated her willingness to negotiate a permanent settlement on the basis of the cease-fire line, with adjustments where necessary, but Pakistan insists on a plebiscite in the valley on the ground that the majority of the people being Muslims, their natural affiliations are towards Pakistan. This dispute has poisoned the atmosphere of relations in both countries and has been the governing consideration of Pakistan's foreign policy. Her membership of the Central Treaty Organisation (with England, Turkey and Iran) and of the SEATO (with America, Britain, France, Australia, New Zealand, the Philippines, and Thailand) and her military alliance with America, are according to the statements of her own leaders meant to strengthen her diplomatic and military position in regard to India, in the controversy regarding Kashmir.

Another aspect of India's external relations which deserves notice is her position at the U.N. and its specialised bodies. India was one of the original members of the United Nations and has from the very first taken keen interest in its work. In matters connected with the fight against colonialism, racial discrimination, development of economically backward nations and similar problems her contribution to the work of these bodies has been specially significant.

What is it that gives to the new age in India—the period after independence—its distinguishing characteristics? How does it differ from the past ages of her history? Though the past is clearly with us everywhere, obviously, it is a new and revolutionary period into which India has passed during these fifteen years of independence. What are its characteristics? The first and most spectacular change is in regard to the character of the state. In all previous periods, India, politically, culturally and from the point of view of ideas, was represented by an elite, a section of the people who either intellectually, by military prowess or land-owning claimed to be the representative class. When we spoke of Indian philosophy, it was a philosophy of the higher castes. When we spoke of the Mauryan, Gupta or Moghul empires, they were of political organisations based on conquest, with power vested in certain classes, from which others were excluded. The great national movement itself was created by a middle class, though in its later stages it reached the masses also. For the first time after independence we have a political structure which embraces the totality of our people, in which power is shared by all and where every effort is made to let all classes participate in national culture. New India is not the India of higher castes or richer classes but of all her sons and daughters.

Secondly, India has at one leap entered the age of industrial civilisation. Her social and economic structure of the future will be determined by new methods of production and distribution as the whole of India has now become one economic unit. Also, this industrial civilisation, being based on scientific advance will push India more and more into the scientific age compelling her people to leave behind them much of what was considered as being characteristic of Hindu culture. The scientific approach though only at its beginning is a significant feature of life in new India.

Thirdly, there is the sense of community. Indian civilisation in the past has been divisive; division of the people into castes and sub-castes, of law into customs and usages, of the country itself into smaller and smaller states. New India is based on a sense of community of shared power and responsibilities and a common emerging culture.

With all this, the identity of India's culture and the continuity of her history are patent enough facts. Neither the partition, nor the great changes introduced in her life have affected India's basic integrity. Behind all the changes that have taken place and the special features introduced into her, one can still see the face of eternal India, striving as ever to carry on the torch of light and to live a life of her own in friendly association with others in this world.

GLOSSARY

Adi Granth: The first book in the *Granth Saheb*—the scripture of the Sikhs.

Adi Varaha: The divine boar which saved the world from sinking into the ocean by lifting it on its tusks.

Advaita: A philosophical term of the Hindus. It means nonduality, identity, especially that of the Brahman, with the universe; of spirit and matter—hence the highest truth.
See *Brahmanas.*

Aitreya Brahmana: One of the two portions attached to the Rig Veda, the other being Kausitaki (Sankhya-yana).
See *Brahmanas.*

Amrit: Nector of immortality; ambrosia, beverage of the gods.

Anjuman: A society; an organisation.

Aranyakas: Treatises composed (or intended to be read) in forests. A religious and philosophical work (in Sanskrit) marking a change from ritualism to the abstract thought of the Hindus.

Arya Samaj: A modern sect among the Hindus (founded by Dayananda Saraswati) based on the Vedas mainly, discarding idolatry and other later tendencies.

Aryavarta: The land of the Aryas, i.e., Hindustan.

Asrama: A stage or period in the life of Hindus. Four Asramas are prescribed: 1. Brahmacharya (the student life); 2. Grahastya (the householder's life); 3. Vanaprastha (the hermit's life); and 4. Sanyas (the beggar's life).

Ashta Pradhans: The cabinet system of government where the number of ministers is restricted to eight.

Asvamedha: A horse sacrifice performed by Hindu kings to imply imperial achievements. For a year, the sacrificial horse was let loose to wander at will, with a protecting army. When passing through a foreign land, the arrest of the horse meant a challenge to the army which immediately gave a fight. Free passage to the horse signified acceptance of the owner's sovereignty. After 12 months of successful wandering, the horse would return to the starting point, only to be sacrificed in the sacred fire.

Atman: Soul, spirit or ego; distinguished as universal or individual. Metaphysical principle of existence in the monistic systems of philosophy.

Avarna: Casteless; one beyond the pale of the caste system—hence an "untouchable."

Avatara: An incarnation. The Hindus believe that Vishnu descends to the earth through mortal forms, from time to time to save it. So far eleven such incarnations are known, the last being *Buddha.*

Avidya: Ignorance, want of learning; illusion.
See *Maya.*

Bania: A professional trader.

Bhakti: Devotion towards the particular deity. Nine ways of expressing it are prescribed. This form of worship and prayer has the largest following because it is the simplest and most appealing to the sentimental mind.

Bharat Varsha: India, the land ruled over by descendants of king Bharat, or the country in which people belonging to the Bharat tribe reside.

Bhasma: Sacred ashes used for smearing on the body throughout the day by ascetics and before beginning a religious function by others.

Bo Tree: The kind of tree under which Buddha got enlightenment. (Hin.: *Peepul,* Lat.: *Ficus religiosa.*)

Boycott: Particularly of British goods, suggested at first as a means to express resentment at the partition of Bengal. Later, used as an item in the non-cooperation programme, with "Swadeshi" as the other side of the weapon.

Brahmacharya: The (celibate) life of a student (before marriage) spent mostly in the house of the preceptor. The first of the four stages in life prescribed for most of the Hindus.
See *Asrama.*

Brahman: The Supreme Being, regarded as impersonal and divested of all quality and action.

According to Vedantins (q.v.) Brahman is both the efficient and material cause of the visible world, the all-prevading Soul and Spirit of the universe, the essence from which all is created and to which all creation is absorbed.

Brahmanas: Prose portion of the Vedas (as distinct from the *Mantras*) dealing with application and use of Vedic hymns for sacrificial purposes. Rig Veda has two Brahmanas, Yajur Veda and Atharva Veda have only one each; Sama Veda has eight.

Brahmo Samaj: One of the religious sects introduced in Bengal during the early British rule by Hindu reformists who wanted to pray to the "formless" without the help of any symbols. In Western India, it is known as Prarthana Samaj.

Brahmins: The first of the four main divisions of Hindu society, their work being mainly confined to "teaching and learning." The other three are: Kshatriyas (warriors—rulers); Vaisyas (traders); and Sudras (menials).

Chapkan (Persian): A long flowing robe of man.

Chauth: One-fourth of the land revenue, collected by the Marathas.

Chettis: South Indian money-lenders. In Burma, they attracted much attention from the local population and from the government.

Chitpavan is a section of Maratha Brahmins. "Konkanastha" is a synonym for "Chitpavan." Almost all leaders (in all walks of life) of Maharashtra, belonged to this section: Ranade, Gokhale, Tilak, Paranjape, Rajwade—all came from the same stock.

Dakshinapath: The Southern Country—beyond the Vindhyas.

Danda: Staff, punishment, used as a symbol of sovereignty; the staff is used to denote judicial authority also.

Dasanami Sanyasis: Sects of Hindu ascetics.

Dasyus: Original residents of India.

Devadasi: Meaning servant (maid) of the gods. In some parts of South India, a custom prevails by which young maidens dedicate themselves to the service of the deities in temples. Abandoning their parental home, they stay in the temples.

Dharma: A very difficult word to be rendered into non-Indian languages. It means righteousness, religious ordinances, rules of conduct, peculiar duties of the individual; while the *Dharma-sastra* is a collection of legal aphorisms.

Dharma-chakra pravartan: Setting in motion the wheel of righteousness of Dharma. It is particularly applied to the first sermon delivered at Sarnath by Buddha explaining his eightfold path to usher in a new order of life.

Dharmashala: A "caravanserai" of the Hindus, built by some donor or by public subscription for the convenience of the travellers. Here passengers can halt for three days, free of charge. Providing such amenities is considered one of the most charitable acts.

Digambar (Jain): One of the two main sects of Jains, whose deities are "without a dress," the other being "Svetambar" with white dress for their gods.

Digvijaya (Sanskrit): Conquest of the (four) quarters. Before assuming imperial authority a king had to conquer rulers of surrounding countries. His conquests were naturally in all directions—hence the term.

Dikpala: Guardian of a quarter.

According to Hindu mythology each of the eight quarters is

guarded by eight regents, each mounted on an elephant.

Dipavali is the festival of lights, in October-November. It is traced to over a thousand years back.

Doab: A Persian word for land between two streams (rivers) in general. It is specifically applied to the country between the Jumna and the Ganges.

Dvija: The twice-born.

According to Hinduism, everyone is a Sudra by birth and is eligible to a higher status only after performing certain rites. Brahmins, Kshatriyas and Vaisyas are said to be twice-born, the first being natural birth and the other religious when initiation takes place.

Fatwa: An order issued by a religious head of Islam, to the public.

Firman: A government order issued by a (Muslim) ruler; a government gazatte of olden times.

Gadi: Throne—the seat of authority in general.

Gayatri is a sacred prayer (from the Rig Veda) to the Sun forming an essential part of the Sandhya performed twice (thrice) by the first three classes of Hindu society.

Ghat: (1) A road on high hills; (2) A range of hills; (3) A series of steps leading to a river bed.

Giri-puja: A festival of worshipping a mountain.

Grantha (Characters): A script used in Tamil-speaking districts for copying Sanskrit books, as the local script was not suitable for the purpose.

Grihastha: A house-holder. The second stage in the life of a Hindu after completion of studies.

Grihya-Sutras: Forming a manual of domestic ritual, these rules guide the house-holder in observing many ceremonies.

Gumathas: Commercial or revenue assistants.

Gunas: Literally, properties. All created things are supposed to have one of the three properties—*Satva; Rajas* and *Tamas.*

Himavat-Setu-Paryantam: From the Himalayas (in the North) to Rameshwaram (in the South)—thus embracing the whole of India.

Hundi: A form of a bill of payment used extensively in India even now by old bankers.

Jagad-Guru: Literally, world preceptor; used to refer to a religious head of the Hindus—particularly the Sankaracharyas.

Jagir (Persian): An assignment of land by a ruler to his feudal chief in return for military service.

Jagirdar (Persian): A feudal chief who holds an assignment of land from a ruler in return for military service.

Jivatma: The individual soul; or the principle of life.
Jubraj (Yuva-Raj): A crown prince, an heir-apparent.
Kafir: A non-Muslim.
Kali: The last (and the present) of the four ages (Yugas), according to Hindu calculation of time, the previous three being *Kreta, Treta,* and *Dvapara.*
Kalpa: An extensively long duration of time—covering millions of human years, supposed to be the lifetime of the world, at the end of which everything would be submerged in water.
Karma: Based on the Hindu conception of re-birth, the law of Karma binds everyone to enjoy or suffer the consequences of his actions in former life. The word is used as synonymous with fate, destiny, and the most oriental expression "*Kismat.*"
Karma Yogi: One who believes in the path of incessant action (one's duty) without expecting any reward. The other paths are: renunciation (sanyas); knowledge (jnyana); devotion (bhakti).
Kayastha: A caste (of the white-collared people) known for its skill in clerical work; even today that reputation is maintained by the people.
Kazi: An administrator of justice, according to Islamic law.
Khalif: The religious head of all the Muslims—inheriting authority from the Prophet.
See *Khalifat.*
Khattri: Corruption of the word Kshatriya—meaning the warrior (ruling) class.
Khilafat: The office of the Khalifa—the Muslim religious head. When after the World War (1914-18) Turkey abolished the Khilafat, an agitation to restore it was carried on by Indian Muslims. It was known as the Khilafat Movement.
Khillat: A robe of honour or of office. It is customary to present suitable robes on ceremonial occasions.
Khuda: Islamic expression for God.
Krishi: Agriculture—enjoined on the Vaisyas—the third of the Hindu four classes.
Kutba (Khutba): The Muslim prayer. The custom was to include the name of the ruler in it; thus showing acceptance of the occupant of the throne as Sovereign.
Left-handed Marga: A section of the Saktas (q.v.).
Linga: Phallus, representation Siva.
Lunar Year: Counting of months by phases of the moon. Between two new moons, the period is roughly 29½ days; so every fourth lunar year, an additional month is calculated to keep pace with the solar years.

Madhyamikas: A school of Nihilists in Buddhism attached to the Mahayana section.

Mahakavya: An epic—a long poem.

Mahaparinirvana: Buddha's death.

Mahaprasad (Sanskrit): Food offered to an idol; (particularly non-vegetarian).

Maharishi (Sanskrit): A great sage.

Mahayana: The greater of the two sections of Buddhism, the other being Hinayana.

Mantra: A hymn or prayer. The Vedas are divided into Mantras and Brahmanas.
See *Brahmanas.*

Maulvis are Islamic priests.

Maya (Sanskrit): Unreality, the illusion by virtue of which one considers the unreal universe as really existent and as distinct from the supreme spirit.

Mimamsa (Purva Mimamsa) is one of the six systems of Hindu philosophy, the others being Nyaya, Vaiseshika, Samkhya, Yoga and Vedanta (Uttara Mimamsa).

Mlechhas: Foreigners; barbarians; non-Aryans.

Moksha (same as Mukti): Emancipation. Freedom from the bondage of birth and death.

Mutt (Sanskrit): The dwelling place of an ascetic; a monastery.

Nataraja: Form of Siva, dancing; the Master-dancer.

Neti: In describing the all-prevading Brahman, Sanskrit pundits used an expression; NETI NETI: "This is not it," "This is not it," suggesting thereby that it cannot be put in any category and that it eludes definition.

Nibandhas are digests containing a synthesis of all dicta of Smriti writers.

Nigantha: Literally, fetter-less. A Jain sect following Parsva and Mahavira.

Nirguna: Devoid of all properties.

Pancham: One belonging to the fifth class—i.e., beyond the four classes of Hinduism; hence an untouchable.

Pan-Islamism: Union of all Islamic countries based on their common religion is yet a dream of many. Modernisation of Turkey, particularly the abolition of the Khilafat, undermined the whole idea.

Parama Bhagavata: A great devotee of Vishnu.

Paramatma: The supreme soul; God.

Parva: Sanskrit term for a chapter.

Peshwa: Persian word for Prime Minister; used particularly for the Maratha prime ministers of Sivaji and his successors.

Prakriti: Nature or matter, as distinct from Purusha (q.v.).

Prasasti: Praise; laudatory terms and expressions used with reference to a ruler.

Prayaschitta: Atonement; expiation; rites prescribed for atonement of sin.

Purusha: The soul or spirit; the active principle in creation as distinct from the passive Prakriti.

Qanungos (Persian): Revenue officers.

Rig Veda: The earliest literary composition of the world by the Aryas, the first of the four, the rest being Yajur Veda, Sama Veda, and Atharva Veda.

Rock Edicts: Inscriptions of Asoka on (flat) surface as distinct from pillar edicts. His thoughts, ideals or achievements were committed to writing for information and guidance of the public.

Rudraksha: A kind of hard bead (seed of a tree) found in Himalayan forests used for rosaries.

Saivism: The sect believing Siva as the Supreme Being, the source and essence of the Universe.

Sakta: A worshipper of Durga, representing the female personification of divine energy. The ritual enjoined on them is of two kinds, the pure or "right-hand" and the impure or "left-hand" ritual (q.v.).

Sankhya: One of the six systems of Hindu philosophy, maintaining dualism.

Sanyasi: An ascetic who has abandoned all worldly possessions and ties; the fourth and the last stage in the life of Hindus.

Sati: A widow who shares the funeral pyre with her husband; the practice of such widow-burning.

Setu (Sanskrit): A bridge; the bridge of rocks from India's southern tip to Ceylon (said to have been built by Rama).

Shariat: The Islamic Law.

Silpasastra: A Sanskrit treatise on architecture.

Sircar (Persian): Government.

Solar Dynasty: Some rulers in ancient India claimed descent from the Sun and were therefore known as belonging to the Solar Dynasty, to which Rama, king of Ayodhya, belonged.

Sramanas: Ascetic (Buddhist) monks or mendicants.

Srenis: Guilds of traders or artisans.

Subaship: Office of the provincial (suba) governor.

Sunyavadins: Those following the doctrine of the non-existence of anything; Buddhists.

Sutras: Aphorisms, extremely condensed and therefore terse sentences. When everything had to be committed to memory (in absence of the art of writing), a concentrated form of expression was indirectly forced on the exponents.

Swadeshi: Meaning, of own country. A movement for popularising home-made things, cloth in particular. It was used as a political weapon, its supplement being "*Boycott*" (q.v.).

Tantrics: Same as Saktas.

Tapasa: Same as Sanyas.

Tathagata: A term of respect used for Gautama Buddha.

Tirthankara: Leading pioneers (24) of Jainism who prepared the path for the progress of that sect.

Trishna: Desire, which according to Buddhism, is the cause of attachment to the objects of desire.

Upanishads: Philosophical treatises, from the Vedas, forming basis of the monistic school of thought.

Ustads: Teachers (experts) in general, of fine arts in particular.

Vaisnavism: That sect of the Hindus regarding Vishnu as the Supreme Being.

Vanik: Same as Bania: A merchant; trader, (Belonging to the third class).

Vanaprastha: The third—herimt stage in the life of a Hindu, preceded by Grahastya and followed by Sanyas.

Varna: A class in Hindu society; they are four; Brahman, Kshatriya, Vaisya and Sudra.

Varnasrama Dharma: A system based on *Varna* and *Asrama* (q.v.).

Vazir (Persian): The Prime Minister.

Vedanga: A subsidiary text of the Vedas.

Vedanta: One of the six systems of Hindu philosophy.

Vedantis: Followers of the Vedanta system of Hindu philosophy.

Veena: A stringed musical instrument.

Vihara: A Buddhist monastery.

Vinaya: One of the three sacred texts of Buddhism, laying down rules and regulations for the monks.

Virastami: Durgastami Eighth day of the bright half of Asvin; two days before *Dassara*.

Vratyastoma: A ritual for re-admitting into the Hindu fold those who have lost caste or who were beyond it.

Yavanas: The Greeks generally. The term is loosely used to denote any non-Hindu.

Yoga: The practice of concentration for controlling the mind.

Yogi: An ascetic in general; one well versed in the practice of "Yoga" in particular. One who practises penance by undergoing all sorts of physical mortification.

Zamindari: In some parts of India collection of land revenue is done through hereditary agents, who in their turn collect it from their tenants. These agents are the landlords—Zamindars, and their office, Zamindari.

INDEX